Knowing God
Doing Justice

Related titles by Anthony Mansueto

Knowing God series:

Restoring Reason in an Age of Doubt, Volume 1 (Ashgate 2002)

The Ultimate Meaningfulness of the Universe, Volume 2 (forthcoming 2011)

The Journey of the Dialectic, Volume 3

Forthcoming in the Theopolitical Visions series (Cascade Books):

The Death of Secular Messianism: Religion and Politics in an Age of Civilizational Crisis (2010)

Knowing God
Doing Justice

VOLUME 4

ANTHONY E. MANSUETO

☙PICKWICK *Publications* • Eugene, Oregon

DOING JUSTICE: KNOWING GOD, VOLUME 4

Copyright © 2011 Anthony E. Mansueto. All rights reserved. Except for brief quotations in critical publications or reviews, no part of this book may be reproduced in any manner without prior written permission from the publisher. Write: Permissions, Wipf and Stock Publishers, 199 W. 8th Ave., Suite 3, Eugene, OR 97401.

Pickwick Publications
An Imprint of Wipf and Stock Publishers
199 W. 8th Ave., Suite 3
Eugene, OR 97401

www.wipfandstock.com

ISBN 13: 978-1-55635-985-9

Cataloguing-in-Publication data:

Mansueto, Anthony E.

    Knowing God / Anthony E. Mansueto.

    vi + 264 p. ; 23 cm. Includes bibliographical references.

    Contents: 1. Restoring Reason in an Age of Doubt. 3. The Journey of the Dialectic. 4. Knowing God.

    ISBN 13: 978-0-75460-853-0 (v. 1)
    ISBN 13: 978-1-55635-987-3 (v. 3)
    ISBN 13: 978-1-55635-985-9 (v. 4)

    1. Ethics. 2. Natural law. 3. Natural law—History. 4. Thomas, Aquinas, Saint, 1225?–1274. 5. Virtues. I. Title.

BT50 M265 2011

Manufactured in the U.S.A.

Contents

1 The Crisis of Values / 1

2 Regrounding and Historicizing Natural Law Ethics / 56

3 The Human Vocation / 99

4 Human Excellence / 134

5 Social Justice / 196

Bibliography / 253

1

The Crisis of Values

THERE CAN BE LITTLE doubt that we are experiencing a fundamental crisis of values—that we have lost our ability to decide rationally what is beautiful, true, good, and holy—and that as a result our civilization is faced with stagnation and even disintegration. Despite a well documented ecological crisis of planetary proportions, developing countries continue to sell off the planet's lungs—the rain forests—and developed countries continue to burn fossil fuels, depleting what Buckminster Fuller called our planetary trust fund, poisoning the air and water, and contributing to a process of global warming which threatens the long-term viability of the ecosystem. The countries of Asia, Africa, and Latin America are forced to sacrifice human development in order to pay interest on an ever-mounting debt, while the United States squanders on luxury consumption resources which might be invested in a way which promotes the full development of human capacities. The religious right talks incessantly about "family values," while the left decries our lack of social responsibility. And yet the market drives us to spend more and more time earning money and less and less time attending to the needs of both family and community.

It is the principal task of universities and religious institutions to lead intellectually and morally, providing the first principles which govern both legislation and personal moral decisions. And yet when the people turn to their natural intellectual and moral leaders for guidance they find both a professoriate and a clergy who are, if anything, more confused than they are regarding fundamental questions of meaning and value. Our professors teach nihilism and despair while our priests are caught between an insipid liberalism which merely counsels that we be "nice" and a fundamentalism which condemns globally every properly human hope and aspiration.

There is, to be sure, a widespread (though by no means universal) consensus that modern ethical theory, both liberal and socialist, is dead. This is partly because of its failure to adequately ground its moral claims and partly because even if those claims could be adequately grounded they are largely empty and formal—merely ways of adjudicating competing claims which offer no substantive moral guidance—no vision of what it means to be an excellent human being or to build a just society. But modernism has yielded not to a richer and more profound moral vision, but rather to a postmodernist relativism which argues that it is, quite simply, impossible, to actually *ground* moral theory and that all attempts to do so are ultimately attempts to legitimate one or another set of social interests. The best we can hope for is an awareness of and respect for the radical otherness of other human beings—informed, presumably, by this deconstructionist critique. Postmodern ethics is, in other words, both groundless and empty—and proud of it.

This crisis of values has been accompanied, furthermore, by a crisis of confidence in humanity itself. It is now all but taken for granted that, even if were to arrive at reliable moral principles, human beings would be unable to act consistently as those principles require. For some this is the consequence of a religious conviction that human beings are marked by a radical sinfulness. For most, however, it is the consequence of what purports to be a scientific understanding of human nature based, variously, on sociobiology, psychoanalysis, and other disciplines. The phrase "it's just human nature" has become a thought-stopping excuse for every sort of moral weakness, individual and collective.

Recent years have, however, witnessed a new turn in the debate, as a number of thinkers have suggested that the failure of modern moral theory derives not so much from its residual foundationalism (its insistence on trying to ground moral claims) as from its secularism, or at least its failure to present a substantive vision of the Good. The most important of these include Alasdair MacIntyre's narrative virtue theory (MacIntyre 1984, 1988), John Milbank's radical orthodoxy (Milbank 1991, 1997, 1999), and Franklin Gamwell's reformed liberalism (Gamwell 1990, 2000). What these alternative theories all share is a commitment to an ethics informed by a substantive and ultimately transcendental doctrine of the Good; they differ in the ways in which they attempt to ground that doctrine. MacIntyre locates the source of all understandings of the Good in culturally specific narratives which present distinctive, compelling visions of human excellence and social justice. These narratives develop by means of a dialectical process catalyzed both by debates within traditions and encounters between them. Milbank goes further, arguing that the contradictions of modernity can be transcended only by revelation, and indeed by specifically Christian revelation which points towards an "Other City," informed by values radically at odds with both the ancient and the modern city, which he regards as little better than an armed camp in which individuals struggle against each other for wealth and power, and in which ethics has become little more than a set of rules for adjudicating this conflict. Gamwell, finally, argues that such rationally arbitrary attempts to reground ethics are inadequate, and proposes instead an ethics rooted in the process metaphysics and "neoclassical theism" of Whitehead and Hartshorne.

This work will argue with MacIntyre, Milbank, and Gamwell that modern (and postmodern) moral theory is fundamentally inadequate and that the current crisis of values can be resolved only on the basis of a substantive vision of the Good. What none of these alternative visions do, however, is to *explain* the moral crisis of modernity (and postmodernity), and the alternatives they offer are all flawed by this failure. By failing to comprehend the social basis of the modern turn, they render themselves unable to specify the conditions for actually transcending modernity. More specifically, I will argue that the modern and postmodern critiques of rational metaphysics and natural law were, in fact, essential preconditions for the rise to power of the two pre-eminently modern institutions: Capital and the sovereign nation-state. In the course of the struggle, philosophers (or rather anti-philosophers) allied with these institutions presented a variety of critiques arguing, variously, that we cannot know transcendentals, that the teleological science on which rational metaphysics had been based is no longer valid, or (most recently) that metaphysics itself is merely a strategy for power and the actual root of modernity and its discontents. The result has been, quite literally, the *demoralization* of society as Capital and State have swept away every authority which might stand in their way. Because MacIntyre, Milbank, and Gamwell fail to comprehend this dynamic, they advance alternatives which leave the authority (or rather the freedom) of Capital and State intact, and which fail to effectively ground an alternative.

Building on three earlier works—*Knowing God: Restoring Reason in an Age of Doubt, Knowing God: The Ultimate Meaningfulness of the*

Universe, and *Knowing God: The Journey of the Dialectic*, I will show that the supposed critiques of rational metaphysics are not nearly as powerful as they claim to be and that it is, in fact, quite possible to rise rationally (through and not around cosmology) to knowledge of a first principle on the basis of which the universe can be explained and human action and human society ordered. I will do the same for the pessimistic anthropology which is currently taken for granted in religious and secular circles alike, showing that human beings are naturally ordered to the Good. This will, in turn, make it possible to reground and revitalize what is, in effect, a natural law ethics. This natural law ethics will differ from earlier variants of natural law theory primarily in its recognition—based on a more historically oriented cosmology and sociology—that it is not only human individuals, but human societies and indeed the universe as a whole which grow and develop towards God and that the moral imperative must be understood to include and obligation to promote that development.

My method, then, will be dialectical in both the Socratic and the Marxist senses of that term. I will show that the critiques of rational metaphysics advanced by modern and postmodern theorists are at radically inadequate *and* that they reflect limited social interests which hold back human development and civilizational progress. Indeed, these two senses of the dialectic are intimately bound up together. Ideas which hold back human development and civilizational progress do so *because* they are inadequate; their inadequacy consists, ultimately, in hold back human development and civilizational progress.

The remainder of this chapter will be devoted to advancing the critique of modern and postmodern moral theory. We will begin situating both natural law theory, on the one hand, and modern moral theory on the other in their historical context. We will analyze the social interests behind the attack on natural law which began in the thirteenth century, and then show how modern—and postmodern—moral theory has served the interests of Capital and of the State. From there we will turn to an assessment of the alternatives offered by MacIntyre, Milbank, and Gamwell. Chapter 2 will turn to the task of actually regrounding natural law ethics in a dialectical metaphysics which can actually answer modern and postmodern critiques. Once this is done we face the challenge of answering modern pessimism regarding human nature. This will be task of Chapter 3, which will analyze and criticize both Augustinian and secular (sociobiological, psychoanalytic, and related) arguments for human depravity.

We will show that such theories violate the test of economy when asked to explain human development and civilizational progress. Evil, both human and cosmic, can more than adequately be accounted for by the fact that the drive towards growth and development, and thus towards the Good, which characterizes everything in the universe must struggle constantly with conditions of finitude, something which often results tragic failures, in choices for lesser goods, and to the eventual emergence of psychological and social structures which embody such orientations, but which also helps point the way beyond fulfillment of our finite human capacities towards authentic union with God.

When this is done we can turn at last to the question of human excellence. Chapter 4 will develop a comprehensive doctrine of virtue, looking systematically at both the acquired intellectual and moral virtues and at what the Catholic tradition historically called the theological or supernatural virtues of faith, hope, and charity and at the higher spiritual perfections. An analysis of the way in which we develop virtue will set the stage for a consideration in chapter 5 of the problems of law and social justice. We will look at the concept of law in general, showing the underlying unity of the concept and its applications in both the sciences and in ethics. We will then turn to the various types of law (eternal, natural, divine, and human) and to the concrete provisions of each. The result will be an ethics which provides ample grounds on which to challenge the market allocation of resources, but which also grounds and defends the principle of subsidiarity and thus such values as decentralization and individual and local initiative. It will point towards a new understanding of democracy as deliberation regarding the common good, at once values based and pluralistic in which there is room for both popular participation and conscious leadership. Finally, it will validate the role in human society of religious institutions, which serve at once as guarantors of natural law and as a catalyst for and guide in the development of our highest, superhuman capacities.

NATURAL LAW

Throughout most of human history, our ideas about the Good have been intimately bound up with our ideas about the nature of the universe itself. Humanity understood itself as an integral part of an organized, purposeful totality in which each element, including both individual human beings and human society taken as a whole, had a definite purpose. This sense of the cosmos as an ordered totality had its roots in the experience of life in a band, tribal, or village community, which formed a kind of microcosm of the universe as a whole, and thus provided the matrix of social relations which permitted the development of such concepts as whole and part, order and law, and eventually the concept of organization (Durkheim 1911, Bogdanov 1928/1980). Indeed, the Hellenic word κοσμος means "right order for the community," in the sense of the traditional order of the village, and the Slavic мир means «village community.» Both mean «universe,» in the sense of the organized totality of being (Bogdanov 1928/1980, Mandel 1968: 30–36, Wolf 1969: 58–63, Hayek 197: 37). The earliest human societies[1] recognized the universe itself as one vast interconnected system, regulated by the "perfect pattern of creation" (Waters 1968) which was less something imposed on the world by a transcendent creator god than something implicit in each and every thing, and above all in the harmonious relationships of all things with each other. This view of the world found its most typical (and most profound) symbolic expression in the cult of the *Magna Mater* who is at once, in the form of Demeter or Tonantzi, the profoundly material goddess of the earth and of its fruits and, as Isis, Sophia, or Sussistinako, the goddess of wisdom, the latent pattern from which all complex organization emerges.[2] Within this

---

1. Paleolithic, Neolithic, and early Bronze Age societies seem to have been of several types. Band societies consist of relatively fluid groups of human beings, generally engaged in hunting and gathering, for whom kinship relations or other formal structures play only a very limited role in defining division of labor, authority, etc. Tribal societies, which may be of a hunter-gatherer, pastoral nomadic, or raiding type, are structured primarily by kinship relations. Communitarian societies layer over this substratum of kinship relations the structures of a village community which brings together many different clans. Authority is increasingly vested in a formal, but not necessarily full time, religious leadership. Archaic societies group several villages around a common sanctuary or temple complex, which the villagers support voluntarily in return for knowledge which helps them to increase the level of agricultural productivity and for moral and spiritual leadership. Many of these societies—especially those which were communitarian or archaic—were also matriarchal or at least matrifocal (Engels 1880/1940, Stone 1976), giving women pride of place in the context of fundamentally egalitarian gender relations.

2. We should keep in mind that the word matter derives from the Latin *mater*, or mother. Originally matter referred simply to the *potential* for being, and thus for complex organization. It was only later, as patriarchy and the warlord state gained hold that this potentiality was transformed into simply a passive capacity to receive form from the outside—from the Father God, or his philosophical reflex: the Idea. In this sense, the

context value is nothing other than κοσμος itself, understood as harmony, order, and the realization by each element in the system of its purpose within the whole.

Gradually this sense of cosmic unity was undermined. Warlord states emerged which sought to enrich themselves with plunder and tribute and by taking slaves rather than by gradually perfecting the arts of civilization. The rise of warfare, which increased the economic significance of men and diminished that of women, undermined the archaic matriarchy, and the matrifocal religious traditions it had nurtured. Human society seemed increasingly out of harmony with the universe, and "form" only something which could be imposed on matter from the outside—as a conquering king imposes order on unwilling subjects (Childe 1851, Lenski 1982, Lerner 1991, Mansueto 1995). But always the village communities conserved some memory of the archaic harmony. The people resisted their oppressors and great teachers arose, prophets who called the people back to fidelity to the cosmic law. This is the layer of wisdom embodied in the prophetic traditions of earliest Israel, in Hesiod's *Theogony* and *Works and Days* and in the earliest layers of texts such as Chinese *Book of Ancient History* and the *I Ching*—texts from which the people continue to derive meaning and hope and moral guidance even today.

All this begins to change with the development of petty commodity production during the early Iron Age, between about 800 and 200 BCE. The market order tends increasingly to dissolve village communities and to make all human interactions simply a means of advancing individual consumption interests. People in a market society experience the world as a system of only externally related individuals—atoms—without αρχη or τελος, or else as a structured but ultimately meaningless system of quantities (prices). This undermines the basis in experience for knowing the Good and thus for the development of a connatural knowledge of God. Whole schools grew up which denied the ultimate meaningfulness

---

communitarian worldview was profoundly materialist, not in the modern sense of denying spirituality, but in the archaic sense of locating the capacity for spirituality within, rather than outside, the self-organizing universe.

Demeter, of course was the great grain goddess of the Mediterranean world and Tonantzi her counterpart among the Nahuatl of Mesoamerica. Isis was the Great Cosmic Librarian of the Egyptians and both in her own right and as the rather more abstract Sophia became the great Mediterranean goddess of wisdom. Sussistinako is the Keres "thinking woman," she who "thought outward into space and what she thought became reality" (Tyler 1964: 89. On the cult of the Magna Mater cf. Stone 1976, Matthews 1991).

of the universe and which reduced morality to a matter of convention or personal preference. Thus the Sophists and Skeptics, the Atomists and Epicureans in the Mediterranean Basin; thus the Caravakas in India and the Legalists in China (Collins 1998).

There should therefore be little wonder that it is in just precisely such societies that we witness the advent of a new way to Wisdom and a new way of grounding ethics: rational metaphysics or the *via dialectica*, which attempts to ascend by means of rational argument to the principle which before human beings knew by means of an experiential and preconceptual knowledge. Between roughly 800 and 200 BCE we witness the development of something like a rational metaphysics in all those centers of civilizational development undergoing a transition to petty commodity production: the Mediterranean Basin, India, China, and Southeast Asia. The resulting metaphysical systems in turn provided a firm foundation for a renewed moral discourse. Plato's Good, Aristotle's Unmoved Mover, the *Brahman* of the Upanishads, the *Tai Ch'i* (Great Ultimate) or *T'ien li* (Heavenly Principle) of the Confucians and the *Wu-Ch'i* (Unlimited) or *Tao* of the Taoists—and, in a very different way, the Buddhist doctrine of *pattica sammupada* or dependent origination—all provide a criterion in terms of which not only can the universe be explained but human action and human society ordered.[3]

---

3. These two periods—the crisis of the tributary social formations of the late Bronze Age and the emergence of petty commodity production during the early Iron Age correspond roughly to Karl Jasper's "axial era" (Jaspers 1953), during which humanity seems to have become suddenly aware that there was something very wrong with the way in which their societies were developing and appealed, for the first time, to specifically *transcendental* principles of value. My approach differs in a number of ways from Jaspers'. First, my periodization is rooted in an analysis of structural changes in the organization of human society. Second, I believe it is useful to distinguish between the still predominantly imaginative language of the prophets of the late bronze age and the increasingly abstract language of the sages of the early Iron Age. Third, I reject Jaspers' implication that prior to his axial age peoples knew nothing of transcendental principles of value. On the contrary, I would argue, they simply saw less contradiction between these principles and the structures of the societies in which they lived, so that their societies, and indeed their rulers, could be credibly regarded as embodying those principles by way of hierocratic and sacral monarchic forms of governance. It is the growing rapacity of the rulers and the alienating impact of emerging market relations which, in two distinct stages and in different ways undermines this sense of unity and *demands* and appeal to the transcendental.

Readers who are unfamiliar with these nonwestern metaphysical traditions may want to consult Chatterjee and Datta 1954, Radhakrishnan and Moore 1957, Yao 2000, Ching 2000, Williams 1989, and Kalupahana 1992.

Sometimes these metaphysical traditions stood on their own, as the case of Confucianism and the more elite schools of Buddhism; more often they merged back with myth and prophecy to form the great religious systems of the long middle ages.[4] In either case they provided a firm foundation for moral discourse.

While there was significant diversity among the resulting metaphysical and religious systems, they all shared a common approach to ethical theory. What one ought to do was determined by the way in which the universe, or indeed reality itself, was organized. Thus the metaphysics of *Esse* or of the "necessary existent" developed by Ibn Sina and Thomas Aquinas and the metaphysics of the Great Ultimate developed by Chu Hsi might pull more towards an ethics of self-cultivation, and the metaphysics *sunyata* or emptiness elaborated in the *Prajnamaramita Sutra* and the Madyamika commentaries to an ethics of detachment, but both systems put forward types of *natural law* ethics in the sense that the moral imperative depends more or less directly on one's understanding of the organization of the universe. The only real exception to this was among the most uncompromising of the monotheists—the Asharites in Islam, for example, and the most extreme Augustinians—who tended more towards a divine command ethics.

Rational metaphysics and natural law ethics did, furthermore, legitimate the emergence of institutions which, while far from perfect, significantly reigned in the rapacity of the ruling classes and which helped redirect resources away from warfare and luxury consumption and towards activities which promote the development of human capacities—the arts, sciences, philosophy, and religion. This pattern was most obvious in those traditions which were most inner-worldly— Confucianism and Islam. The Confucian ideal of the sage king transformed successive dynasties of warlords into civilized rulers who at least part of the time ruled with the interest of the people in mind and thus

---

4. As I have argued elsewhere, the global middle ages should be understood to begin not with the sack of Rome in 476, which was an event of only regional importance, but rather with the completion of the Silk Road around 200 BCE, which integrated most of Eurasia into a global petty commodity economy governed by a shifting network of large territorial empires. At the ideological level this is the point at which the age of "prophets and sages" gives way to the age of systematic metaphysics and theology of the sort represented by Neoplatonism and Aristotelianism (as the basis of either neopagan or monotheistic theologies), of the Hindu *darshanas* and the Buddhist metaphysical schools, and of Confucian-Taoist scholasticism in China (Collins 1998).

made China the most advanced civilization on the planet. The Islamic institution of the *zakat*, similarly, because it shifted the tax burden from the poor to the rich and centralized the resources necessary for civilization building, allowed a marginal group of desert traders to liberate most of the Mediterranean Basin and much of Africa and Asia from what was left of the Roman Empire and from successor warlord states and build the planet's second most advanced civilization in just two centuries. But even more otherworldly religions such as Buddhism and Christianity ended up by transforming the world they rejected. One need only consider the social reforms instituted by King Ashoka in India, the role of the medieval papacy as a guarantor of natural law or the role of monasteries in both traditions as engines of economic development.[5]

There were, to be sure, limitations to this approach. Humanity seemed but a limited and insignificant element in the great cosmic system, and as a result natural law doctrine tended to emphasize harmony with the pre-existing order of the cosmos rather than humanity's potential to contribute to the cosmohistorical evolutionary process. The prophetic and philosophical movements which created the natural law traditions, did not, furthermore, wholly transcend the patriarchal structure of the warlord states which they were resisting. Even as they called humanity back to the archaic harmonies, they tended to treat this harmony as something imposed on matter from the outside.[6] This "idealistic" tendency left the tradition open to authoritarian deformations. The advantages of natural law ethics over later divine command, liberal, and "postmodern" value theory should, however, be obvious. Unlike these doctrines, natural law theory offers a substantive vision of what it means to be an excellent hu-

---

5. Presenting a rigorous argument for the claims made in this paragraph is the focus of my forthcoming work *Knowing God: The Journey of the Dialectic*. For a briefer argument see my "The Journey of the Dialectic" in *Fealsunacht* 1 (Mansueto 2000) and "Seeking Wisdom and Doing Justice" in *Seeking Wisdom* 1 (Mansueto 2003), as well as *Spirituality and Dialectics* (Mansueto and Mansueto 2005).

6. Mary Daly (Daly 1984) makes a convincing case that the Aristotelian tradition represents a patriarchal appropriation and deformation of an archaic "gynocentric" wisdom. Similar research is needed into humanity's other wisdom traditions. There were, to be sure, a few exceptions to this patriarchal pattern. The Joachites of Southern Europe, the Radical Aristotelians of what is now Northern France and Belgium—David of Dinant, Amalric of Bena, and Siger of Brabant—and certain of Rhineland mystics, especially Meister Eckhardt, all interpreted the tradition in a way which was materialistic, in the sense of recognizing the self-organizing capacity of matter, and/or panentheistic so that the patriarchal-idealist dynamic was suppressed or at least restricted.

man being, and of what sort of society cultivates such excellence, a vision rooted in rational knowledge of our own nature as human beings and of the nature of the universe which we inhabit. Right, virtue, and justice, are not something imposed on human beings from the outside, but rather the realization of our own latent potential for the Good.

THE AUGUSTINIAN REACTION

The metaphysical foundations of natural law ethics have, however, come increasingly under attack over the course of the past 750 years. Indeed, there is no discipline which has been more uniformly derided for a longer period than rational metaphysics. Of the ancient and medieval sciences which have now fallen into disrepute, even astrology and alchemy get better press. Declared impossible (at least as it had traditionally been understood) by Kant (Kant 1781/1969), its assertions were determined to be logically meaningless by Ayer (Ayer 1937). Even the materialist wing of the dialectical tradition has turned against metaphysics, arguing that the universe can be explained adequately in terms of purely material principles (Engels 1880/1940), while others argue that "modern science" has determined the universe to be ultimately meaningless (Krause 1999). Finally, beginning in the middle of the nineteenth century a diverse group of philosophers—or rather antiphilosophers (Kierkegaard 1848, Nietzsche 1889, Heidegger 1928/1968, Ayer 1937, Arendt 1958, Levinas 1965, Derrida 1967/1978)—began to argue that metaphysics,[7] quite apart

---

7. The terminology here is tricky. Most of the critics of a rational ascent to first principles of explanation and action have, at least since Heidegger, called the discipline they criticize "metaphysics" or "ontotheology," and used another term for their own doctrine of the self disclosure of Being, the laws of motion of matter, etc. (ontology, dialectics). A few, however, (e.g., Levinas) call the discipline that they criticize it by some other name (e.g., ontology), and reserve the term metaphysics for their own doctrine. The Marxist tradition presents particularly difficult terminological problems. Some Soviet philosophy, for example, explicitly rejects metaphysics on the grounds of one or another version of the cosmological critique, but advances just precisely the sort of universal explanatory-causal theory which Heideggerrian critics call metaphysical. This is especially true of Bogdanov and Deborin who, as we will see, actually tended to a materialist pantheism. Other Marxists, (e.g., Bhaskar) use the term metaphysics in the disciplinary sense to describe a general inquiring into being, while eschewing the incipient materialist pantheism of the Soviets for an ontology centered on negativity, contradiction, and absence (Bhaskar 1993). Still others reject the term entirely, counterposing it dialectics (Mao 1937a/1971, Amin 1988/1989, 1999).

For the purposes of this book "metaphysics" means any attempt to ascend rationally to a first principle of explanation and action. This includes immanent principles, such as the

from whether one believes it to be epistemologically possible or impossible, scientifically founded or not is, in fact, at the very root of a plethora of social evils, from technological domination through patriarchy, imperialism, and totalitarianism to atheism and despair. It is not only, or not so much, that we no longer *can* do metaphysics as that we never *ought* to have tried in the first place.

The result of this "crisis of metaphysics" has also been a crisis of the natural law ethics which depends on it. Without a substantive doctrine of the Good, or some other substantive principle of value, it is simply impossible to do natural law ethics.

What is the basis of this attack? John Milbank (Milbank 1991, 1999) provides an important clue, pointing to the Scotist doctrine of the univocity of being as a critical turning point in this regard. Thomas and most of his Platonist and Aristotelian predecessors had understood the difference between God and the universe as qualitative. God is *esse*, the power of Being as such; contingent or created beings participate in this act of Being. This at once rendered everything sacred—because everything participates in the divine act of Being—and rendered impossible and even ludicrous the idea of a human assault on the throne of heaven. We call this an analogical metaphysics. If, however, the difference between God and the universe is *quantitative*—if both exist in the same way, and differ only in that God is infinite and everything else finite, then it is quite possible for human beings (and especially for humanity collectively) to become divine simply by means of building power. We call this a univocal metaphysics. There is thus a contradiction, which is foreign to the Thomistic tradition, between divine transcendence and human self-development. For those who understand God as infinite power, human self-development, if not in itself wrong, can easily over-reach itself and become rebellion against divine sovereignty, and thus cannot become the basis for an ethics. Thus the turn, which we see in marked form in Scotus (Boler 1993, Ingham 1993), towards a divine command ethics. For those less concerned with divine sovereignty (even if they remain theistic in some sense) the human drive to *become* God by understanding and gaining control of the

---

"laws of motion of matter" where they are conceived in such a way as to order all things to an end—e.g., the development of increasingly complex forms of organization. It does not include doctrines which, while treating of being in general deny the existence of such a first principle. Doctrines which, like Bhaskar's, argue for a purely negative first principle (absence) sit right on the borderline of our definition.

universe becomes the basis for a new civilizational ideal. This is, in fact *the* civilizational ideal of modernity, liberal and socialist. In this sense, the turn towards a univocal metaphysics *defines* the modern alternative between fundamentalism and (liberal or socialist) modernism. From this point of view modernity (and postmodernity) are not so much about a rejection of metaphysics as they are about a shift from an analogical to a univocal metaphysics.

What Milbank fails to do is to explain why the new doctrine of the univocity of being emerged and gained currency in the first place. In order to answer this question it is necessary, first of all, to point out that while Milbank is quite correct to date the emergence of at least a partial consensus in favor or a univocal metaphysics to the fourteenth century or later, the turn in fact begins much earlier. Graham MacAleer (MacAleer 1996), for example, has shown a similar concern with human over-reaching in the ethics of Anselm of Canterbury. This is especially significant in light of the fact that it is Anselm, above all, who puts forwards a "quantitative" concept of God as "that than which nothing greater can be thought." I have shown elsewhere that his ontological argument is convertible[8] with a mathematical proposition known as Zorn's Lemma (Mansueto 2002b), which has never been proven. Similar concern for divine sovereignty can be found in Stephen Tempier's condemnations of Aristotelian science in 1270 and 1277 (Duhem 1911). And it is, of course, easier to arrive at a strong doctrine of original sin on the basis of a univocal metaphysics, which cannot help but pit human beings against God and against each other, than on the basis of an analogical metaphysics which does not. Because of this I am inclined to believe that the doctrine of the univocity of being is rather deeply embedded in the whole Pauline and Augustinian tradition, even if Augustine himself, and some medieval Augustinian thinkers such as Bernard and perhaps Bonaventura at times transcended it.

Let us explore this thesis in greater depth. Augustinian philosophy begins with a critique of skepticism, something which would seem to place him squarely in the party of meaning and hope and which he himself no doubt saw as an extension of the work of Socrates and Plato. Augustine argues in essentially the same way Descartes would later. It is quite possible that our senses deceive us, but in order to be deceived we

---

8. The term "convertible" is a technical term in Thomistic philosophy. It means that two terms refer to the same thing under a different aspect.

must first exist (Augustine, *The City of God* 11:26; Descartes. *Meditations*). This means that there is at least *one* thing we know with certainty, thus defeating the program of the radical skeptics.

This initial success, however, raises the specter of solipsism, which is avoided only by proceeding more or less immediately to an argument for the existence of God. The basic thrust of the argument is simple. We have in our minds the idea of God—that is, of Being, which is infinite, perfect, necessary and so on. Clearly this idea does not arise directly from the rational self-knowledge we have in the *cogito* or from whatever vague knowledge we may derive from the senses, since in both cases the knowledge in question is of a finite system. But the idea must come from somewhere, indeed it must come from something capable of producing the idea of infinite, perfect, necessary Being. But only Being itself could explain the presence of this idea. Thus we have an immediate rational intuition of God. This knowledge of God then guarantees the objectivity of our knowledge of finite systems, which are either seen in the mind of God, or for those more concerned to safeguard divine transcendence, such as Augustine himself, in a divine light which bathes the intellect, revealing the intelligible properties of things just as natural light reveals their sensible properties. Indeed, the fact that we know anything changeless and eternal, such as the Pythagorean theorem or other mathematical formalizations, was for Augustine evidence of an eternal light which made such knowledge possible, and thus evidence for the existence of God. Later Augustinians (Anselm. *Proslogion*) added to this what eventually became known as the ontological argument:

1. God is that than which nothing greater can be thought.
2. When we hear this idea we already have it in our intellect.
3. But it is greater for something to exist in reality as well as in our intellect as for it to exist in our intellect alone.
4. God, therefore, must exist.

Or, in Descartes' version:

1. God is perfect.
2. Perfection includes existence.
3. Therefore God exists.

The question, of course, is the extent to which the resulting metaphysics is univocal. We should concede, to begin, that Augustine's theory of knowledge, while it has serious deficiencies (Mansueto 2002b) is not incompatible with an *analogical* metaphysics centered on objective, transcendental principles of value. On the contrary, what we "see" in the divine light might well be God understood as Being, Beauty, Truth, Good, Integrity, etc. This is at least one possible reading of Plato's position in the *Republic*, it is almost certainly the position of Hellenistic Neo-Platonism, both pagan and Christian, and it is clearly what Augustine was aiming at. Nor is it surprising that Milbank would qualify this approach to knowledge of God as *theological* rather than as a strictly autonomous, rational metaphysics. Thomists have always criticized the illumination theory for its failure to distinguish clearly between natural and supernatural knowledge.

But something else is up with Augustine, something which is more apparent in the *City of God* and in the polemics with the Pelagians and the Donatists than it is, say, in his more strictly philosophical writings or in the *Confessions*. Indeed, in order to understand Augustine, we must remember his characterization of the supreme Good as *Tranquilitas Ordinis*. There may well have been an Augustine who was passionately in love with Being as such, and who read his own promiscuous youth as a misguided attempt to find in contingent beings what only Being itself could give him. But there is also the Augustine who was a member of the provincial ruling classes at once disillusioned with the Roman Empire and frightened by its collapse and desperately searching for a new principle of order. And it is this Augustine who dominates the later Augustinian tradition—who sees in the love of creatures not a sacramental participation in the love of God but a threat to the dignity of the divine sovereign, who regards human beings (in love as we are with ourselves and other creatures) as thus marked by original sin, and who ends his live in utter despair regarding the prospects for the human civilizational project. It is this Augustine who, despairing of the possibility of an actually virtuous clergy vested religious authority in office rather than excellence and despairing of the possibility of an actually Christian society argues that the conquest and indeed the enslavement, of the "lovers of pleasure" by the "lovers of honor" is actually a good thing, because it supplies for them at least a measure (albeit never a salvific measure) of discipline (Augustine 429/1972).

Augustinian Christianity, we should remember, never really found a following in its original, North African home. The Church's repression of the Donatists—something accomplished with no small aid from Augustine—left Libya, Numidia, and Mauritania ripe for the Arab conquests. Nor did Augustinianism ever really sink deep roots in Celtic or Latin Europe. Popular Catholicism has always been at least semi-Pelagian. There were, however, two groups which found Augustinian doctrine attractive. Augustinian political theology provided those Germanic warlords who were anxious to settle down with at least a limited and conditional legitimation of their authority—as guarantors of the temporal order.[9] It also provided the Roman hierarchy with a separate and, in a sense, superior claim to authority which was not, however, dependent on real spiritual excellence. The warlords kept order; those who held a priesthood on the basis of office mediated the divine grace which alone made salvation possible.

In this sense it is possible to argue that Augustine's metaphysics functioned as both univocal and analogical. The concern for order pointed towards a univocal metaphysics which legitimated the authority of the Germanic warlords, who restrained the power of Satan on earth just as Christ, the Heavenly King, had bound Satan in Hell. The concern for sacramental grace, on the other hand, pointed towards an analogical metaphysics, in terms alone of which the whole concept of sacrament made sense.

Later Augustinian theology develops both aspects of Augustine's thought. One can find in Bonaventure's teachings on divine illumination an echo of the Platonic Augustine who was passionately in love with Being and desperately searching for a way to know Her. The doctrine of the *ratones seminales* also speaks of the presence of the divine in the created. Bernard, similarly, shows an understanding of the dynamics of love which only a true lover of Being could have developed. Even so, it is central to

---

9. The Germanic peoples, according to Georges Dumezil (Dumezil 1952) appear to have had no permanent, full time priesthood. Authority belonged to those warriors who could, by their shear prowess, gain the support of loyal followers with whom it was expected they would share the spoils of battle. It is quite natural, therefore, that they tended to give priority to the temporal over the spiritual authority and eventually theorized Jesus as a sort of triumphant warrior sharing freely with those who placed their faith in him the "booty" of his war with Satan—salvation and eternal life. This fully Germanic Christianity incubates, as it were, during the Middle Ages and comes into its own only with Luther.

Bonaventure's agenda, to limit the role of human reason in knowledge of God and of intermediate causes in the production of creatures and Bernard, like Augustine, pits the love of God against the love of creatures in a way which calls radically into question his Catholic sacramentality. Both are well on their way to being world-hating Protestants.

Medieval Catholicism was, in fact, characterized by an equilibrium between these two metaphysical perspectives, as it was by a sort of stalemate in the struggle between Church and State, papacy and empire. In the twelfth and thirteenth century, however, this struggle intensified and the stalemate was eventually broken in favor of the State—and of an entirely new force, the emerging bourgeoisie. In order to understand this we must remember that Europe was essentially a backwater the largely undeveloped if perhaps not underdeveloped periphery of the Afro-Eurasian world system. One measure of this is the relative size of European universities and those elsewhere. The size of universities measures the capacity of a society to support people in activities which do not contribute directly to material production, and thus their capacity to generate a social surplus product. In 1250 the largest university in Europe was that at Paris, which had roughly 600 students. During roughly the same period the Islamic university at Timbuktu—by no means the largest in *Dar-al-Islam*—had 25,000 (www.timbuktufoundation.org/university.html).

Europe had been growing rapidly, however. Feudalism, whatever its limitations, did allow peasants to keep a part of what they produced and thus encouraged innovation in agriculture. The alpine plow, the three-field system, and greater use of animal and water power led to an increase in agrarian yields from about 4:1 in 500 CE to about 9:1 in 1000 CE. Population increased accordingly, as did the portion of the population which could be employed in nonagricultural activities. The guild system, meanwhile, because it regulated prices meant that craftsmen could compete only on the basis of quality. The result was a developing craft production which eventually allowed Europe to enter the global market as an exporter of dyed wool clothe and other craft goods (Anderson 1974).

On the one hand, this made Europe (and not merely its Mediterranean Rim), a real civilizational center for the first time. Human beings developed an intense sense of their own creativity and thus their participation in the creative life of God. In the rural areas this found expression in the Benedictine ethos of *ora et lavora*; in the cities it provided a constituency for the Aristotelian philosophy imported from *Dar-al-Islam*, and especially for the metaphysics of *esse* which Thomas borrowed from Ibn Sina and made the centerpiece of a fundamentally new theology. While the clergy, much of which was allied with local warlords, was ambivalent regarding these developments, the papacy embraced Thomism which, among other things, provided a more adequate philosophical and theological foundation than did Augustinianism for the developing claim that the hierarchy generally and the papacy in particular enjoy an "indirect authority" over temporal rulers as guarantors not only of revealed truth and divine law, but also of the natural law, so that laws which violated the rational norms of justice could be overturned and rulers who consistently violated them removed (Innocent III, *Sicut universitatis conditor, Verabilem fratrem*; Boniface VIII, *Unam Sanctum, Clericos Laicos*; Thibault 1971). The Thomistic metaphysics of *esse*, furthermore, provided a far more adequate foundation for Catholic sacramental theology by making everything, in so far as it *is*, a real participation in the life of God.

At the same time, the expansion of the areas under cultivation led, by the middle of the twelfth century if not earlier, led to land shortages. These were not so much *absolute* shortages in the sense that the carrying capacity of the land was being pushed, but rather relative shortages engendered by feudal landholding patterns. The law of primogeniture, followed in varying degrees by most European warlord families, meant that nearly the whole of a lord's land was bequeathed to his eldest son. Dowries were provided for daughters and perhaps for a second son who chose to enter a monastery or who was able to obtain a senior clerical post. The other sons were sent to be trained as knights and to serve as retainers for other lords. The lived in their lord's castle as "knights bachelor" until such time as their lord was able and saw fit to grant them a fief, after which they could settle down, marry, and have children. The difficulty is that as the land under cultivation was extended so too was the land which was already enfoefed. This meant more knights bachelor—and what amounted to a sort of aristocratic gang problem, as these armed, unmarried young men did what such men have always done, preying on women and peasants and generally undermining the social order.

Many aspects of medieval culture can be traced to efforts to address this problem. The codes of chivalry were no doubt, at least in part, an attempt to control armed men by ideological means. But a shortage of land and a surplus of armed men in the long run could only mean one thing: pressure for conquest. This dynamic was already becoming signifi-

The Crisis of Values

cant in the eleventh century with the beginning of the crusades and with the Norman conquest of Britain. These "greater crusades" were eventually extended to al-Andalus, to Africa, to the Americas, and to Asia.[10]

These conquests had two results. First, they gradually improved the position of Europe in the global trade networks and provided the "first installment" as it were in the primitive accumulation of capital, which led eventually to the emergence of an authentic bourgeoisie and to the industrial revolution. Second, wars of conquest helped bring into being strong monarchies which gradually put forward claims to sovereignty which were hitherto unheard of in Europe. Indeed, it is *only* in those regions of Europe which were touched significantly by these conquests that we see early developments in the direction of the sovereign nation states: England, which was formed by the Norman Conquest of Britain, France, where the monarchy played a leading role in organizing the crusades, and Spain, which was the product of the *Reconquista*. Elsewhere state formation lagged, sometimes well into the nineteenth century.

It was above all the emerging monarchies and elements in the clergy close to them which sponsored the continued development of Augustinian philosophy and theology. And the result was to bring to the fore the *implicit* univocity which had always been latent in Augustinian metaphysics. Thus the attacks on Aristotle and Thomas by Stephen Tempier, who was allied with the emerging French monarchy, and by Robert Kilwardy, his English counterpart, on both the Radical Aristotelians and on Thomas; thus Scotus, whose Franciscan movement was, we must remember, objectively aligned with the Empire and against the Popes. The monarchies were assisted—and eventually overtaken—in this struggle by the emerging bourgeoisie, which also needed to be "emancipated" from natural law if it was to prosecute its struggle for profit and for the accumulation of capital without restraint.

The univocal metaphysics which defines modernity radically altered the underlying problem facing ethical theory. For an analogical metaphysics there is, quite simply, no contradiction between the full development of my capacities *properly understood* and the full development of every-

---

10. The institutional and ideological continuity between the crusades, the *Reconquista*, and the conquest of the Americas is well established. Ramon Guttieriez (Guttieriez 1990) for example points out that the office which financed pacification of the Indians in New Mexico in the seventeenth century was called *la cruzada* and that the Spanish regarded the indigenous peoples of the Americas as "Moors."

thing else in the universe. This is because what all things seek is, quite simply, the undivided and inexhaustible power of *esse* as such. Ethics is all about understanding properly what we seek. For a univocal metaphysics, on the other hand, the universe is a zero-sum game. While it is *possible* for me to grow and develop in ways that do not take away from others, it is also quite possible for the development of two systems, even when rightly understood, to come into conflict. Ethics is more about containing human over-reaching than it is about combating ignorance.

For medieval thought this problem was framed in terms of the *casu diaboli*, the "case of the devil" (MacAleer 1996). The question was, quite simply, how Lucifer, who had a clear vision of the divine good unclouded by sensuality, could possibly have chosen a lesser over a higher good. The answer given by more Augustinian thinkers, such as Anselm and Duns Scotus (Boler 1993, Ingham 1993), is that he did not. He chose exactly as a good Aristotelian would have advised: he chose to *be* God, a choice which led him into fatal rebellion against his rightful divine sovereign. This is taken to show that, at least under some circumstances, choosing the full development of one's capacities can, in fact, be sinful.

This reasoning led Scotus—who advanced the most complete and consistent form of this ethics—to make a distinction between the *affectio commodi* and the *affectio justiae*. The first seeks its own development, the second what is right. When my development comes into conflict with that of another, I am obliged to do as God commands, loving my neighbor as myself and God above all.

Just what loving my neighbor as myself means is, to be sure, open to question. Some contemporary thinkers (MacAleer 1996) see in Anselm, whose analysis is similar to that of Scotus, the basis for a postmodern ethics of *caritas* understood as respect for the radical otherness of the Other, not unlike that elaborated by Levinas (Levinas 1965). This approach is coherent with much Lutheran ethics, which stresses the centrality of the message of divine forgiveness, and with some contemporary Catholic teaching, which focuses on respect for the human person. The Reformed tradition, on the other hand, has given the notion a more activist reading. Consider, for example, Jonathan Edwards' claim that true virtue consists in a love of benevolence towards Being in General, an ethos reflected in practice in an active commitment to social reform (Edwards 1765/1957).

There are a number of difficulties with this approach to ethics. First, its analysis of the *casu diaboli* is flawed, just as one would expect it to be given the faulty univocal metaphysics on which it depends. Lucifer was not wrong in wanting to be God; he simply misunderstood the sense in which this was possible and the proper way of achieving it. To become God *essentially* is quite impossible for any contingent being; the line between *esse* as such and contingent being is absolute and cannot be crossed. What we can do is to become God *intentionally* and *accidentally* by means of *knowing God*, both theoretically, through philosophy and theology, and connaturally and experientially through the just act. This later love, which is the basis of infused contemplation and of the beatific vision, comes when we love God and our neighbor with God's own love and thus partake in the divine nature itself. Another way of putting this would be to say that we become God to the extent that we share in God's creative activity, something which promotes—in fact constitutes—our development *and* that of others. Lucifer sins first, as we do, in the intellect, precisely by his option for a metaphysics which permits essential divinization, which leads him to believe that he can become God simply by amassing knowledge and power and thus mounting an assault on the throne of heaven.

Second, it is a mistake to see in an Augustinian ethics, whether Catholic, Lutheran, or Reformed, a real alternative to secularism. On the contrary, the moral problematic constituted by a univocal metaphysics is the very foundation of secularism. This point requires some further elaboration. Thomistic ethics, and indeed most of the broadly "natural law" systems which dominated Silk Road societies, regarded the intellectual and moral virtues as closely associated with each other. More specifically wisdom, understood as knowing first principles or the ends of human life, together with prudence, knowing the means to those ends, were regarded as conducive to moral excellence. Knowing the higher good, and knowing how to pursue it, at once made that higher good more vivid, and informed us regarding the practices necessary to overcome bad habits and develop good ones. This is not to suggest that the wise do not sin, but there was a presumption that those who devote their lives to seeking and teaching wisdom will in fact be globally more developed human beings than those who devote their lives to warfare or moneymaking. This gave clerics, monastics, and scholars the moral authority necessary to hold rulers and merchants accountable before the court of justice, and in general tended to subordinate the secular to the religious without in anyway denying that the secular, too participates in the life of God.

Augustinian moral theories, on the other hand, radically divide intellectual development from moral virtue. Wisdom may help us understand what is right; it does not directly help us to act justly. This, in turn, reduces masters of wisdom to a purely ministerial role, and strips them of even indirect authority over temporal rulers. And even where there has been an attempt to develop an institutionalized mechanism for identifying the "elect" or "morally superior" the criteria used inevitably place the laity on a par with the clergy, or perhaps even give them an edge. Thus, in the Reformed tradition, evangelicals have contested with liberals for nearly four centuries over the relative importance of internal criteria such as a convincing narrative of a conversion experience, or external criteria such as usefulness to the community. But lay Christians are every bit as capable of conversion or productivity as are the clergy. The effect has been to undercut efforts on the part of the clergy to hold temporal rulers—and more importantly the bourgeoisie—accountable for their injustices. This is a lesson which Jonathan Edwards, who combined a Reformed theology with a high view of the role of clergy in society, learned the hard way.[11]

This is not to suggest that an Augustinian ethics provides no criterion on the basis of which either warfare or moneymaking can be criticized. On the contrary, many radical Christian critiques of social injustice have been motivated by an Augustinian ethics of *caritas*. The difficulty is that *either* this critique leads to a sort of holy war of annihilation *or* it is blunted by credible critiques of the moral character of the revolutionaries themselves. What Augustinianism fails to do is to ground credible intellectual moral authorities who can hold potential oppressors accountable *without* a resort to holy war.

MODERN MORAL THEORY

Liberal Theory

RATIONALISM

Given this analysis, it should not surprise us to find that the boundaries between divine command ethics anxious to protect the sovereignty of God

---

11. Edwards, who spent the early years of his ministry leading revivals among the youth of the Connecticut River Valley, who were frustrated by the lack of access to land and thus given to some mild antisocial behavior, was eventually removed from his pulpit by his own (now adult) converts when he began challenge their efforts to grab Indian land (Tracy 1980).

and modern liberalism are not nearly so well-defined as contemporary secular moral theorists are apt to claim. It is interesting, in this regard, to look at modern rationalism, which represents a kind of middle position between earlier forms of divine command ethics and later liberalism. We have already shown that Descartes, for example, begins at exactly the same point as Augustine, with an immanent critique of skepticism which, with some generosity, we might say he borrowed. Modern rationalism, however, has tended to pull away from the illumination theory in favor of an attempt to ground knowledge on what it claims are analytically self-evident first principles from which rational deductions can then be made. Thus Descartes, after proving his own existence and that of God, argues that a perfect being would not have created us with faulty senses, thus grounding the validity of sense data and evading the necessity of an appeal to divine illumination. This shift does not, however, alter the way in which Descartes grounds moral judgment. Like Duns Scotus he argues that morality is ultimately dependent on the divine will (Descartes 1641/1998). God could have created a universe governed by any moral norms which he wished. That He created one ordered to human excellence and human happiness is the result of a free and sovereign choice on His part. This virtue and happiness is furthered by means of knowledge of God, of the soul, and of the physical universe. Knowledge of God is knowledge of the principle which creates and governs all things. Knowledge of the soul is knowledge of our capacity to transcend the material world. Knowledge of the physical universe allows us to manipulate and control the world for our own benefit, while teaching us subordination to the divinely sanctioned laws by which it is governed. Similar reasoning can be found in Malebranche (Malebranche 1674/1980, 1684/1977, 1687/1980), somewhat radicalized and in Rosmini (Rosmini 1841/1993), somewhat moderated. It should not surprise to discover that Descartes was favored over Thomas in seminaries which operated under the *de facto* control of the French absolutist state, which was anxious to protect is autonomy from Rome (Thibault 1971). Descartes' divine sovereign looks far more like a heavenly monarch than like a spiritual father dedicated to the development of his children. What is demanded by his ethics is, quite simply, submission to the will of God on no ground other than its infinite power. That this power may endow us with certain rights, or manifest itself in a loving manner, does not alter the underlying dynamic which is, in the final analysis, every bit as relativistic as the most extreme postmodernism. And it is far from clear why command by a powerful being, even a singularly powerful being, makes something obligatory. By this reasoning what Hitler commanded would at least have been *more* obligatory than the silent pleas of his victims.

Similar, if more moderate tendencies towards a divine command ethics are evident in Leibniz. Leibniz argues that the universe is composed of distinct monads, some rational and some not, which are maintained in a pre-existent harmony by the coordinating activity of God, who is at once the author and sovereign monarch of the universe. The Good consists first and foremost in this harmony, which produces pleasure for all rational creatures, and right action is action which is in accord with and helps to promote it. Indeed, humanity seems to play a critical role for in Leibniz in God's plan for the perfection of the universe. We thus find here a more dynamic conception of both the universe and of humanity than we saw in Descartes. Indeed, Leibniz clearly aims at rebuilding something like the old Aristotelian teleology on the foundation of the new mathematical physics. This physics does not, however, allow such a conclusion. Rather than an organic conception of the universe as growing naturally towards God, Leibniz gives us a universe of monads directed externally by God towards a perfection in which they remain always and forever subjects. Leibniz is careful to avoid making explicit the voluntarist implications of his approach, but they are inevitable. Indeed, it is not difficult to see in Leibniz and implicit justification for royal regulatory power during the era of emerging capitalism.

We find a rather different implementation of the rationalist program in Spinoza. Spinoza begins with a number of definitions and axioms and—skipping over the *cogito* entirely—proceeds through analysis of the idea of substance (something which can be conceived in and through itself, independently of any other conception) to a proof of the existence of God and of the identity between God and the universe. All particular systems are simply modifications of God; thought and extension are those two of the infinite divine attributes of which we are able to conceive (Spinoza 1675/1955). The difficulty, of course, is that Spinoza, unlike the Augustinians, has not really answered the skeptics. How do we know that "substance" exists at all? The analytic argument presented in Proposition VII of Part One of the *Ethics*—that existence belongs to the notion of substance—simply begs the question. What Spinoza actually proves here is that if anything exists at all, something exists necessarily—and is, therefore, divine. He has not, however, shown that anything exists. Spinoza's real answer to the question comes only in Part Two, Proposition XVIII, where he acknowledges that *we* know that something exists because our bodies are modified in certain ways by other bodies. Our knowledge of the universe, in other words, derives from sensation of finite particulars, from which we *infer* the existence of God.

Once again, the difference between God and finite modes is purely quantitative. God is at once infinite and the whole; the modes are finite and particular. There is no sense here that God *is* in anyway different from particular things.

It is thus not surprising that Spinoza's ethics is first and foremost an ethics of *power*. "To act absolutely in obedience to virtue is in us the same thing as to act, to live, or preserve one's being (these terms are identical in meaning) in accordance with the dictates of reason on the basis of seeking what is useful to one's self" (Spinoza, *Ethics,* Part IV, Proposition XXIV).

There are, to be sure, aspects of Spinoza's doctrine which have lead some to regard him as a mystic. "The highest endeavor of the mind, and the highest virtue, is to understand things by virtue of the third kind of knowledge" (Spinoza, *Ethics,* Part V, Proposition XXV). By the "third kind of knowledge" Spinoza means an intellectual intuition in which we grasp the very essence of God. "The intellectual love of the mind toward God is that very love of God whereby God loves himself . . ." (Spinoza, *Ethics,* Part V, Proposition XXXVI). What this intellectual love of God produces, however, is more a recognition that God, as the whole, is more worthy of love than any individual mode, coupled with a sort of Stoic resignation to the condition of finitude. The moral status of competing claims is still based, ultimately, on the power of the system making the claim.

Empiricism

It is only with the empiricists that we make the transition to a moral theory which contemporary scholars would recognize as fully liberal. In considering the implications of empiricism for ethical theory, however, it is necessary first of all to distinguish between the moderate empiricism of a thinker such as Locke, who argues that knowledge begins with the senses, but allows intellectual operations such as the comparison, combination, or separation of ideas derived from the senses, so that we can make inferences from sense data, and the two very different sorts of radical empiricism advanced by Berkeley and Hume.

Berkeleyan empiricism or subjective idealism leads directly and necessarily to a divine command ethics. Indeed, George Berkeley saw himself as vindicating religion against the attacks of the materialists (Berkeley 1710). Berkeley says that we know *nothing* except what we experience. But experience occurs *inside*, not *outside* the mind. This led him to the conclusion that "to be is to be perceived." But what does this do to things which are not currently perceived—to the famous tree which falls in the forest with no one to hear it? Berkeley must resort to the idea of an Ultimate Observer—God—who guarantees the possible objects of sensation by perceiving them when we are not. Variations on this theme have been developed in the present period by information theoretical "physical idealists" such as Frank Tipler, who attempt to resolve the dilemmas of quantum cosmology by reference to an ultimate observer.[12]

From here, a divine command theory follows necessarily. Indeed, in so far as everything is an idea in the mind of God, everything is, in effect, a result of divine action. Similar ideas can be found in Jonathan Edwards and other New Divinity men anxious to find a philosophical foundation for Reformed Theology. Not only is the Good a result of divine decree, but so is our response to it, for which we are nonetheless morally responsible because it is *also* what we will (Edwards 1754/1957–1989).

The moderate empiricism of Locke, on the other hand, leads to a moderate divine command ethics in which moral norms are derived not so much from divine revelation, but from certain facts about the relationship between God and the universe. Locke, we will recall, allows

---

12. According to quantum theory, subatomic particles (and by implication the universe, which is composed of such particles) cannot be described in terms of their position and momentum, but only by a wave function which describes the relative probability of various "quantum states." According to one interpretation (the so-called "Copenhagen interpretation") this wave function is "collapsed" when an observation is made and a definite value given to position, momentum, and so on. The alternate "many worlds" theory suggests that the wave function never collapses and that all possible values are in fact realized, so that the universe branches out into an infinite number of worlds, each corresponding to a specific quantum state of each particle. Tipler synthesizes these two approaches, arguing that all possible values of the quantum wave function describing the universe as a whole exist mathematically, but that only those which permit observers exist physically (the Berkeleyan criterion) and that all those which permit observers evolve necessarily to an "Omega point" which is, in effect, Berkeley's Ultimate Observer (Barrow and Tipler 1986, Tipler 1994).

us to make inferences from sense data, something which allows us to demonstrate the existence of God using something like a cosmological argument (Locke 1690/1995). Human beings, because we are created by God, are His property. We must not, therefore, harm others or restrict their freedom. Indeed, we cannot even dispose freely of our own lives and freedom. Our very condition of servitude towards God thus defines our liberty with respect to other human beings. God also created us with the capacity to make things our selves. By mixing our labor and thus our lives with the soil (or any other raw material) it becomes our own, subject to no higher claim but God's. Government is instituted to protect and defend these fundamental rights to life, liberty, and property, and may do nothing for any other purpose. It is to natural rights theory, and not to natural law, which most U.S. "conservatives," who use natural law language, such as Supreme Court Justice Clarence Thomas, actually owe their allegiance (Locke 1690/1967).

Where Berkeleyan subjective idealism leads to an ethics of unlimited divine sovereignty; moderate Lockean empiricism leads to an ethics in which divine sovereignty guarantees our freedom from each other. In either case it is still all about power.

The radical empiricism of Hume (Hume 1777/1886, Hayek 1988), on the other hand, takes us into entirely new territory. Humeans generally begin by granting that we can perceive "facts" and "events." But since such things as "structures" and "causal relationships" are not direct observables, they deny their objectivity. All we are really seeing is a "constant conjunction" of phenomena. Assuming that all knowledge derives ultimately from the senses (and thus ruling out the ontological argument), and in the absence of an authentic doctrine of causality, it becomes quite impossible to argue for the existence of God, whose name can thus no longer be invoked to sanction moral norms. Indeed, the whole notion of truth and value becomes radically relativized. Some ways of organizing our experience are better than others only because they lead to practices which work. Ideas which work survive; those which do not die out. Survival value is not, however, the same thing as truth value. There is no claim, especially among contemporary Humeans such as Hayek, that ideas which work also correspond in some sense to the way in which the universe is organized. Science is reduced to little more than tried and true tradition and any attempt to rise above science to first principles is ruled out.

The same is true, from this point of view, with morality, which is simply a way of talking about what pleases us. This notion can be developed in a number of different ways. Hume himself, and many thinkers of similar temperament, argued for the existence of a sort of moral sensibility which led us to take pleasure in benevolent conduct. It is actions which are pleasing to this sort of preference in particular which we call moral. Later Humeans, such as F. A. Hayek (Hayek 1988), argue that there is a sort of natural selection for social practices which have survival value. It is these practices which are conserved and become part of a moral tradition. Utilitarianism of the Benthamite or Millian variety takes pleasure as the standard of morality and then argues that there is a moral obligation to promote "the greatest good for the greatest number." This can be determined by means of the operation of market forces, by democratic decision making, by the activity of expert planners, or by some combination of these three methods.

What all these variants of empiricism share is an identification of the moral with personal preference. It is simply a question of whose preference rules—God's or our own—and of how we know what those preferences are. As we noted above in the case of rationalist ethical theory, it is not at all clear why something that is preferable should also be obligatory, even if the preferences in question are those of God or Tradition or the People. To put the matter differently, they offer us no real guidance as to what is actually Good, and thus fail to answer the question which is at the heart of the contemporary crisis of values.

Social Contract Theory

The emptiness of modern moral theory is most apparent in social contract theory, which makes morality purely conventional, cutting it loose even from such considerations as utility or survival value. For Rousseau the "state of nature" is characterized by absolute moral neutrality. The law of nature commands nothing more than self-preservation. This is, however, quite impossible apart from civil society. Because of this human beings come together to form a social compact in which they alienate their natural liberty in return for the security of the political order. In the process, however, they bring into being a new collective being, a General Will which is the authentic arbiter of the moral. Human beings, on entering into civil society, are transformed from amoral individuals into moral beings and citizens dedicated to whatever the General Will commands.

If this sounds a bit like a Calvinist conversion experience, it is no accident. Rousseau was born in and formed by the Calvinist city of Geneva. It is simply that, as the universe has come to seem less and less meaningful and order more and more something created rather than discovered, human beings have replaced God as the authors of the moral order.

Social contract theory shares the same difficulties as the other theories we have analyzed thus far. It is not at all clear why an arbitrary decree, whether of God or of the People, should be morally binding. Neither tyranny nor mob rule are adequate forms of government for rational animals.

CRITICAL IDEALISM

Ultimately neither rationalist nor empiricist approaches to philosophy proved convincing. Having to prove the existence of God in order to validate the reliability of sensation seems to violate the principle of economy, while the empiricist insistence on beginning with sensation turns out yield conclusions no less exotic than those of the rationalists. By the end of the nineteenth century science, ethics, and religion all seemed to be in jeopardy.

It was just precisely this situation which motivated Kant (Kant 1781/1969a, 1781/1969b). Kant recognized that both empiricism and rationalism had run into dead ends. Rationalism had proven itself incapable of escaping the prison house of the *cogito* (at least on an authentically rationalist basis), while empiricism had "demonstrated" (his main point of reference in this regard being Hume) that very little is actually given in sensation. The effect was to call into question the foundations of science, of ethics, and of religion. It was these foundations which he wanted to secure as best as possible, given the limits on human cognition which the rationalists and empiricists had already discovered.

Kant begins by making a distinction between two types of judgments: analytic and synthetic. In analytic propositions the predicate is already contained in the subject; analysis merely draws it out (e.g., All triangles have three sides). Synthetic propositions, on the other hand, join ideas which were previously separate (e.g., The chair is red). Prior to Kant, it was taken for granted that analytic arguments are *a priori*, and that synthetic arguments are *a posteriori*. The judgment that all triangles have three sides requires no observation; we conclude directly from the definition. The judgment that the chair is red, on the other hand, is possible only after we have observed the chair and determined its color. What Kant proposes is that there is another sort of synthetic argument, the synthetic *a priori*, which provides the solution to his problem. Synthetic *a priori* judgments join two ideas prior to any observation, by showing that they are the condition of any possible experience. Kant claims that we make this kind of judgment all the time in mathematics. The idea of "7" is not, he claims, contained in the ideas of "3" and "4," nor is the idea "shortest distance between two points" (which is quantitative) contained in the idea "straight line" (which is qualitative). The same is true of physics. The conservation of matter for example involves not an analysis but rather a synthesis of ideas. But in none of these cases are the judgments based on observation. We make the judgment prior to any observation whatsoever.

What Kant concludes from this is that knowledge is not so much a matter of conforming our minds to objects as it is of conforming objects to our minds. He did not mean by this that the object is created by the mind, and therefore exists only within it, but rather that we know the object only as it is structured for us by the operation of the intellect. What the mind does is to take the manifold data of experience and impose on it a unified structure which makes thought possible. The forms of intuition, space and time, structure our actual sensory experience; the categories of the understanding—quantity, quality, relation and mode—structure the way we relate experiences to each other and form them into a unified whole.

What this does for Kant is to establish a sort of foundation for mathematics and science. Universal and necessary knowledge is possible in these disciplines because everyone organizes and unifies the given data of the senses in the same way. The same is not, however, true for metaphysics. Because the intellect unifies rather than abstracting, we cannot conclude to anything supersensible. Concepts such as the self, the cosmos, and God, which Kant calls the transcendental ideals, reflect nothing more than the drive of the intellect to unify our experience perfectly. These ideas do not, however, correspond to any possible object of experience and we thus have no basis on which to claim that they correspond to anything outside the mind. Indeed, when we try to treat the transcendental ideas as if they were objects of experience, reason runs into contradictions or antinomies from which it cannot extricate itself. Thus the interminable debates regarding freedom and necessity, the finitude or infinity of the universe and its infinite divisibility or reducibility to simple parts (atoms), and the existence or nonexistence of God.

It is on this basis that Kant rejects the historic arguments for the existence of God. The ontological proof he rejects out of hand. Being, he points out, is not a real predicate which can be deduced by analysis of some other predicate, such as "than which nothing greater can be thought" or "perfect." We know something actually exists only by observation. But he goes on to reject the cosmological and teleological arguments as well. The cosmological argument, he points out, turns on extending the category of causality, by which the understanding orders sensible experience, to the supersensible realm—a move he claims is illegitimate. Similarly, the teleological argument argues from the presence of cosmic order to the notion of an orderer who is, however, beyond any possible experience.

Unable to conclude to a first principle, Kant had to seek some other way in which to ground ethical judgments. Here, too, Kant turned to *a priori* reason. Like science, ethics is grounded in the *a priori* structure of human reason. Just as the mind unifies experience under the forms of the intuition and the certain definite categories of the understanding, so it seeks to unify our action under a single, internally consistent and universal principle, the categorical imperative: "Act only on that maxim whereby you can at the same time will that it should become a universal law." From here, Kant does on to argue that in order to follow this principle through consistently, we must assume (though we cannot prove) freedom of the will, immortality and the existence of God.

There are a number of difficulties with Kant's approach. If space, time, quantity, quality, relation and mode are structures imposed on experience by the mind, rather than characteristics of objects given in experience and abstracted by the intellect, then it is difficult to understand why these forms and categories have such powerful survival value. Put slightly differently, this is fundamentally the Hegelian critique of Kant (Harris 1991, 1992). Our ideas are, after all, a part of the world—one might even say that they are the world's own consciousness of itself. That these ideas structure our experience and forge out of disparate sensations a unified totality does not mean that the unity and structure is something *imposed*. It might equally be something *discovered*—or, to use Hegelian language, something implicit which has been made explicit and brought to conscious certainty of itself. Indeed, this is both the simpler and more powerful explanation. It is simpler because it does not require us to postulate a unifying drive in the mind, complete with forms and categories. It is more powerful because it explains why these forms and categories have survival value: they reflect (albeit perhaps selectively and imperfectly) the way the universe is actually structured. Or, if we do think of the action of the mind as a unifying drive, then this drive itself is not simply postulated, but itself explained as part of a larger tendency of matter towards form, a drive which takes a new and important step in the transition from diffused and disorganized sensory experience to organized categorical thought (Harris 1991, 1992).

Kant's strategy for regrounding science, ethics, and religion, finally, leaves him vulnerable to criticism from cultural relativists. Kant claims that the forms of the intuition and the categories of the understanding are universal structures of the human mind. But is it really true that all human beings order the data of the senses in the same way? This seems increasingly difficult to maintain given the growing evidence that diverse languages and cultures embody fundamentally different concepts of space, time, quantity, quality, relation, and mode. This criticism might seem to compromise even further the realism we are attempting to defend, but we will see that it is in fact quite possible to reconcile a moderate sociological relativism with an underlying philosophical realism strong enough to ground science, metaphysics, and ethics. For Kant, on the other hand, who grounds science and ethics in the universal structure of human reason, any concession to relativism spells disaster.

In the final analysis, Kant can be understood as a response to the realization that we have no immediate intuition of intelligibles—that we cannot see "turtle" the way we see *a* turtle, and that we cannot see God in any meaningful sense at all. This is of course the very point we made in our critique of rationalism and objective idealism. The absence or darkness of vision, however, is not absence of knowledge. The human mind is limited and must make do with concepts which are not in any sense an intellectual vision. These concepts do, however, nonetheless provide the basis on which we can advance to an authentic knowledge of God—and demonstrate the possibility and reasonableness of a revelation which begins to close the gap between our desire to see and the dark and indirect knowledge we have through the medium of the concept.

Modern Dialectics

The crisis of Aristotelianism at the end of the middle ages did not mean the end of dialectical theory. On the contrary, we have already seen that Spinoza and Leibniz advance a sort of "abbreviated" dialectics, which attempts to ascend to first principles on the basis of the new mathematical physics. Later attempts at a similar ascent had to grapple not only with mathematical physics, but also with the experience of the industrial revolution, capitalist development, and the democratic upheavals of the eighteenth and nineteenth centuries. The result was a new dialectics which understood not only individual organisms but humanity and ultimately the universe as a whole developing towards ever higher degrees of organizations, so that it appeared as itself a sort of dialectical ascent, a struggle for growth and development which was also, therefore, a struggle for the Beautiful, the True, the Good, and the One. The foundational work in this regard is, of course, that of Hegel (Hegel 1807/1967, 1817/1990, 1830/1971).

The question, of course, is whether or not this modern dialectics represents an authentic solution to the contradictions of modern moral theory generally. Let us examine it in some detail. Hegel overcame Kant's scruples about our ability to know "things in the themselves" and thus to rise rationally to a first principles by showing that the forms of intuition and the categories of the understanding (*Verstand*) are not merely ways of organizing experience imposed from outside "the world," but rather stages along the way in the universe's own struggle for self-understanding. While limited, they also point beyond themselves, through the process of self-consciousness and the struggle for recognition to what he calls Reason (*Vernunft*) which actually comprehends the underlying Concept or Idea which externalizes itself in the world and of which it is the highest realization. The mechanistic outlook of modern mathematical physics is relativized as the consequence of looking at nature through the categories of the understanding (*Verstand*), which can see only external, mathematically formalizable relationships. Reason (*Vernunft*) recognizes in Nature the external manifestation of the Idea. The cosmohistorical process is simply the gradual, often contradictory realization of this principle. Human civilization is "God's march through history."

This in turn allows Hegel to ground ethics in much the same way as Aristotle and Thomas had before him. Value consists above all in the unfolding of the Idea—the realization of its latent potential—through the progress of human civilization, which terminates in absolute knowledge or fully adequate comprehension of the Idea. This is reflected in the social order in a fully rational organization of all human institutions. Here we are very close, at least, to an historicized natural law ethics.

Why did Hegel's synthesis fall apart? The answer to this question is complex, because Hegel's system is an unstable amalgam of monarchic conservatism and modern over-reaching. On the one hand, in struggling to endow history with meaning, he also ended up legitimating what was clearly a backward, semifeudal Prussian state. This had the effect of making the revolutionary generations of 1830 and 1848 suspicious about the whole enterprise of rational metaphysics, which they classed with religion as a means of reconciling in thought or imagination contradictions which in fact had to be resolved in reality, but it also prevented Hegel himself from framing a clear moral imperative, for fear that if he said that things should be other than they are he would end up reverting to the condition of the Unhappy Consciousness for which the Good is always and only located in the Beyond, and thus abandoning historical dialectics altogether. Ethics, for Hegel, is reduced to an enterprise for finding the hidden ethical meaning in institutions which seem outwardly to be fraught with injustice and contradiction—to find the Reason, which is the "rose in the cross of the present." The difficulty, of course, is that the Prussian state with which Hegel reconciled himself did not and could not actually resolve the contradictions of emerging capitalism, but rather functioned as a kind of immanent Beyond. Citizenship and service to the political common good, compensated for, but did not remove, the individualism and alienation of civil society and the marketplace.

At the same time, Hegel's attempt to reground religion ends by advancing claims which can only be regarded as idolatrous. For Hegel, human beings not only *know* God, we know God *absolutely*, and know Him in our consciousness of our own role in the historical process. We are, in fact, nothing other than God become conscious of Himself. This is not only absurd, since even if it *were* possible for human beings to become God essentially rather than just intentionally or accidentally, we are clearly very far from having done so; it also absolutizes something contingent and finite.

Both of these problems were the result of Hegel's immanentism. While modern dialectics, unlike Augustinianism and Liberalism, conserves the analogical metaphysics of the Aristotelian tradition, it treats the boundary between contingency and necessity as permeable. Specifically, it confuses rational autonomy and the collective Subjectivity of humanity as author of its own history with Necessary Being, which is something quite different.

The Marxist "reversal" of Hegel can be understood—and in fact has been historically understood—in either of two ways: as making explicit Hegel's univocal, immanentist metaphysics, so that language about God becomes superfluous in what is, nonetheless, essentially, a materialist pantheism, or as a rejection of metaphysics altogether in favor of the claim that the only meaning in the universe is that which we humans create. The first alternative is represented by Engels, whose *Dialectics of Nature* (Engels 1880/1940) sets human historical progress in the context of a larger process of cosmic evolution, and much of the Soviet tradition including, especially, Bogdanov and Deborin. Here matter is regarded as itself possessing the properties of the Hegelian Idea, being self-organizing and containing in itself the potential for the full dialectical scale of forms. History—cosmic and human—is fundamentally about the realization of this latent potential. Various social forms are evaluated on the basis of their capacity to promote the development of increasingly complex forms of organization. The result is, in effect, a historicized natural law ethics (Meikle 1985, Daly 2000). In its most radical manifestations this tradition was quite explicit in its rapprochement with religion and metaphysics. Bogdanov's circle included God-builders like Gorky and Lunacharsky, who saw socialism as the means to realize humanity's age-old desire to *become God* (Rowley 1987). Deborin was criticized by Stalin because his concept of matter was regarded as excessively idealist (Joravsky 1966). Indeed, some Soviet thinkers during the Khrushchev era made quite explicit the link between their understanding of Marxism and the materialist pantheism of the Radical Averroists (Dahm 1987).

This reading of Marx ran up against both theoretical and practical problems. On the one hand, Engels' *Dialectics of Nature* seemed to conflict with scientific results which point instead to a cosmic heat death. This led most Western Marxists to abandon the dialectics of nature altogether in favor of the view that humanity, through the medium of its labor, *creates* the only meaning which is possible in an otherwise hostile and meaningless universe. Socialism is legitimated as, in effect, an imperative of practical reason in an ethics which, try as it might to be Hegelian keeps slipping back into Kantian formalism. Some, like Bernstein, made this move explicitly. Others, like Lukacs and Fromm, returned to Kant surreptitiously, by attempting to ground moral claims on the basis of an historical dialectics cut off from nature, thus reintroducing the antinomies between pure and practical reason, nature and history. The result looked something like a humanistic existentialism, and it is not surprising that this trend eventually merged with existentialism in the work of the later Sartre. Althusser, who argued that this amounted to return to an essentially petty-bourgeois position (i.e., the standpoint of an historically impotent moralism), abandoned ethics entirely, and attempted to refocus Marxists on the scientific tasks which Marx had set for them, while rejecting both the cosmohistorical metanarrative of dialectical materialism and the humanism of Western Marxists as nothing more than legitimating ideologies.

In the Soviet Union, on the other hand, materialist pantheism was regarded as a political threat because it threatened to constitute an intellectual and moral leadership outside of and above the party. There was, indeed, at first just such a leadership centered on the (competing) schools of Bogdanov and Deborin in the Institute of Red Professors and the Communist Academy. After Stalin's rise to power, however, these organizations were merged into the Academy of Sciences and reduced to the status of a support staff, with the role of ideological leadership reserved to the Central Committee of the Communist Party—i.e., to a political organization.

Neither the market nor the state can tolerate the existence of intellectual and moral authorities which call them to account. Modern moral theory is fundamentally an attempt to make the world safe for these two institutions. In the process, of course, it has also made the world *un*safe for humanity. As capitalism and socialism both slipped ever more deeply into crisis in the late twentieth century the poverty of modern moral theory became more and more apparent. The result, however, has not been a renewal of authentic moral discourse, but rather a regression into an ever more explicit nihilism and despair.

THE CURRENT SITUATION IN ETHICAL THEORY

Neomodernisms

INFORMATION THEORETICAL NEOLIBERALISM

The current situation in ethics is dominated by three main trends, two of which represent attempts to shore up and one of which claims to represent a fundamental break with, modernity.

The dominant trend, or at least the official ideology of the dominant strata of the bourgeoisie is clearly neoliberal theory of the sort represented by F. A. Hayek (Hayek 1988). Hayek adopts an explicitly Humean epistemology and ontology, but recasts it in information-theoretical terms. We know only facts and events and patterns of facts and events, which alone can be taken to be really real. He also accepts the currently fashionable cosmology, according to which the universe consists of elementary particles which interact randomly, with those structures which are stable surviving and those which are not disintegrating. Human interactions are no different. Human beings learn by experience, struggling under conditions of scarcity to realize their self-interests, developing and trying out new practices. Those which work are conserved; those which do not work are discarded. The result is an accumulated body of tradition. Hayek argues that spontaneous forms of organization such as language, the family, and the marketplace, precisely because they capitalize on this dynamic of random variation and natural selection, and thus tap into the dispersed knowledge of diverse individuals, work better than any sort of centralized planning apparatus. The economy, human society, and indeed the entire universe is one vast information processing system which analyzes practices and forms of organization, determining which work and which do not, while rewarding the former and punishing the latter.

It is interesting to note that Hayek's theory, unlike earlier forms of radical empiricist liberalism, makes room in advance for an alliance with the religious right. While himself an atheist, Hayek includes religion among the spontaneous institutions which have proven their survival value over time, thus laying the groundwork for an alliance with the religious institutions against the state and the secular intelligentsia.

Hayek's theory can be attacked at any of a number of levels. We have already criticized empiricist epistemology and atomistic cosmology in detail in other works (Mansueto 2002b, Mansueto and Mansueto forthcoming). Here it should suffice to note that the distinction, central to his theory, between truth value and survival value, is simply incoherent. Ideas work because they comprehend, albeit imperfectly, the way the world actually is. But if we can understand the underlying structures of things in themselves, then we may be able, at least in principle, to ascend to a first principle of explanation and of action, and thus to some criterion of judgment other than survival value. Hayek, furthermore, never directly addresses the dialectical critique of the market order, but concentrates, rather on his own critique of centralized planning. This works in the absence of a moral criterion which might suggest to us that the arts, sciences, philosophy, and religion are more important than designer jeans and sports cars, but once we have ascended to such a principle, we must confront the possibility that even with all of its many failings, centralized planning may actually do a better job than the marketplace of promoting human development.[13]

Dialectical Critical Realism

The principal critique of Hayek from the left has been put forward by Roy Bhaskar (Bhaskar 1989, 1993). Bhaskar begins by mounting a systematic critique of positivist epistemology and metaphysics. Bhaskar begins by making what amounts to a transcendental argument for the reality of those objects of scientific knowledge historically affirmed by the dialectical tradition, but denied by the positivists ("society," "social structures"). Specifically, he argues that structures are, in fact the condition of possibility of the "facts" and "events" to which Humeans would reduce reality (Bhaskar 1989: 62–65). He does not, however, then argue for an ascent through knowledge of these structures to a positive doctrine of Being. On the contrary, he argues that the difficulty with all hitherto existing dialectics, including those of Hegel and, to some extent Marx, has been an insistence on the positivity of Being—i.e., on the priority of Being over Non-Being. Even where the category of contradiction is introduced as a determination of being itself, as it is in Hegel and Marx, the priority of the positive leads inevitably to closure of the cosmohistorical process and the collapse of Being into an undifferentiated expressive unity. In the case of Hegel, because of his idealism and spiritual monism, this lead to a reconciliation with the status quo of a still semifeudal Germany. In

---

13. This does not, of course, mean that we should rest content with a forced choice between market and plan. On the contrary, there are other options, which we will explore in greater detail in a later chapter.

the case of Marx it led to the claim that history terminates (or, what is the same thing, that prehistory terminates and history begins) with the achievement of communism, a doctrine which was easily mobilized by the Stalinist state to close-off further progress not only beyond, but actually towards communism. Bhaskar proposes instead to give priority to the category of absence which he claims is the condition for the possibility of physical systems of any kind, being implied by spatio-temporal extension, physical interaction, and thus motion, and which is the driving force of human society from the demanding cry of an infant distressed at the absence of the mother, through the most sophisticated demand for the "absenting of constraints on the absenting of constraints" and thus for the full development of human capacities (Bhaskar 1993).

Bhaskar gives this notion of "absenting constraints" concrete content through his proposal for an "explanatory-critical social science." He begins by pointing out that the subject matter of the social sciences includes not just social objects, but also beliefs about those objects. Some of those beliefs, he argues, are false, and if one can explain the falsity then, other things being equal, one can move to "a negative evaluation of the *explanans* and a positive evaluation of any action rationally designed to absent it" (Bhaskar 1993: 261–62).

What Bhaskar is doing here, of course, is to make explicit and rigorous the ethics which is implicit (and not always consistent) in Marx's social scientific and ideological-critical work, while extending it beyond the scope of Marx's specific analyses, which were confined to a study of the capitalist system. Thus Marx's critique of political economy, as a critique of beliefs about capitalism, not only shows those beliefs to be flawed, but shows them to be rooted in the capitalist order itself, of which it is an ideological reflex. The critique of political economy thus becomes a critique of capitalism and a mandate for social transformation. Similarly, he suggests, critiques of sexist and racist ideology imply critiques of women's oppression and imperialism, and provide a mandate for emancipation.

Bhaskar's approach is, clearly, far superior to Hayek's. Grounded in a solid epistemological realism, it provides a basis for distinguishing between true and false and from there going on to criticize structures which give rise to false judgments and thus stand in the way of effective action on behalf of human development. Bhaskar's position is, furthermore, self-correcting. He is able to do for aspects of Marx's theory, and certain claims of later Marxists, what Marx himself did for bourgeois political economy, thus limiting the tendency toward dogmatism and ideological legitimation of structures which once promoted social progress but which may have outlived their usefulness.

Implicit in Bhaskar's ethics, however, is the assumption that effective action on behalf of human development is somehow a moral imperative. But this, precisely, is to assume what must be demonstrated. Bhaskar does take some tentative steps towards showing that human beings have a drive towards such development, arguing that the drive towards universal human autonomy is implicit in the infant's "primal scream" (Bhaskar 1993: 264) and that it becomes explicit through hard experience of what Freud called the "reality principle," which teaches us the extent to which and the real conditions under which our desires can actually be realized. What this does not do, however, is to tell us just what a fully developed human being *is*. Indeed, Bhaskar seems to remain scrupulously agnostic on this question. He gives us no basis, for example, on which to prefer investment in liberal arts education over the production of luxury automobiles except, perhaps, the claim that the latter is not sustainable or does not work in the long run due to economic or ecological limitations. But this is quite different from showing that the former is intrinsically preferable. Desire remains the watchword of Bhaskar's ethics, standing in for the absent Good, just as absence stands in for Being itself.

The symptom which allows us to diagnose Bhaskar's disorder is an ambiguity in his language. While he often uses the language of human development or human flourishing, in his more rigorous formulations he always reverts to the term "autonomy" or "freedom." And it is indeed this latter value to which his argument actually concludes. Bhaskar abbreviates his ascent to first principles intentionally, precisely because a more substantive doctrine of the Good would undermine his ultimately libertarian agenda. His whole enterprise, in fact, can be read as an attempt to show that contrary to the claims of Hayek and his camp, the market order neither advances human freedom nor promotes the long-term survival of the species. Neither, in other words, answer the primal scream schooled by the reality principle. In the process, though, he comes to accept the criteria fixed by the bourgeoisie and agrees to contest the issue on their terrain.

Even so, might not Bhaskar win on bourgeois terrain? Not with the weapons currently at his disposal. The judgment of the peoples of the former Soviet bloc against socialism was first and foremost a judgment against the fact that it did not allow them to freely pursue their own self-interests, which they had come to understand in narrowly consumerist terms. The judgment against the new market order is, rather a judgment against the failure of the market to support certain higher-order aspirations which were well-funded under socialism—the desire to dance, to paint, to teach, or to engage in research. While these aspirations can be recast in terms of freedom, it remains necessary to show that the freedoms or aspirations which socialism makes possible or fulfills are higher than those made possible or fulfilled by capitalism. And for this we need a principle of value higher than freedom.

Postmodernism

The currently hegemonic trend in the secular academy is deconstructionist postmodernism, of the sort represented by Foucault, Derrida, Lyotard, and the like. Deconstructionist postmodernism is defined by its explicit rejection not only of metaphysics, but of foundationalism of any sort. According to this view moral judgments are always and only ungrounded and must be owned as such—or else become instruments of a perverse will to power.

This trend can, we have shown (Mansueto 1999, Mansueto and Mansueto forthcoming), can be traced back to the medieval Augustinian reaction. But it is not until the middle of the nineteenth century, with Kierkegaard (Kierkegaard 1840/1941), that we find philosophers beginning to make arguments against philosophy as it has historically been understood—not simply restricting the scope of human reason, but actually arguing that the *via dialectica* is itself a path to perdition. For Kierkegaard the very attempt to construct a system excludes the possibility of discovering God, because in rendering the universe intelligible it rules out in advance the encounter with another free personality—human or divine. God is known only in the radical inwardness of human subjectivity, only after we have despaired of the effort to comprehend and organize the world on the basis of some principle accessible to reason. Kierkegaard quite explicitly subordinates the ethical, understood in a roughly Kantian sense as a concern for duty, to the religious, understood as a concern for relationship (Kierkegaard 1843/1971).

What we have here, of course, is simply an attempt to draw out fully and completely the implications of traditional Lutheran doctrine, a doctrine which itself, as we have already shown, is simply an attempt to draw out fully and complete the implications of the Augustinian critiques of Aristotle developed in the Late Middle Ages. And we already know what Luther counseled with respect to the political authorities: submission. And this is not just the result of some failure of nerve on the part of an otherwise heroic rebel. It is a necessary logical implication of his larger theology. God freely offers forgiveness to those who will humbly accept it in faith. Any attempt to build a just society will corrupt the Christian message of divine forgiveness; any attempt to make the state more "Christian" in the sense of being more forgiving will let evil run amok. The authority of the state thus remains unaccountable to any higher authority.

Kierkegaard is one font of the political-theological critique of metaphysics; the other is Nietzsche (Nietzsche 1889/1968). At first no two figures could seem more different: the radical Christian and the prophet of the anti-Christ. And certainly their *explicit* reasons for rejecting metaphysics are nothing if not diametrically opposed. Kierkegaard (who continues in the tradition of the Augustinian reaction) rejects metaphysics as a manifestation of human pride and the will to power; Nietzsche rejects it precisely because it represents a retreat from the raw struggle for power which, in his mind, is the only real principle which governs the universe—an attempt on the part of the weak-spirited to hide from "the world as it is" in the name of "the world as it should be," a search for some pre-existing pattern of organization on which to depend rather than a bold struggle to organize the universe ourselves, as best we can, in full knowledge that our efforts will, in time, be swept away.

What is rejected by Kierkegaard and Nietzsche both, however, is the presence of a meaning immanent in human activity and in the universe generally which, however, points beyond itself to an intrinsically meaningful ground. Both ultimately regard meaning as a function of power. For Kierkegaard this power is always and only the power of God before which the only proper human response is one of radical submission. Nietzsche, on the other hand, scorns such submission and counsels us to join the eternal struggle in which meanings are created and destroyed.

These two strains flow together in the work of Martin Heidegger, where we find the first really complete and rigorous statement of what becomes the postmodernist critique of metaphysics. Heidegger's work is notoriously complex and obscure and has been buried in layer upon layer of commentary, so that it becomes difficult to say anything about him

The Crisis of Values

without risking exposure for some scholarly *faux pas*. This complex of defensive ramparts, however, in fact conceals a cluster of relatively simple claims. Heidegger's early critique of metaphysics, set forth in *Problems of Phenomenology* (Heidegger 1927) and *Being and Time* (1928) focuses on the failure of thinkers, beginning with Plato, to grasp the distinction between Being and beings, and instead attempts to theorize Being as the beingness of beings—i.e., it thinks Being in entitative terms. Where the pre-Socratics, according to Heidegger, were able to think the self-manifestation of Being, something he associates with the term φυσις or nature, Plato and Aristotle increasingly use the language of μορφη (form) and ενεργεια (actuality). Form, and especially the Good or the "form of forms" is, for Plato, what really *is* and that in terms of which this world of appearance must be explained and judged. Aristotle goes even further down this road, arguing that it is form which actualizes matter, bringing things into being. Rather than simply allowing Being to manifest itself, to present itself as a question, it is reduced to something other than Being, something which can be comprehended—and once comprehended, used to ground our own process of making, our own process of bringing into being. Indeed, as Heidegger points out, the very notion of μορφη derives from the language of the craftsman: it is the look or appearance given to something by its producer. Ενεργεια, similarly, is rendered in German as *Wirklicheit*, from the root for work. Metaphysics thus grounds technology, and the larger technological mode of relating to the world.

Later (Heidegger 1941) Heidegger modified both his historical analysis and his philosophical position. Increasingly identifying ancient Greek and German romantic thought, he claimed to hear in Plato and Aristotle echoes of the earlier Greek aleqeia or unconcealment of Being and located the crystallization of metaphysics in the "translation" of Greek thought into Latin, the language of road builders and empire makers, a crystallization which is completed in the Middle Ages when Being is identified with the supreme maker, the Christian Creator God. This process culminates, of course, in Thomas, who is the supreme philosopher of the "ontotheologic," the universal causal-explanatory system in which Being is simply an instrument for explaining and ultimately manipulating entities. Modern metaphysical theories, such as those of Descartes and Hegel—or for that matter Marx—differ only in giving human rather than divine subjectivity or labor pride of place. Nietzsche's claim that the world is just the "will to power" is simply the culmination of this long metaphysical tradition, and offers just one more formulation of the first principle.

Being, for the later Heidegger, manifests itself in a people only through the voice of the few who help it to discover its "god," a sort of mythos under which Being is revealed. "[T]he essence of the people is its 'voice.' This voice does not, however, speak in a so-called immediate flood of the common, natural, undistorted and uneducated 'person.' The voice speaks seldom and only in the few, if it can be brought to sound" (Heidegger 1934/1989: 319). "A *Volk* is only a *Volk* if it receives its history through the discovery of its god, through the god, which through history compels it in a direction and so places it back in being. Only then does it avoid the danger of turning only on its own axis" (Heidegger 1934/1989: 398–99).

In this regard Heidegger remains close to Kierkegaard, seeing humanity as a passive instrument of Being rather than an active creator of meaning. After the "turn" in his thought, however, Heidegger also becomes more interested in analyzing the historical process by which Being is unconcealed—or by which it "withdraws" leaving the world subject to *techne* and to the will to power—than he is in the existential analysis of *Dasein* (human being or literally "being-there") as an opening to Being. While the historical process is treated here simply as a product of Being's unconcealments and withdrawals, the effect is, nonetheless, to reinstate the Nietzschean focus on the nexus between power and meaning, while endowing this nexus with an ontological legitimation which makes the forcible irruption of meaning in history no longer the product of finite human organizing activity, but rather an epiphany of Being itself. It is this notion of the historical destiny of the people as an unconcealment of Being, by Being, which made Heidegger vulnerable to the appeal of Nazism, which appeared to him as the possible occasion of just such an unconcealment.

After its first complete formulation in the work of Heidegger, the political-theological critique of metaphysics developed in a number of apparently very different directions. Levinas (Levinas 1965) argued that Heidegger's continued use of the language of Being perpetuated the effacement of the Other in the interests of power and domination which had characterized the whole Greek philosophical tradition, which he refers to as "ontology" and advocates a new "metaphysics" rooted in confrontation with the radically Other, the victim, in which alone we can discover—

but never conceptually possess—God. This line of reasoning has been taken up by Latin American liberationists, explicitly by Miranda (Miranda 1972, 1973) and Dussel (Dussel 1998), and more loosely and eclectically by others, for whom the encounter with the poor and oppressed becomes the unique privileged hermeneutic key for reading the scriptures—and reality in general.[14]

The "democrat" Hannah Arendt does not frame her argument in terms of a critique of metaphysics, but the link to the thought of her fascist lover (Heidegger) is readily apparent. At the very core of Arendt's political theory is a sharp distinction between labor, work, and action. By labor she means the physical, biological, and economic processes which are necessary to sustain life. Labor leaves nothing behind except life itself, and perhaps the freedom of another (the master) to engage in work or action. By work she means the process of producing objects which possess some permanence, serve some purpose beyond themselves, and which are executed in accord with some pre-conceived plan. Work is an intrinsically teleological process. By action she means the disclosure of the subject in relationship with other subjects—a process which unlike labor or work directly presupposes the presence of others, which, consequently has a characteristic frailty, and the outcome of which is always uncertain (Ardent 1958). Arendt criticizes the entire tradition of Western political philosophy from Plato though Marx, which, she says, understands politics as a form of fabrication or work rather than as the quintessential form of action.

> Plato and Aristotle elevated lawmaking and city building to the highest rank in political life ... because they wished to turn against politics and against action. To them, legislating and the execution of decisions by vote are the most legitimate political activities be-

---

14. It is often supposed that this hermeneutic is compatible with or even builds on the sociological reading of the scriptures advanced by Gottwald, Pixley, and others, which points out the origins of many strains in the Jewish and Christian traditions in the struggles of oppressed. Actually, however, the two hermeneutics are quite opposed. According to the sociological reading proposed by Gottwald, for example, the cult of YHWH emerged not out of some "encounter with the oppressed," but rather out of an encounter *by* the oppressed with their own historical power, a power which, if we accept the theological reading proposed by Judaism and Christianity, was a real participation in the power of the living God. Gottwald's reading is a reading from the standpoint of the oppressed, or at least one which attempts to recover something of this standpoint; the readings proposed by the Latin American disciples of Levinas are readings from the standpoint of a guilt-ridden elite.

> cause in them men "act like craftsmen:" the results of their action is a tangible product, and its process has a clearly recognizable end. This is no longer, or rather, not yet action (πραξις) properly speaking, but making (ποιησις) which they prefer because of its greater reliability. It is as though they had said that if men only renounce their capacity for action, with its futility, boundlessness, and uncertainty of outcome, there could be a remedy for the frailty of human affairs. (Ardent 1958: 195)

The tradition which Arendt criticizes, of course, reaches its consummation in the work of Marx, for whom the transformation of the working class from mere makers of physical objects, into the conscious makers of history, constitutes the highest possible level of human development.

The link between making and metaphysics is located for Arendt as for Heidegger in the Platonic doctrine of forms or ideas, though Arendt focuses on the term ειδος rather than μορφη. She notes that according to Aristotle, Plato himself was the one to introduce this term into philosophical usage and that Plato (*Republic* X) explicitly uses an analogy with craftsmanship to explain the doctrine.

Is there any difference between the critiques of metaphysics advanced by Heidegger and Arendt? Absolutely. For Heidegger the critique of metaphysics makes way for the disclosure of Being, something which he makes quite clear takes place first and foremost in the historical destiny of peoples. This is especially true after the "turn" in his thinking, when he becomes less and less concerned with the existential analysis of *Dasein* and more and more concerned with the historical conditions for a new unconcealment of Being. For Arendt, on the other hand, the critique of metaphysics clears the way for a disclosure of the subject in action, to other like subjects, from whom there is some possibility of recognition. Thus the pull in Arendt's theory towards a broadly "democratic" politics. Note, however, that both share a common rejection of work, and of the historical movements which have regarded work or creativity as a privileged opening to understanding Being itself: i.e., Catholicism and dialectical materialism. We should note as well that Arendt's "democratic" politics is fully as elitist as Heidegger's fascism: it is only those who have been freed from the necessity of labor and from the obsession with work who are really capable of public life.

The most radical expression of the political-theological critique of metaphysics is, of course, that advanced by the postmodernists. There are many varieties of postmodernism, but for our purposes the most relevant is undoubtedly the deconstructionism of French philosopher Jacques Derrida (Derrida 1967/1978). Derrida develops his position dialectically, accepting the Heideggerian critique of all earlier metaphysics and Levinas' critique of Heidegger. But he then goes on to point out that Levinas, as well, is unable to escape the "violence" of metaphysics. In finding God in the face of the Other, do we not efface the difference and specificity of the Other as surely as if the Other (and his suffering) were reduced to a necessary expression of the divine first principle, an object of divine providence, of a vanishing moment of the human historical process? What Derrida suggests is that violence is unavoidable: there is no escape. The best that we can do is to unmask the violence embedded in our own discourse and that of others in an effort to contain the damage.

More recently deconstructions have "found religion" (Derrida 2001), discovering that deconstruction is possible only from the vantage point of something "undeconstructible," i.e., justice, and arguing for "messianicity without messianism," a kind of purely negative theology which acknowledges that God is, in fact the condition of possibility of moral judgment and of a moral universe while treating both as something which always and forever "to come." "Weak theologies" (Caputo 2006) go a bit further, rereading the Christian story, centered as it is (in their version) on the defeat of the crucifixion rather than the triumph of the resurrection, in a way which makes it embody just such a messianicity.

The social basis of postmodernism is complex, drawing, on the one hand (like the Augustinian reaction from which it partly derives) on the sponsorship of warlord and later imperialist interests and, on the other hand, on elements in the humanistic intelligentsia disillusioned with the ability of modern dialectics to make good on its promise of inner-worldly divinization.

In all cases the political valence of the critique is the ultimately the same. Where modernism attempts to enlist the people in the great project of understanding the world in order to control it, in the hope of a kind of innerworldly self-divinization, postmodernism counsels what amounts to either active participation in or submission to the inevitable violence of history, whether understood as reflecting the mysterious hand of God, some new unconcealment of Being, or simply random configurations of power relations. All variants of postmodernism are, furthermore, based on a false identification of the univocal metaphysics of modernism with the analogical metaphysics which emerged from the Axial Age and the Silk Road Era and which, we have seen, have a very different import. There are other options besides the false alternative between control and submission—between the vain and ridiculous claim to comprehend exhaustively the divine essence and the radical rejection of meaning characteristic of postmodernism.

Postmodernism is, furthermore, characterized by profound internal contradictions. If values are purely and simply the product of human social action, and lack any ground in the structure of being as such or the nature of the universe, then any claim to universal authority on the part of a particular moral vision (including a critical, emancipatory vision) must be regarded as a claim to power on the part of the social class, ethnic group, or gender group which developed the vision. Postmodernists set themselves the task of "deconstruction": of unmasking claims to universality and showing them up for what they are: claims to power. More specifically, postmodernists argue for the conservation of "difference" and are thus at the forefront of struggles for multiculturalism, gender equality, etc.

There is, however, a fundamental contradiction at the heart of the postmodernist position. If there is no universal standard outside of the array of competing moral systems developed by different cultural traditions, then on what basis can we argue with moral authority that diversity, the preservation of difference, and "multiculturalism" are values? The matter is complicated by the fact that many, if not most, of the cultural traditions which postmodernists are anxious to defend against the totalitarian hegemony of "Western Civilization" in its Christian-conservative, market-liberal, or secular-socialist forms in fact differ very sharply with postmodernism regarding the fundamental question of the meaningfulness of the universe. For we have seen that the concept of cosmic unity and order, to which postmoderns are so allergic, is in fact the unifying idea of all human civilization. And some non-Western traditions—e.g., Islam—are every bit as capable of intolerance as Christianity and its secular residues. So who is the real adversary of Hopi communities trying to conserve the "pure pattern of creation," of Africans living in *ujamma* (cooperative) villages, or of religious Zionists on their *kibbutzim*? More generally, we should point out that postmodernism gives us neither a positive vision of the Good nor any method of adjudicating the competing claims of rival individuals, social classes, ethnic groups, gender groups, etc. As such, we must say that it fails as a moral theory.

BEYOND POSTMODERNISM?

But what of the three alternatives we mentioned at the beginning of this chapter? Might they not offer an alternative to both modernist triumphalism and postmodernist nihilism and despair. That is certainly their intent. As we noted above, these theories all share is a commitment to an ethics informed by a substantive and ultimately transcendental doctrine of the Good; they differ in the ways in which they attempt to ground that doctrine.

MacIntyre locates the source of all understandings of the Good in culturally specific narratives which present distinctive, compelling visions of human excellence and social justice. These narratives develop by means of a dialectical process catalyzed both by debates within traditions and encounters between them. This dialectic draws out the implications and limitations of existing views and drives towards increasingly more adequate formulations. Narratives compete with each other in an ongoing dialogue. Those which are able to incorporate the insights of other narratives without compromising their own integrity tend to win out; those which are incorporated or which cannot find adherents lose. He makes no attempt, however, to ground his ethics in a rational metaphysics, the impossibility of which he seems to accept, even as he embraces "narratives" developed by thinkers who, like Augustine and Thomas, were nothing if not metaphysicians.

MacIntyre sees his theory as an extension of Socratic, Platonic, and Aristotelian dialectics. Indeed, he claims to represent the vanguard of a Thomistic revival. Nothing, in fact, could be further from the truth. What we have here, rather, is a return to the moderate sophism of a Protagoras against the extremism of a Gorgias or a Callicles—a moderate, "constructive" postmodernism pitted against the deconstructive radicalism of Derrida and his allies. In the final analysis the ground, such as it is, remains the same: tradition and social convention. Indeed, in the light of MacIntyre's attempt to join Thomistic philosophy with Augustinian theology on the basis of an epistemology and (absent) metaphysics which both would have rejected, it is probably most accurate to it regard him as an intellectual heir of the French traditionalist Joseph de Maistre, who in the wake of the French Revolution gave a rightist spin to the same conventionalist morality which, in the works of Rousseau, had been one of the touchstones of the Revolution.

This return to traditionalism is made explicit in the work of John Milbank (Milbank 1991, 1999). Milbank, as we have seen, shows a profound and subtle grasp of just what it is that is actually wrong with modern metaphysics—i.e., its univocal rather than analogical doctrine of Being—which makes it a philosophy of power and of violence. At the same time, however, he rather treats this univocity as the inevitable characteristic of any autonomous metaphysics. The only way to transcend metaphysics, and thus modernity, is theologically. Indeed, Milbank is quite explicit in claiming that only Christian theology offers adequate safeguards against modern nihilism. Writing in the shadow of Heidegger and Derrida, Milbank regards the whole dialectical tradition as ultimately grounded in an ontology of violence in which will is pitted against will. This is illustrated for him not only in modern theories of class struggle, but also in the older dialectical ethics of Socrates, Plato, and Aristotle. Even Plato's ideal state, he claims, is an armed camp, and Aristotle's whole concept of virtue is really just transformation of a fundamentally military ethic of heroism. Indeed, Aristotle counsels his students to be haughty to those beneath them in station and to make sure that others depend on them.

Against this ontology of violence, Milbank proposes an ontology of peace, the carrier of which is the Christian Church which, following Augustine, he calls the "Other City," founded on different loves. Milbank argues that when we recognize Being as difference, we learn a nonpossessive love which at once cancels and preserves the distance between persons. This is the creative love of God, who brings into Being creatures different from Himself and authentically free, and who calls us to love each other in the same way. There is, Milbank argues, no way to ground this ontology dialectically; indeed to try to do so is to yield to the very ontology of violence which seeks truth through struggle and contradiction.[15]

There are a number of difficulties with Milbank's approach. First, he seems to me to fundamentally misread Plato, Aristotle—and indeed most ancient and medieval metaphysics whether "Western," Indian, and Chinese. As we demonstrated earlier in this chapter, these doctrines rep-

---

15. Graham MacAleer advances a similar ethics based on a reading of Anselm's *De casu diaboli*, where the fall of the Devil is attributed precisely to his desire to become God—precisely the motive behind the dialectical ethics of virtue, even in Thomas (MacAleer 1996). One might see Levinas, who grounds ethics in an encounter with the face of the radically Other, as thinking in much the same vein.

resent an authentic attempt to ascend to a first principle which is always acknowledged to be radically beyond exhaustive rational comprehension. The resulting ethics is, furthermore, very far from that of an armed camp. On the contrary, the metaphysical traditions which emerged from the Axial Age and the Silk Road Era are uniformly optimistic about the possibility of knowledge and habituation to promote right conduct and give the leading role in human society not to the strong but rather to the wise. Second, Milbank's approach fails to address the radical skepticism engendered by both the spontaneous dynamics of the market system and by the conscious polemics of the bourgeoisie. In short, while it might be satisfying to those who already believe, it does nothing to combat the hegemonic nihilism and despair of our time.

Both MacIntyre and Milbank clearly offer visions which are informed by an ethos radically at odds with that of capitalism and modernity generally, but like the religious existentialists and postmodernists they leave the people ideologically disarmed. They represent the perspective of clerics disillusioned with capitalism and modernity but disconnected from and perhaps a bit frightened of the only forces which might actually bring about real change: the organized working class and peasantry.

We turn now to a consideration of Franklin Gamwell's reformed liberalism. Gamwell's position is, in many ways, closest to our own, precisely because he argues for both a teleological approach to ethics and for the necessity of grounding ethics in a theistic metaphysics. His approach to metaphysics is, however, radically at variance with our own, and we need to consider its merits.

Gamwell approaches the problem of metaphysics from within the transcendental tradition which traces its lineage to Kant. By a transcendental approach to metaphysics, we mean any approach which argues by means of an analysis of the conditions or presuppositions of human subjectivity. Thus Kant, for example, argued that human subjectivity was inconceivable apart from what he called the "forms of intuition"—space and time—and the "categories of the understanding"—quality, quantity, relation, and mode. Kant, however, regarded the idea of God, along with the ideas of the self and the world as what he called transcendental ideals—ideas we naturally use to organize our experience of the world, but which are not actually preconditions of any possible experience. For this reason he ruled out rational metaphysics in the traditional sense of the word.

Transcendental theism accepts Kant's basic approach, but argues against him that the idea of God is, in fact, a precondition of or implicit in all acts of human subjectivity. There are many different types of transcendental theism. The most important is undoubtedly the Transcendental Thomism represented by Karl Rahner and Bernard Lonergan. According to Rahner for example every existential judgment we make—every judgment that some particular thing exists, contains a "nonthematic preapprehension" of *esse* as such and thus of God (Rahner 1957). Lonergan (Lonergan 1957), similarly, argues that God as Being is the object of our constitutively human unrestricted desire to know.

Gamwell, while he occasionally makes gestures in the direction of the ontological argument and Thomas' third way (Gamwell 1990: 165–68, 176–78), is actually closer to Kant than most transcendental theists, in that he looks for the foundation of his argument in an analysis of practical reason. He begins from the fact that every human choice, simply because it involves a judgment of better or worse, makes implicit reference to some "comprehensive variable in accord with which all actualities may be compared" (Gamwell 1990: 168), or some principle against which their relative worth can be measured (Gamwell 2000: 13–58). Such a comprehensive variable, in turn, "implies a comprehensive actuality of which all other things are parts" (Gamwell 1990: 168). Following Hartshorne (Hartshorne 1949) he calls this actuality the "divine relativity" a term which, he shows, is convertible with creativity (Gamwell 1990: 169, 178ff., 2000: 122–31, 139–49).

Where Gamwell differs from the Transcendental Thomists is in his characterization of the nature of God. While his argument closely tracks Thomas' fourth way and while he makes some reference to the Thomistic principle of the convertibility of the transcendentals, he rejects the idea that God is outside of space and time on the grounds that this is a purely negative determination and thus not, strictly speaking, comprehensible (Gamwell 1990: 175–76, 2000: 107–22). For Gamwell, as for Hartshorne, God is the supremely temporal individual.

On the basis of this metaphysics, Gamwell is able to derive a well-defined moral imperative: act in such a way as to promote the divine good, understood as maximum future creativity. He follows the Platonic and Aristotelian tradition in tracing wrong action to the limited character of human knowledge, which means that lesser goods are sometimes known more vividly than higher goods, but he rejects the Aristotelian identification of virtue and happiness, arguing that there may well be a contradiction between our own future creativity and that of others and ultimately the maximal future creativity of the universe (Gamwell 2000: 59–104, 131–39).

There are a number of difficulties with this approach. First, transcendental arguments for the existence of God are not really decisive. The fact that the idea of God (whether understood as the Thomistic *esse* or as Hartshorne's divine creativity) is in fact a condition of any possible knowledge and is implicit in each and every human choice, does not necessarily imply that God in fact exists. Second, attempts to rise to the idea of God in a way which, like the transcendental argument, evade rather than passing through cosmology, are inevitably religiously unsatisfying and lead to otherworldliness of a sort which leaves them open to the critiques of Feuerbach, Marx, Nietzsche, and Freud. Third, in spite of its otherworldliness, the transcendental approach fails to challenge fundamentally what is arguably one of the principal characteristics of modernity: the notion that human subjectivity is the proper point of departure for all philosophical reflection. By taking subjectivity as its starting point, transcendental theism (classical or neoclassical) implicitly imports into its system the whole complex of principles and values which constitute modern liberalism. To put this another way, by using subjectivity as the foundation for theology and ethics, transcendental theism rules out in advance the possibility that subjectivity might be called into question.[16]

Finally, Gamwell's concept of God as "supremely temporal" reflects a similar failure to subject modernity to serious criticism. Gamwell's failure to engage the issue of analogical predication means that he not only fails to understand what is meant by the claim that God is eternal, but also and more seriously that he (perhaps accidentally) falls into the trap of a univocal metaphysics. This is reflected above all in his claim that virtue and happiness are not the same in human beings. This is because a univocal metaphysics implies, more or less necessarily, a "zero-sum" view of the world in which the maximal future creativity of one person or system may

16. For a detailed consideration of this problem see Hans Urs von Balthazar's *Love Alone* (von Balthazar 1968) or John Milbank's work (Milbank 1990, 1999). Von Balthazar makes the same criticism, to be sure, of the cosmological approach favored in this work. The criticism applies, however, if and only if the God to which such a cosmological argument points exists in the same way as the world She explains, i.e., if the resulting metaphysics is univocal, and cannot therefore call our assumptions about that world radically into question. This need not be the case.

detract from that of others or even of God. It is just precisely this zero-sum worldview which is shared by both the liberal and the Augustinian traditions which are constitutive of modernity. As we will see, if God, and thus "Being" or "creativity," is understood analogically, then the moral imperative is not so much to maximize creativity or Being (our own or others) but rather to maximize our *participation* in an indivisible and uncreated power of creativity of Being. Our own authentic participation in this power is never in contradiction with the similar power of others nor does it take away from the Power of God who draws all things to Herself.

This brings us to the problem of the social basis and political valence of "transcendental" theism. What this trend does is to recognize the fundamental necessity of an ontological ground to any coherent science, ethics or religion—and thus to the full development of human capacities. They argue further that, *contra* Kant, God is a condition for any possible experience and for any act of human choice, and not merely, as Kant claimed, a moral postulate. But they fail to transcend the realm of the subject which is first and foremost the realm of the marketplace and the bourgeoisie.[17] It is little wonder that at the political level the resulting theologies tend, on the one hand, to legitimate action to restrict and modify the operation of market forces in accord with general moral principles without, however, advocating a real break with the market order. For this reason it is legitimate to speak of "liberal" Protestantism and "liberal" Catholicism. Put differently, transcendental theism makes room for God in bourgeois society, on the condition that God not call the basic structure of that society into question. This is reflected in Gamwell's political theory, which opens up the possibility of democratically-directed state intervention in the market, but which also makes agnosticism about fundamental questions of value the cornerstone of the political order, providing effective constitutional protection for bourgeois right.

• • •

Where does this leave us? It should be clear at this point that the only reliable way to ground moral judgment is in an authentic metaphysics which ascends dialectically to a first principle of explanation which is

---

17. The standpoint of subjectivity is the standpoint of the bourgeoisie because for the bourgeoisie meaning and value are constituted by the individual human subject: they are ultimately grounded in individual preference.

also, at the same time, a first principle of action. Only such a metaphysics can give us a criterion by which we can not only find the market allocation of resources wanting, but also make judgments regarding the relative merit of different claims on resources in the context of a postmarket social order. But is such a metaphysics possible? I will argue that it is. A return to metaphysics, however, involves addressing prior epistemological and cosmological questions. This is the task of the next chapter, which will show that epistemological and metaphysical realism is, in fact compatible with a recognition of the social determination of knowledge, which will argue (on the basis of recent developments in the sciences) for a teleological cosmology, and which will show that metaphysics is in fact the cure and not the cause of the modern disease. The next chapter will also sketch out a metaphysics adequate to the task of grounding a radically historicized natural law ethics. Specifically we will show that any attempt to actually explain, rather than to merely describe, the universe necessarily terminates in something very much like ibn Sina's Necessary Existent or Thomas' *Esse* as such, which can be shown to be convertible with the Beautiful, the True, the Good, and the One—i.e., with transcendental principles of value. Things have value to the extent to which they participate in Being, so that the entire universe becomes a dialectical scale of values (Harris 1991, 1992).

We turn, now, to the problem of constructing a metaphysics adequate to the task of grounding a historicized natural law ethics.

2

Regrounding and Historicizing Natural Law Ethics

WE HAVE ALREADY DEMONSTRATED in the last chapter the superiority of natural law ethics to other approaches. We have also shown that such an ethics requires, if it is to be credible, a firm metaphysical foundation. It is our task in this chapter to supply such a foundation. In the process of doing this we will show that natural law ethics need not be static or ahistorical, but that on the contrary lends itself naturally to a dynamic and radically historical view of the universe.

There have, historically, been three principal objections raised to the dialectical metaphysics on which natural law theory was historically founded. The first objection, which we addressed in the previous chapter, concerns not so much to the possibility of metaphysics generally or of a dialectical metaphysics in particular, but rather the political-theological valence of metaphysical doctrines as such. According to this view metaphysics lies at the root of the modern diseases of technological manipulation and state terror. We have seen that this claim is based on an historical confusion between the traditional, mostly analogical, metaphysical systems of the Silk Road Era and the univocal and immanentist metaphysical systems of the modern era. The second objection is epistemological and claims that we cannot know about the sorts of things metaphysics claims to understand, and which we have shown to be foundational for a natural law ethics: i.e., essential natures, first principles, etc. The third objection, which is cosmological or physical, claims that the universe is not in fact organized in such a way as to point to the existence of transcendental first principles, so that even if we could *do* metaphysics (and not all proponents of this critique deny its possibility) the result would at best be a general science of the laws of motion of matter as such, of the sort elaborated by Engels and the dialectical materialists, which might tell us *how* to promote the development of complex organization, but not *why* we should do this.

Our task in this chapter will be to shore up the epistemological and cosmological foundations of metaphysics, and then sketch out briefly what the metaphysical foundations of a radically historicized natural law ethics might look like.

THE EPISTEMOLOGICAL FOUNDATIONS OF DIALECTICAL METAPHYSICS

Sensation

We have already addressed, in the previous chapter, the principle problems with the various theories of knowledge which have been put forward in order to show the impossibility of dialectical metaphysics. What we need to do here is to explain our alternative. Any such discussion must begin with a defense of the validity of sense data as a gateway to authentic knowledge. According to St. Thomas, all knowledge begins with the senses (Thomas, *Summa Theologiae* I, Q 78, a 3, 4). The five external senses gather data, while the internal senses transform that data in such a way as to produce a rudimentary knowledge of the material world. The data we gain through the senses are formed into coherent images by the *sensus communis*. This is the capacity which allows us, when observing a room, to see walls, chairs, desks, carpets, etc., and not just an undifferentiated feed of data regarding color, light, and shadow, etc. These images may be stored in the memory and reorganized by the imagination, so that we are able to produce images of things which presumably do not exist, such as unicorns and Klingons. Finally, the internal senses involve what Thomas called the estimative faculty. This is the ability to make judgments regarding the proper response to some stimulus prior to any knowledge of intelligible universals. Sensation is possible, for Thomas, because the organs of sensation share a common material nature with things sensed. We will see that this concept of connaturality becomes even more important at the level of intellectual knowledge.

It turns out that this traditional Thomistic account of sensation is strikingly compatible with recent results in the developing science of neuropsychology. The key here is the capacity of the organism to form internally an image (what Thomas called the *phantasm*) of the objects of its experience. It is from this image that abstraction will take place.

While the way in which this happens still remains largely mysterious, recent neuropsychological research in fact appears to be giving us far more than we actually need to refute those who are skeptical about the senses and to establish something like the historic Aristotelian and Thomistic doctrine of the image or phantasm. Signals from the sense organs are relayed along neural fibers to the early sensory cortices—those parts of the brain which seem to be largely responsible for sensation. There they form what Antonio Damasio calls "topographical representations" (Damasio 1994: 98–99). Certain patterns of electrical activity in the brain appear to correspond to certain objects of experience. Experiments regarding sight in monkeys have even found that there is actually a resemblance between the pattern of, say, a grid which is shown to the monkey and the pattern in which the neurons fire (Damasio 1994: 104)—though how this would work with highly complex visual images, or with the other senses, is not clear. These images are then stored not, to be sure, in the form of topographical representations, but as what Damasio calls "dispositional representations." These dispositional representations are modifications of the brain structure which tell certain neurons to "fire" under certain definite conditions. Some dispositional representations encode innate knowledge. These are stored in the hypothalamus, the brain stem, and the limbic system and contain commands related to biological regulation. Those which interest us here, however, those encoding acquired knowledge or memories, are stored in the higher cortices.

When images are recalled, what happens is that these dispositional representations cause neurons to fire, producing a rough facsimile of the original topographic representation. But this is not all that happens. All of our experiences are intimately bound up with feelings—what the Aristotelian tradition calls the passions. The same is true of all of our decision-making processes. Even the most rationalistic among us never really sit down and analyze options in an emotional vacuum. Indeed, were it not for the powerful emotions which accompany the sight of a large truck turning onto the highway just a few dozen feet ahead of us, while we are traveling at sixty miles per hour, we would not long survive to consider such matters as the nature of sensation. Damasio, following William James and others, points out that these passions always involve body states (Damasio 1994: 129). Try to imagine desire or anger without that quickening of the heart—somehow slightly different in the case of each passion. It is impossible. The implication is that our memories—our dispositional representations—store not only images but also body states, which are recalled along with the image, setting our hearts racing and our blood surging and, perhaps, engorging certain members and creating a complex affective or, to use a more Thomistic term, "passional" context for our decision making. It is this capacity not only to form and store and recall images, but to link them to body-states or passionate responses to our perceptions, and to store and recall those states and those links which constitute what Thomas called the "estimative faculty."[1]

Contemporary neuropsychology, in other words, far from suggesting that the old Aristotelian and Thomistic understanding of sensation is outmoded is, in fact, developing an account which is remarkably similar. What happens in the act of sense-perception, as in the simpler act of sensitivity, is that the organism undergoes a structural modification—it takes on a new form, that of the object perceived. This modification does not degrade the organism but rather, because it is linked to body states or passions through complex dispositional representations, helps it to maintain its integrity and to realize its latent potential. The new form is a perfection, a second degree of actuality of the body which, in addition to its own form, can take on myriad others—though at the level of sensation these are still particular forms. The soul is not yet capable of becoming "all things." Similarly, it becomes ordered to its own good, which implies the Good in itself, but cannot yet intend this higher end, but only serve it implicitly with the humble but beautiful service rendered by the animals simply by being what they are and seeking and desiring what they need to live.

Before proceeding any further it might be well to point out that this approach to the problem of knowledge provides a powerful answer to the objections of skeptical empiricists and critical ideals (Hume 1777/1886,

1. The reader may object that the neurobiological results we have cited could *also* be interpreted to lend credence in varying degrees to sociobiological, behaviorist, or other approaches to learning and knowledge, depending on where the line between innate and learned knowledge is drawn. This is correct, in so far as these trends also acknowledge a relationship between what we experience (the image) and the real world. But even at this stage in the argument we should note that the Aristotelian and Thomistic account of the internal senses is far more developed, and more nearly compatible with the results of neurobiology than, say, Lockean empiricism, which treats the mind as a blank slate, and allows no role for the soul in *producing* the image. In the later stages of our argument, where we analyze the process of abstraction, and the role of the image in this process, we will differentiate our position, and the Aristotelian tradition generally, more clearly from moderate as well as radical empiricism.

Kant 1781/1969) regarding the reliability of the senses. It is, on the one hand, quite clear that our sensory apparatus is selective in what data it collects and in just how it fashions that data into images. A dog experiences me differently than a monkey would—no color, mostly smells. Human sensation, like all other animal sensation, privileges some data over others and thus gives an incomplete image of the object. There is also no real reason to believe that a one to one or "onto-" relation exists between our images and the objects to which they correspond. At the same time, the fact that animal sensation appears to have survival value suggests that it conveys some real knowledge of the animal's environment. The phenomena of error and disappointment, furthermore, suggest that we are, in fact, capable of distinguishing between perceptions which convey real knowledge and those that do not. We do not always "see what we want to see," and when we do the illusion does not last for long. And even radical skeptics are hesitant to treat perceptions affected by brain lesions and other disorders as simply another point of view or a window into an alternate reality.

Intellect

EMPIRICISM

Human knowledge does not stop with sensation, but advances to knowledge of intelligible truths. We not only recognize cats, in the sense of knowing that they are different from carp and require a different response; we know *what* they are. We can grasp the form or underlying structure of things, and, if the system in question is sufficiently simple (this is clearly *not* the case with cats) represent it mathematically and then manipulate the resulting formalisms according to the rules of logic to generate new conclusions. We can even, Thomas argues, rise to the first principle, God or Being itself, and show that this principle is convertible with the Beautiful, the True, the Good, and the One, providing a ground for judgments of value.

The question, of course, is just how we do this. There are many thinkers who, especially in the light of advances in neuropsychology and information theory, attempt to explain the intellect exclusively in terms of "information processing" taking place in "neural networks." Let us pause at this point and ask how much of the intellect we are able to explain on the basis of this approach—and what kind of intellect is possible if we restrict the intellect to the operation of the brain. Intelligence, given what we have said so far, is going to consist largely in the development of a complex system of interconnections, made possible by the development of the higher neocortex, between the images produced and stored in the lower sensory cortices. Ideas, in other words, are simply associations between images. If we add to this network of neural relationships complex interconnections with the hypothalamus and other subcortical regions responsible for biological regulation, we get an approximate definition of the "will" and its relationship to the passions. If passions arise because of dispositional representations which associate sensory images with body states, the will exists because of dispositional representations which associate *relationships between images* with body states. Thus, the *passion* of maternal love might consist in a link between the image of a new born baby and a body state which pre-disposes us to care-taking behavior. Love understood as an act of the will would link the same body state with a complex of relationships between images which includes images of babies (perhaps with bloated stomachs and large searching eyes), aid workers distributing grain, and ourselves writing checks.

We must, however, be cautious here. It is one thing to say that even our most complex ideas and appetites can be broken down into relationships between images stored in and processed by the nervous system, and quite another thing to say that they can be adequately explained in these terms, or that they are "nothing more than" this. A turtle swimming ashore to lay eggs (Mayr 1988) is certainly a chemical system, and both her motion and whatever cognitive processes are involved in moving her clearly involve many complex chemical reactions. But the chemistry doesn't explain why she comes ashore; or why in general the eggs are laid on land rather than at sea. The same is true of intellect. Thinking the idea of God may involve relating myriad bits of data (or images) to each other and, at the physiological level, the establishment of complex neural networks, but that is not *why* people have the idea of God. It is only *how*. Indeed, we shall see that it is only a *part* of how. In both cases there is a higher level of organization at issue, the emergence and operation of which cannot be explained adequately in terms of the lower levels.

Rationalism

But thinkers who separate the intellect entirely from matter and specifically from the internal and external senses—the rationalists and the critical and objective idealists—also err. To say that the intellect simply draws out the logical implications of analytically self-evident propositions, or that it "sees" intelligibles in the divine light of eternal reason is to separate intellectual knowledge from its passional context, which is just precisely what tells us it is knowledge of something real and important. The passional context of knowledge means that it already takes place in a teleological context; our bodies are ordered to the fulfillment of certain needs which are necessary if they are to survive and reproduce and grow and develop. That the intellect itself involves an "ordering to," and not simply an "ordering" means that the act of the intellect cannot be understood exclusively in terms of what is happening inside the human mind. Berkeleyan subjective idealism, in other words, which identifies being with perception, is excluded. Nor are matters helped much if we specify in addition that intelligence involves "meaning" in the sense favored by contemporary information theory (Tipler 1994), i.e., a relationship between symbols and something in the environment. The relations between symbols and the environment must be structured in such a way as help the organism survive. And this, as we showed above, involves the notion that the symbols encode real knowledge about the environment. The image, in other words, already contains the universal, whether or not the organism in question is capable of abstracting it. Intellect is ordered through the image to the universal embodied in the image, which tells us what it is an image of, and thus how we ought to react to it, and through the universal to the Truth, which is affirmed in the judgment that the particular perceived with the senses, really *is* an example of the universal known in the concept. It is this ordering to the Truth which makes the intellect such a powerful tool for the survival and development of the organism.

Reconciling Dialectical Realism with the Sociology of Knowledge

The finite intellect thus knows only by turning to something outside itself. This something cannot be God, who we know only mediately, by inference from particulars. It must, therefore, be the data of the senses or, as we have specified above, the image or "phantasm" produced by the brain in response to stimuli received from the external sense organs. Thomas, following Aristotle, understands the process by which we grasp intelligible truths encoded in these images as one of "abstraction." A faculty called the "agent intellect" illuminates the images or "phantasms" we garner from experience and abstracts from them their intelligible essences. The passive or potential intellect then takes on the form of the thing known, thereby "becoming" it "intentionally" (Aristotle, *De anima* III, Thomas, *Summa Theologiae* I Q 85, a 1, 2, and *De Veritate* 2:2, Maritain 1937, Peifer 1964).

Now Aristotle, who first advanced the idea of the agent intellect, left its status rather ambiguous. On the one hand, the intellect is a power of the soul, which is the form of the body, and would appear to be something individual. On the other hand, as an immaterial principle, the intellect was individuated by its species, suggesting that there was, in fact, only one intellect for all of humanity (von Steenberghen 1980: 29–74). Ibn Sina (Avicenna) regarded intellection as a fundamentally divine activity and treated the agent intellect as the last of the intelligences which emanates from the unmoved mover. This agent intellect was responsible for creating the forms of all material objects and for "informing" the individual "potential intellects" of each individual with the essence of the objects it experienced. Later commentators, such as Ibn Rusd (Averroes) went further, arguing that not only the agent but also the passive intellect is one—that we know universals not with individual minds but with a single collective mind which, in effect, does our thinking for us, using individual human animals essentially as data collectors.

To claim the unity of the agent and even more so of the passive intellect seems bizarre and contrary to experience. We appear, for better or worse, to do our own thinking and to have different ideas from other people. It also creates serious theological problems, calling into question personal immortality and moral responsibility, among other things. Still, the doctrine captures something important about the nature of human knowledge of universals—that it derives from our participation in a reality larger and higher than ourselves and distinctly different from, even as it builds on, our animal endowments. Dante (Alighieri. *De Monarchia*), who had been influenced by the Latin Averroists but rejected metaphysical monopsychism, stressed that it took humanity as a whole, collectively, to realize the full potential of the human intellect. He thus implicitly recognized knowledge as a social reality which develops over time and which is bound up both with the structures which organize human civilizations and with the larger struggle for a just social order which makes possible the full development of human capacities (Gilson 1968: 167).

Dante's approach suggests it might indeed be possible to join a dialectical sociology and a realist metaphysics of knowledge after all.

It has become clear from the study of human cognition that, whatever the role of biological factors, the development of the intellect depends on, even as it contributes to, the emergence of ever more complex forms of social organization (Durkheim 1911/1965, Bogdanov 1928/1980, Luria 1974/1976). This suggests that what Aristotle called the agent intellect is, in fact, nothing other than human society. This way of understanding the agent intellect provides an interesting solution to the problem of its unity or multiplicity. The social system is both one and many. It is "one" in the sense that it is ultimately a single interconnected system, prior to the individual, which informs his/her particular intellect from the outside. It is many both in its internal diversity and in the sense that it is internalized, and internalized differently by different individuals, so that however dependent we are on our social context for the basic forms of our thought, there is no group mind which is doing our thinking for us. But the development of higher degrees of abstraction depends in part at least on the development of more complex forms of social organization, and might be held back by deformations in the social structure.

Just how this works becomes clear when we consider a second concept from the Thomistic theory of knowledge, i.e., the idea of connaturality. The basic idea here is simple: that like knows like. We have already seen how this informs the Aristotelian-Thomistic theory of sensation. But Thomas develops the idea further, and suggests that it is the key to intellectual knowledge as well. His starting point here is the Jewish concept of *da'ath elohim*. Generally translated "knowledge of God," the prophets continually identified *da'ath elohim* with ethical conduct (e.g., Hos 4:1–2; 6:3). The idea is that in the just act we know God experientially and nonconceptually, because in that act we share in the divine nature—i.e., we become connatural with God. This forms the basis for the Catholic doctrine of "caritative wisdom," the nonconceptual wisdom which characterizes the highest levels of mystical experience, where acting with a perfect divine love and justice, we in effect become divine ourselves and in knowing our own act know God in Her essence (Thomas *Summa Theologiae* II, Q 45, a2, Maritain 1937).

It follows from this insight that anything we live or do, we, in a certain sense, become and thus know. Thus Thomas argues that the person who has prudence, temperance, fortitude, or justice, knows these virtues even without studying philosophy of theology. But this means that by living *in* a definite social structure we in effect *live* that structure and become con-

Degrees of Abstraction

natural with it and thus know it pre-conceptually and experientially. This preconceptual knowledge then illuminates the images we garner from our sense experience and allows us to perceive certain aspects of their intelligible structure—but not others which remain opaque because we have not yet lived them.

In order to see the explanatory power of this theory we need first to distinguish between the various degrees of intellectual knowledge[2] and ask why certain degrees or forms of knowledge seem to predominate in some societies rather than others. The Thomistic tradition has, following Aristotle, historically distinguished between total and formal abstraction, and between the three degrees of formal abstraction, *abstractio totius, abstractio formae,* and *separatio*. Total abstraction simply abstracts from the individual to the class of which it is a member, without concluding to an authentic definition. Total abstraction would thus leave Fido and Rover behind in favor of a vague idea of "dog" which associated a name with a cluster of images. Formal abstraction, on the other hand, actually rises to the concept of a thing. The first degree of formal abstraction, *abstractio totius* abstracts from individualizing matter, i.e., it leaves behind Fido and Rover to rise to the notion of "dog" (e.g., as a specific form of carnivore with a snout, social hunting, etc.). For Thomas as for Aristotle this sort of abstraction is especially characteristic of physics, but it is, of course, employed by all of the sciences. *Abstractio formae* abstracts from matter as such, in order to render the form fully intelligible. For Thomas as for Aristotle this is the sort of abstraction which is characteristic of mathematics. One leaves behind the orbits of the particular planets in order to rise to their intelligible form, which is that of an ellipse. The third degree of formal abstraction, which he calls *separatio*, which is characteristic of first philosophy or metaphysics, "separates" the act of existence from not

---

2. Readers should note that the question of the degrees of abstraction is quite controversial in Thomistic circles and that this account is simplified at best. For a fuller treatment cf. Mansueto 2002b, as well as Cajetan, *In De Ente et Essentia, Prooemium*, Q 1, n 5., *De Nominium Analogia* 5; John of St. Thomas, *Ars Logica* II, Q 27, a 1; Maritain 1937, 1951; Simmons 1959; Maurer 1964, Pugh 1997. I find the distinction between total and formal abstraction as outlined by the Dominican commentators problematic, because I am unsure of the possibility of a classification without some element of definition and of a clear definition which is not strictly formal. I thus prefer a simple threefold classification of the degrees of abstraction as total, formal, and transcendental.

only the matter but also the form, and judges that existence is possible apart from matter, and that there is indeed something which exists apart from matter, namely God or Being itself (Thomas, *In Boethius De Trinitate* Q 5.). This final degree of abstraction I call transcendental, because in rising to the idea of Being such it also rises to the transcendental properties of Being, i.e., those properties of Being which pertain to things simply in so far as they *are*, rather than because of *what* they are (Thomas, *Summa Theologiae* I Q 5, 6, 11, 16; Reith 1958: 122ff.). Traditional enumerations of the transcendentals include Beauty, Truth, Goodness, and Unity. This is the sort of abstraction which is involved both in scientific explanation, which shows why something is and why it is the way it is, as well as in the metaphysical ascent to God. Clearly it is also this sort of abstraction alone which allows us to conclude to principles of value.

We should point out that the distinction made in German Idealism between "*Verstand*" or Understanding and "*Vernunft*" or Reason is in fact convertible with the distinction between formal and transcendental abstraction. *Verstand* grasps merely the external relationships among phenomena, through the media of categories (logical wholes, mathematical formalisms) whereas *Vernunft* penetrates their inner essence and comprehends their organizing principle. For Kant, of course, such a grasp of the organizing principle is possible only for practical reason, which grasps the principles of our actions; for Hegel, who regards Spirit as the Idea become conscious of itself as it emerges from its self-externalization in nature, *Vernunft* is, in fact the principle of the natural as well as the social worlds, both of which can be comprehended in their totality (Hegel, *Encyclopaedia* para 467 *Zusatz*). Hegel gives as an example of *Verstand* Kepler's laws of planetary motion. The existence of the planets, their nature as planets, and their motion are all given; there is no necessary relationship between these givens and the laws of motion themselves. This does not mean that Kepler's laws are without value. "Understanding . . . is a necessary moment of rational thinking" (Hegel, *Encyclopaedia* para 467 *Zusatz*). Before we can advance to *Vernunft* we must first "separate the essential from the contingent" (i.e., the general or universal from the particular) and advance to a rigorous definition. Kepler's discovery thus merits "eternal fame" (Hegel, *Encyclopaedia (Outline)* para 212). But the categories in terms of which the laws are framed can themselves be comprehended only by the higher faculty of *Vernunft* which, having grasped the Idea, can then return to derive from it "the concepts of space and time, the moments whose relation is motion" (Hegel, *Encyclopaedia (Outline)* para 212). Dialectical materialism makes a similar distinction between degrees of intellectual knowledge, though the terminology used is less regularly and consistently. Marx, for example, distinguished between bourgeois political economy, which grasped only the external relations between commodities, and his own critique of political economy which penetrated their inner essence (Marx 1863/1971: 500).

There is more at issue here, however, than simply penetrating beneath the phenomenon to the organizing principle. This organizing principle is, for both Hegel and Marx, a principle of motion or of development. Once one has grasped the inner logic of something, one has also grasped its internal contradictions and thus the conditions for its supersession by a still more complex form of organization. Thus in Hegel's "critique of mechanics" a rational comprehension of space, time, and motion is also, at the same time, a grasp of the rational necessity of the "elementary particle," the existence of which is implied by these more abstract categories. And in Marx's critique of political economy, comprehending capitalism means comprehending the crisis tendencies which lead ultimately to its dissolution and supersession by a higher form of organization, i.e., socialism. Where *Verstand* can only describe change, *Vernunft* comprehends it. In this sense as well *Vernunft* is like the Aristotelian-Thomistic *separatio* or what I have called transcendental abstraction, which grasps the principle which draw all things into Being.

Now if we look at the historical development of human thought, it rapidly becomes apparent that while totalization is nearly universal, a reflex of the division of even the simplest human societies into *taxa* (clans, phratries, tribes, etc.), formal abstraction develops only in market societies. Thus, a fully abstract mathematics develops for the first time in Greece in the sixth century, a period which witnessed the rapid development of petty commodity relations as the emergence of a specialized agriculture centered on wine and oil production led to an explosion of trade coupled with rapid economic differentiation (Anderson 1974). Mathematical formalization, furthermore, becomes the ideal of knowledge only in societies which, like our own, are characterized by generalized commodity production. The apparent absence of formal abstraction on premarket societies is also attested by Luria's research in Uzbekistan in the 1920s, where he found that peasants from remote villagers, unlike those who were participating in collective farms, show little or no ability to solve simple problems requiring formal reasoning. This is hardly surprising. In a market economy society presents itself as a system of quantities (prices) and people soon begin to view the universe as a whole in much the same way.

The historical development of transcendental abstraction presents us with a far more complex picture. Most communitarian societies clearly have something like a capacity for transcendental abstraction, as is attested by the elaboration of myths which involve imaginative representations of something like a transcendental first principle. Consider the Keres *Sussistinako*, or Thinking Woman, who thinks out and brings the universe into being. This capacity to rise to knowledge of the organization principle of the universe rests on the day to day experience of life in a community in which every person has a definite function in service to a common end, an experience which makes it possible to theorize the ultimate purpose of the universe as a whole. The struggles of oppressed peasant communities against the warlord states of the tributary epoch seem to have further developed this capacity. Thus *'El yahwi sabaoth yisrael*, El who brings into being the armies of Israel, is soon recognized as *yhwh*, the causative power of Being itself, who is also creator of heaven and earth (Gottwald 1979: 682, 825).

At the same time, this sort of transcendental abstraction is without benefit of formalization. Philosophy, which depends on both formal and transcendental abstraction, emerges only in market societies. But here we run into a paradox. As market relations penetrate into every sphere of life and traditional village communities dissolve, it becomes more and more difficult for people to see any global purpose in society—or indeed in the universe. The capacity for transcendental abstraction atrophies. Philosophy, we will argue, emerges as a form of resistance to this dynamic, an form of defense of the sapiential dimension of human knowledge against the nihilism generated by the market order—and thus of humanity's higher capacities generally against their degradation by consumerism.

From Hermeneutic Circle to Dialectical Spiral

Does not this solution, though, open the floodgates for relativism and undermine the possibility of any authentic knowledge of universals? If society *is* the agent intellect, are not the universals to which it concludes merely social products; artifacts of the way particular societies organize themselves; useful, perhaps, for understanding the customs and mores of the societies in question but hardly a window on the organization of the universe, much less on God and the transcendental principles of value?

The answer to this question turns on our earlier analysis of the nature of sensation. Once we have established that the images we garner from the senses really do encode information about the organization of the universe, and that intellectual knowledge is based on an abstraction from the senses, and is not merely the free creation of a disembodied intellect (human or divine), then we must acknowledge that the ideas we abstract from these images have, at the very least, some connection with reality. The strength of this connection can furthermore be tested in practice. Incorrect ideas simply do not work. There can be no doubt that human societies, like the sensory systems of various animal species, are finite and can reveal only part of the systems which they perceive. There is, furthermore, no doubt that the part of reality which is revealed by these structures is selected by the needs of the social systems in question, just as animals develop those senses which serve their adaptive strategies. But abstractions which help a society to survive and flourish must disclose something important about the way the universe really works, just as well adapted sensory systems disclose something important about an animal's environment. Ideas and systems of ideas which lead to stagnation and decline are probably flawed in some way. Ideas, in other words, develop on definite material bases (the human nervous system) and are formed by definite structural principles (those of the society in which they are produced). They are, nonetheless, ordered to the Truth, even if they also serve particular social interests. Indeed, their ability to serve those interests, and the viability of those interests themselves, is constrained by their relationship to the Truth.

But there is more. The *interest* served by all ideas is, ultimately, Being as such. This is what all things seek, each in their own way: minerals in thermodynamic stability, plants in nutrition, growth, and reproduction, animals in sensation and locomotion, and human beings in pleasure, wealth, power, love, and knowledge. Even conquest and exploitation are, ultimately, ways of seeking Being, however misguided. Incorrect ideas, furthermore, simply do not work, at least in the long run. And so in understanding the social basis and political valence of ideas we read them as strategies in the pursuit of Being, and evaluate them as such.

From this vantage point it becomes clear that recognition of the role of social structures in shaping our ideas, including our metaphysical ideas, is by no means opposed to the agenda of epistemological and metaphysical realism—even to a strong realism which claims to be able to rise to the idea of God and of the transcendental principles of value. Ideological criticism which points out the social basis and political valence of metaphysical ideas is, rather, an integral part of the dialectic of ascent by which we discover what the Truth is and indeed that it Is. Demonstrating that a particular set of ideas (e.g., the Aztec belief that the universe came into being through divine self-sacrifice and had to be sustained by continuing human sacrifice) legitimates particular social interests (that of the Aztec warlords and their priestly allies) does not by itself demonstrate that the ideas in question are wrong. But when we understand that the Aztec empire fell, and how, including the ways in which Aztec religion was implicated in the fall, we are at least one step closer to knowing that the Aztecs were (at least partly) wrong after all, as well as to gaining some insight into what does in fact create and sustain organization (social or cosmic). A definitive judgment, of course, is possible only at the End, which we can never know with certainty and in advance. But the cumulative judgments of history, harvested by ideological criticism, do in fact gradually give shape to at least a rough and ready knowledge of what Is, and thus to some criterion for judgment. Metaphysics is, in fact, epistemologically possible.

THE COSMOLOGICAL FOUNDATIONS OF DIALECTICAL METAPHYSICS

Once the epistemological problems facing us have been resolved, it is then necessary to demonstrate that the universe is structured in such a way as to point to a transcendental principle of value. This means confronting head on the problems of both Aristotelian science, on which the earlier dialectical metaphysics and natural law theory depended, and the picture of the universe bequeathed to us by modern science.

As we have already noted, Aristotle's physics was rejected for two different sets of reasons, one scientific and the other theological. We have already considered the theological critique of Aristotelian physics in the previous chapter, in our analysis of the Augustinian Reaction of the thirteenth century. For now let us concern ourselves with the scientific problems which confronted Aristotelian physics in the late medieval and early modern periods. These, in turn, fall into two categories: theoretical and empirical. First, Aristotelian physics lacked a unified theory of motion. Aristotle's scientific strategy, and that of his medieval commentators, centered on explaining things in terms of their ends or purposes. The universe was drawn into being and set into motion by the attractive power of the unmoved mover, the effects of which were mediated to the sublunar realm by the intelligences which governed the various heavenly spheres. The sublunar realm, in turn, constituted a hierarchy of lesser goods, each of which motivated the growth and development of the various grades of material being: the cultivation of intellectual and moral virtue for human beings, new and more pleasant sensations and graceful and powerful movement for animals, nutrition, growth and reproduction for plants, stability of form for minerals, and the possession of the basic planetary qualities (hot, cold, wet, and dry) for the elements. The entire universe is thus understood as an organism striving for God.

But how does one explain teleologically a decaying corpse or a thrown javelin? These processes do not seem in any sense ordered to the perfection of form. Thus Aristotle had made a distinction between natural motion, which is driven by teleological attraction, and violent motion driven by impressed force. This in turn led to a distinction between the celestial realm, where all motion is natural, and the sublunar realm where both kinds of change occur. This undermined the theoretical unity and elegance of the system.

Second, Aristotelian science had considerable difficulty coming to terms with new empirical evidence which contradicted specific aspects of existing Aristotelian physics, even if they did not touch its underlying logic. Thus Galileo's experiments with falling bodies contradicted the Aristotelian claim that heavier bodies will fall faster than those which weigh less, and the observations of Copernicus and Tycho and the celestial mechanics of Kepler suggested that the heavens did not, in fact, form the hierarchy of nested spheres required by Aristotelian physics (Murdoch and Sylla 1978, Grant 1978, Pedersen 1978, Lindberg 1992).

There were two ways to resolve this problem. One would have been to generalize the concept of teleology in such a way as to accommodate the reality of violent motion, and to abandon the particular cosmological models developed by Aristotle in order to save the principle of teleological ordering. There were powerful reasons to take just precisely this approach. Aristotle and his interpreters had, after all, already implicitly shown that the only complete explanation is a teleological explanation.

This is because a complete explanation must terminate in a principle which (directly or indirectly) explains everything else while being self-explanatory. Such a principle must be necessary, infinite, and perfect (and thus divine), and it must cause exclusively by the attractive power of its own perfection (otherwise it would be in motion itself and would thus require some other explanatory principle, resulting in an infinite regress) (Aristotle, *Metaphysics* 1071b–76b, Thomas, *Summa Theologiae* I, Q2).

This was not, however, the road taken—largely for the political theological reasons outlined in the previous chapter. Teleology was abandoned altogether, and (though this was never acknowledged, or perhaps, even really recognized) the possibility of a complete explanation along with it. Instead, an attempt was made to develop increasingly general mathematical formalisms which describe motion (now conceived exclusively as change in place). Thus the whole history of mathematical physics, beginning with the special theories of Galileo and Kepler, up through the "first unification" by Newton, and each of the successive generalizations and unifications: Hamiltonian dynamics, Maxwell's equations, relativity, quantum mechanics, and most recently quantum cosmology. By supplementing quantum mechanics with thermodynamics we can explain chemical interactions. Molecular biology is, in turn, rapidly reducing biological processes to their chemical underpinnings, while sociobiology claims to demonstrates that all human interactions, even the most complex, are merely an attempt on the part of our genes to reproduce themselves. The appearance of complex organization is simply the result of random interactions, which accidentally generate structures which are more thermodynamically stable and are thus conserved by natural selection.

Modern science is presented to the general public as if it were a unified system which provides us with a comprehensive explanation of the universe without recourse to "metaphysical" principles and without internal contradictions. It is also, often, presented as having resolved once and for all the question of the existence of God and of the ultimate meaningfulness of the universe. Thus the common "wisdom" of our time, holds that the universe came into being as the result of a "quantum fluctuation," is governed by chaos and contingency, yields complex organization only as a result of random variation and natural selection, and will either continue to expand endlessly, so that the interactions which lead to complexity become less and less frequent and eventually cease altogether, or else collapse in a "big crunch" in which life and intelligence and civilization are lost forever. In such a universe meaning and value are at best temporary and fragile constructs of the human individual and human society—and at worst illusions which cover a weak-hearted inability to confront the darkness and the abyss. And such a universe hardly requires for its explanation (indeed would seem to *exclude*) a principle infinite, perfect, necessary, and thus divine. Only such a principle, however, can ground meaning which is ultimate in character. All else is partial and contingent.

And yet "modern science" is in crisis—and has been almost since its inception—because of a complex of internal contradictions. Indeed, while it has certainly made significant contributions to our understanding of the universe and even greater contributions to technological development, modern science has shown itself no better able than its Aristotelian predecessor to advance a unified theory of motion. On the contrary, the mathematical-physical description of the universe is characterized by three fundamental contradictions which no theory thus far proposed has been able to overcome, i.e., the contradictions between:

1. relativity and quantum mechanics,
2. dynamics generally and thermodynamics, and
3. thermodynamics and evolutionary theory.

The first of these contradictions derives fundamentally from a difference in the mathematical formalisms used by each discipline. Relativity, which describes both the underlying structure of space-time and the behavior of gravitational interactions, assumes that change is continuous—i.e., that space and time are infinitely divisible and that objects can move (and energy thus be transferred) in arbitrarily small quantities. Because light moves at a finite speed and nothing moves faster, relativity forbids instantaneous signaling, while at the same time insisting that in order for one part of a system to affect another some sort of signal must be exchanged. Relativity, in other words, conserves a very strong concept of causation. At the same time, the recognition that light moves at a finite and constant speed implies that space-time has a dynamic structure which depends on the relative motion of observers and their proximity to massive bodies. Quantum mechanics, on the other hand, which was developed to describe electromagnetic interactions and which has been extended to describe the weak and strong nuclear interactions as well, treats the universe as a discrete order in which energy transfer and thus movement are quantized. While quantum formalisms are fully deterministic, some quantum phenomena seem to imply something other than a classical concept of causality. And quantum formalisms, in so far as they describe the evolution of systems in space over time conserve an essentially Newtonian understanding of space-time. Even sophisticated string-theoretical formalisms fail to resolve these difficulties.

Above and beyond these purely theoretical difficulties, the amalgam of relativity and quantum mechanics which dominates physical cosmology has run into increasing empirical difficulties. The application of relativity to cosmological problems, for example, has historically depended on the assumption of cosmic homogeneity, but observational data has been building for some time which suggests that the universe is anything but homogenous, and may well be structured at the very largest scales.[3] Most cosmological models, furthermore, predict that the quantity of matter in the universe should be at least close the value necessary to eventually halt cosmological expansion. Current measurements, however, suggest that this is not the case, something which has led cosmologists to postulate the existence of invisible "dark matter," for which we have no direct evidence. Recent observations have, furthermore, led to the discovery of stars older than the universe itself is supposed to be. And big bang models consistently make incorrect predictions regarding the basic ratios of such elements as Deuterium, Helium, and Lithium (Lerner 1991).

These contradictions notwithstanding, relativity and quantum mechanics have far more in common than either does with thermodynamics. The first two disciplines describe processes which are reversible using formalisms which do not distinguish a well defined arrow of time; the second describes irreversible change. While it is not, strictly speaking, true to say that relativity treats time as "just another dimension," (the negative sign on the time term in the Minkowski metric means that the temporal dimension still behaves differently than the spatial dimensions), no purely mechanical formalism can adequately describe irreversible change. In order to understand this simply assume any simple system of point particles with mass—e.g., the solar system. Now assume, variously, Newtonian, Hamiltonian, relativistic, or quantum descriptions of

---

3. If indeed there is a largest scale. It is the assumption of cosmological homogeneity, we will remember, which leads (via the solutions to Einstein's field equations) to the conclusion that the universe must be finite. But if it turns out that the universe is not infinite, then there is no largest scale, but only an ascending hierarchy of structured systems.

that system—i.e., descriptions in terms of position, mass, velocity, spin, charge, etc. Allow that system to evolve over time, then pick two arbitrary states of the system. You will not be able to tell simply from observation which state came first and which second. This is not true in the case of thermodynamic descriptions. If someone showed you a picture of a warm house on a cold winter day with all of the doors and windows closed and an internal temperature of 20° C, while outside the reading was -20°C, and another with the doors open and the readings now nearly the same, you would be constrained to assume that either the first picture was taken before the second, or that there had been some outside intervention into the system—e.g., the family living in the house returned to find the doors open and the heat off and rectified the situation.

This is not to say that the question of time is not important for relativity and quantum mechanics, but the questions pursued by these disciplines are not questions which arise from our day to day experience, but rather questions which are generated by the formalisms themselves: questions such as time dilation and the possibility of time travel. Thermodynamic time, on the other hand, is the time we fight on a day to day basis, the time which, "like an ever-flowing stream, bears all her sons away"[4] and which is a mark of the finitude of all material systems.

But if thermodynamics is able to theorize irreversible change, the change which it theorizes is always and only dissipation and disintegration, and the one of the principal discoveries of the past two hundred years is the reality of evolutionary change, of a development at least locally from lower to higher degrees of organization. Thermodynamics, which is our only theory of irreversible change at the fundamental physical level says that this really ought not to be possible, being ruled out by such basic principles of thermodynamics as the Second Law and the Boltzmann Order Principle (Prigogine 1977, 1984). To say that the principle of self-organization is supplied by natural selection is not really adequate. Natural selection, as biologist Lynn Margulis puts it, plays the role of editor, not that of author, in the evolutionary process. In rigorous formulations of the Neo-Darwinist theory, first of all, it is random variation and the recombination of genes, not natural selection, which is supposed to generate variety. And random variation turns out not to supply anything like the level of innovation necessary to explain evolution-

---

4. The reference here is to Isaac Watts' hymn "O God Our Help in Ages Past."

ary change. Complex systems theorist Ilya Prigogine has shown that "the time necessary to produce a comparatively small protein chain of around 100 amino acids by *spontaneous* formation of structure is much longer than the age of the Earth. Hence, spontaneous formation of structure is ruled out ... according to the modern theory of self-organizing systems, classical arguments concerning the 'coincidental' realization of a complex living system cannot be employed" (Zimmerman 1991).

Molecular biologist Barry Hall, similarly, has found that the bacterium E. coli produces needed mutations at a rate roughly 100 million times greater than would be expected if they came about by chance. Nor can random variation and natural selection account for the fact that evolutionary changes often seem to occur rather suddenly, rather than in gradual increments, as the theory of natural selection would suggest. A retina or a cornea, after all, without the rest of the organ, would have no survival value by itself, and would be unlikely to be preserved in future generations.

Above and beyond these specific contradictions, there is a more fundamental difficulty which has begun to affect mathematical physics, an issue at which we have already hinted in some of our earlier discussions. This is the problem of cosmological fine-tuning: the fact that some twenty fundamental parameters, including the relative strengths of the four fundamental forces and the relative masses of the four stable particles, are fixed in just precisely the way that would be necessary in order to make possible the development of stars, and thus the heavy elements and hospitable habitats, required for the evolution of life and intelligence. Even slight variations would lead to a lifeless universe.

Given this situation, the time has come to ask whether modern science is any better able than its Aristotelian predecessor to offer a unified theory of motion. The contradictions cited above suggest rather pointedly that it is not. Perhaps it is time to consider the road not taken: an expansion of the concept of teleology so that it can accommodate chaos and disintegration, and thus dispense with the dualisms inherent in Aristotle's original formulation. And this is precisely the direction implicit in the work of a number of physicists and biologists who are (sometimes in spite of themselves) rediscovering the necessity of teleological explanation to a complete science, and gradually helping to reground a teleological cosmology. One need only mention the work of such diverse thinkers as David Bohm (Bohm 1980), Benjamin Gal-Or (Gal-Or 1986), Ilya

Prigogine (Prigogine et al 1977, 1979, 1984, 1989; Eric Lerner 1991), Rupert Sheldrake (Sheldrake 1981), and Lynn Margulis (Margulis and Fester 1991). Recognition of the radical interconnectedness of all things, of the fine-tuning of key physical constants, which seem to be fixed in just such a way as to make possible the development of complex organization, life, and intelligence, and of the tendency of all matter to develop towards increasingly complex forms of organization: these are the marks of a resurgent teleological science which has not yet broken through the bonds of the hegemonic mathematical physics, but which will ultimately make such a break not only possible but necessary.

I have argued elsewhere (Mansueto forthcoming) for a new teleological research program which would build on the work of these thinkers and not so much displace mathematical physics as supplement it. Mathematical physics offers us a rigorous description of the *how* the universe works, but only a teleological science can tell us *why* it is the way it is, and ultimately why it *is* at all. Such a teleological science would explain things in terms of three factors:

1. the material conditions under which they develop, which constrain the availability of various resources (raw materials, energy),
2. the dominant structure, which determines how these resources are used, and
3. teleological attractors, both local and universal, appropriate to the level of organization in question.

At any given point existing structures at once facilitate and constrain development, so that the teleological drive towards higher degrees of organization, and thus a higher ontological grade, sometimes comes to conflict with the existing structure, which is then burst asunder and replaced by new forms more conducive to growth. This process takes very different forms at different levels of organization (physical, biological, and social). It is at once necessary, operating with iron-clad certainty towards the long-term development of higher degrees of organization, and radically open, proceeding along lines which can never be completely predicted, constrained only by what is logically possible, and by certain general conditions, which are embodied in fundamental physical law, which are necessary to the existence of any sort of organization whatsoever. The process terminates only in a form of organization which is infinite, perfect, necessary, and thus divine—i.e., in Being itself, which is the attractor on which the process also radically depends and from which it derives its ultimate meaning.

Even in such a rudimentary and schematic form, a teleological approach has considerable explanatory power. Within the framework of such a science, for example, cosmological fine-tuning finally begins to make sense, and indeed can be seen to affect more than just a few key physical constants. Spatial and temporal extension themselves, for example, turn out to be the condition of any possible organization, which after all implies difference and thus separation as well as unity and ordering to a common end. The existence of various types of physical interactions (gravitational, electromagnetic, strong and weak nuclear), similarly, make it possible for the elements within systems to relate across space and time. Indeed the relative strengths of these forces seem fixed just precisely in order to make the development of more complex organization possible. But even physical principles which have been the cause of much pessimism and despair, such as the Second Law of Thermodynamics, turn out, when properly understood, to serve the cause of teleological progress. Without dissipation and disintegration established structures would last forever, making growth and development essentially impossible. Physical systems, in other words, are structured in just the way necessary to make higher, biological and social forms of organization possible. Those who hear echoes of the Aristotelian concept of matter as the potential for form would not be wrong.

At higher levels of organization the teleological dynamic becomes more explicit. Some physical systems are structured in ways which permit them to conserve their form, which constitutes the higher degree of participation in being which Aristotle called the mineral soul. Such systems are also characterized by a chemical holism which means that they have distinctive properties which make them more than the sum of their parts in a way which is not true of mere mechanical ensembles. Biological systems, on the other hand are actually organized, i.e., structured in such a way as to promote an end, namely their own survival and reproduction. In maintaining themselves in hostile environments which would undermine many mineral species, and in reproducing themselves, living organisms achieve a higher degree of participation in being than mere physical or mineral systems. Social systems finally, are not only organized but also have the capacity to organize, i.e., through labor to contribute to the creation of new and more complex forms of organization.

In a sense, in the absence of this new science, our argument necessarily remains incomplete. But its outlines are already sufficiently clear for us to discern clearly the direction in which it points. Everything in the universe is, in fact, ordered to an end, and that end is nothing other than Being as such. Everything seeks that end in the way appropriate to its essential nature and to extent of its capacities. For physical systems that means retaining their forms—i.e., seeking out thermodynamic stability. For biological systems that means nutrition, growth, and reproduction, and, in the case of animals, sensation and locomotion. For human beings it means understanding the Being in order to add, through our labor, to the beauty and complexity of the universe. Even systems which are not themselves organized in a purposeful manner (i.e., physical systems) are structured in such a way as to make the development of complex organization possible. And even laws, such as the accursed Second Law of Thermodynamics, which seemed to those who discovered it to imply the ultimate meaninglessness of the universe, can be understood instead simply to mean that the universe has a way of disciplining her children and requiring them to exert themselves with ever greater strength, and has provided herself with a way of making room for new and more interesting forms of organization. If this understanding of the universe can be sustained as we implement our teleological research program, then the cosmological foundations of an historicizedrational metaphysics and natural law ethics will be well established.

TOWARDS A NEW DIALECTICAL METAPHYSICS

What will such a metaphysics look like? It must be said, that there will not be just one metaphysics which meets the criteria outlined above. In this sense John Milbank is quite wrong to lump together all non-Christian metaphysical systems under the heading of "impersonal religions which celebrate fate or the void" and to identify them with the nihilism of modernity (Milbank 1999:32). Metaphysics, while it is indeed a science, in the sense of offering a principle which, among other things, explains the world, is hardly an *exact* science. There may be many different ways of capturing partly and roughly, but still in a way which promotes human development and civilizational progress, the first principle which Thomas called *Esse*, which Chu Hsi called *T'ai Ch'i*, (the Great Ultimate) and which

Nagarjuna called but also *prajnaparamita* (surpassing wisdom). What follows is merely an outline, an attempt which is frankly rooted in the dialectical tradition which emerges from Socrates, Plato, and Aristotle, and in the originally Jewish understanding of God as YHWH (as the power of Being as such), but which has also attempted to learn from other traditions. Hopefully it will seem credible; a complete argument will have to await a later work.

One of the most striking results of the our analysis of the current crisis of the sciences has been to focus attention on both the *relational* and the *teleological* character of the universe. And yet it seems as if these characteristics point in very different directions metaphysically. Is there not, after all, an irreducible conflict between the metaphysics of *substance* developed by Aristotle and his followers (or, what is really the same thing, the Confucian metaphysics of the Great Ultimate) and the metaphysics of *relation* advocated by most of the Buddhist systems and by Nagarjuna's Madyamika school most especially? In the one school we have an attempt to explain—and ground—the reality of the things we experience in a first principle which is its own ground, a project which is completed in the identification by ibn Sina and Thomas of the Aristotelian unmoved mover with the God revealed in Exodus. In the other school we have in Nagarjuna a ready acceptance of the infinite regress of causes which to the Aristotelians seems so abhorrent and a conclusion that, because everything is ultimately dependent on everything else, nothing has *inherent* existence in the sense which ibn Sina and Thomas, for example, assign to God. These are, taken at face value, two incompatible doctrines which cannot and ought not to be harmonized.

But matters look rather different if we focus on *Thomas* rather than Aristotle and the fully developed Mahayana Buddhism of The T'ien Tai or Hua-yen schools rather than the early doctrines of Nagarjuna. From this point of view both doctrines look rather like competing ways of coming to terms with a *common* reality: the fact that what Thomists call *contingent* being is always and only dependent on and ordered to something outside itself, and that the ground of things consists not in self-possession but in a radical generativity. Put differently, we might say that being, in the sense of contingent being, means *being related*. And once we have recognized this, we also recognize that the Thomistic metaphysics of *Esse* is quite incompatible with any notion that form or structure gives things being. Rather, each of the various grades of being—mineral, vegetable, animal, rational—and each of the specific forms of these grades of being are merely *ways of being related*, ways of seeking Being as such.

This leaves, of course, what looks like a more fundamental difference and one not so easily susceptible to resolution, between the Thomistic claim that Being *Is*, and the Madyamika claim that *nothing* has inherent existence—a difference which would seem to entail a whole complex of practical differences, between, for example, an ethics centered on the cultivation of virtue and an ethics of detachment. But here too matters are more complex. In fact the whole Socratic tradition up until ibn Sina was quite reluctant to identify the first principle with Being. Thus Plato speaks of the first principle as "the Good," which he says is "beyond Being." Aristotle, while he sometimes falls into the trap of saying that it is form which gives contingent things their being, does not even really attempt to define the Unmoved Mover. Later Neo-Platonists speak of the first principle as the One, again "beyond Being." The Christian Neo-Platonist Dionysus the Areopagite went even further, stressing the need to complement the *via positiva* which ascends to God rationally by means of affirming things of Him, with a *via negativa* which ascends by means of denying things of God. This reluctance to characterize the first principle as Being may well be the result of the fact that these thinkers all because they understood being as substance or self-possession and recognized that such a principle could not, in fact, be the source of all that is. Ibn Sina and Thomas, on the other hand, put forward a doctrine which is, in fact, radically different from any notion of Being as substance or self-possession. *Esse as such* is first and foremost a radical creativity which lives by sharing itself. Thomas' most common image of God is that of a craftsman. Much the same is true of the image we find of the Buddha in later Mahayana texts, such as the *Saddharmapundarika* (Lotus) Sutra. Here Buddhas do not pass over into *paranirvana* or complete extinction, but rather generate *Buddhaksetras* or Buddha-fields—what amount to entire cosmic regions, the quality of which is dependent on their level of merit they have accumulated. We live in *Saha*, the Buddha-field of Sakyamuni, which is not an especially pure place, largely due to his limitations by comparison with other Buddhas, such Amitayus (as well as to our own limitations). What Buddhas do, according to these later Mahayana schools, is to create and teach, ripening sentient beings who will themselves eventually become creators and teachers (Williams 1989: 224–25).

A Buddha, of course, is not a first principle. One can, however, find hints of something like a doctrine of the first principle as creativity in Nagarjuna himself.

> The *prajnaparamita*
> Is a real dharma, not an inverted view...
> The Buddhas as well as the Bodhisattvas
> Are able to bring benefit to all.
> *Prajna* serves as mother to them.
> It is able to give birth to and raise them.
> The Buddha serves as father of beings.
> *Prajna* is able to give birth to the Buddha.
> This being so, it serves for all
> As the grandmother of beings...
>
> The *prajnaparamita*
> Is comparable to a great fiery blaze.
> It cannot be grasped from any of four sides.
> There is neither grasping nor not grasping.
> All grasping has already been relinquished.
> This is what is meant by being ungraspable.
> It is ungraspable and yet one grasps it.
> It is just this which is meant by "grasping."
> *Prajna* is characterized by indestructibility.
> It goes beyond all words and speech.
> Fittingly, it has nothing upon which it depends
> (Nagarjuna. *Treatise on the Great Perfection of Wisdom Sutra*)

It is not surprising that *prajnaparamita*, personified as a sort of wisdom goddess, became the center of powerful popular cults in Nepal and Kampuchea!

What all this suggests is that there is more common ground between the fully developed forms of the great metaphysical traditions than has generally been allowed. What follows is clearly more Thomistic than Buddhist, but it reflects an attempt to incorporate insights from the Buddhist tradition—especially a focus on the relational character of being. It also reflects an attempt to anticipate somewhat the results of the teleological research program which we proposed in our section on cosmology and it thus differs from traditional Aristotelian and Thomistic metaphysics in that it understands the universe as a whole, and not merely individual organisms as growing and developing towards God. In this regard it reflects the influence of Errol Harris' vastly under-appreciated work, which shows that the whole universe develops along what he calls a dialectical scale towards God.[5] It is presented not as something definitive, but rather as an opening to further discussion.

We consider first the shift from a metaphysics of substance to a metaphysics of relation. It is one of the ironies of history that an economic system marked by the most rapacious egoism should teach us about the radical interdependence of all things, but this, precisely is the great lesson of the capitalist era. Markets emerged spontaneously as a result of the development of new specialized technologies, first in agriculture and later in handicrafts; ancient slavery and later capitalism developed when those who were profiting in the marketplace used coercion to try to liberate themselves from the imperative of serving the Common Good, something which, Marx demonstrated, is quite impossible in the long run. As first goods and services, then labor-power, and finally capital have become commodified, humanity has been forced to recognize the principle (which certainly holds with equal force in nonmarket societies) that everything depends on everything else. Petty commodity production, under which goods and services which would have been produced anyway were brought into relation to each other created the basis in experience for the recognition of the external relatedness of all things—that everything depends on everything else for its behavior. Generalized commodity production, under which market forces determine what commodities are produced, created a basis in experience for the recognition of internal relationality,

---

5. Harris is a British Hegelian and, like most Hegelians, was not in active dialogue with the Thomistic revival. As a result he fails, to the best of my knowledge, to take an explicit position in the debate between a univocal and an analogical metaphysics. It seems to me, however, that he develops Hegel's ideas in a way which avoids at least the greatest dangers of a univocal metaphysics—making it explicit, for example, that all finite systems are exemplifications of the organizing principle of the universe (God) but that no finite system—or indeed even the whole at any given moment—is ever a fully adequate exemplification of this principle. The result is at once to name what is sacred in each and every thing while at the same time to recognize that God transcends the universe in something more than a purely quantitative manner. See especially Harris 1964, 1991, 1992.

Furthermore, regardless of how one evaluates his approach to this question, Harris stood for many years against the rising tide of nihilism and defended when it was most unpopular the idea that metaphysics must be grounded in—but also govern—the special sciences. Harris also developed considerably the idea of the relational character of being (Harris 1987). His work is not addressed explicitly in the critical sections of this book only because, some real differences notwithstanding, we have absorbed so much of it that—along with the contributions of Maritain, Lukacs, and Mary Dale, it permeates the whole.

the fact that the cosmos is a system not only in the sense that the behavior of its constitutive elements is radically dependent on the behavior of all the other elements in the system, but also in the sense that the essential nature, indeed the very existence, of these elements is determined by their interrelationships with each other, so that they are best conceived not as elements at all, but rather as relations. Being is, at the most fundamental level, a *system of relationships*, from which it is possible to abstract certain *nodes* which therefore *appear* particular, but which exist, and can thus be comprehended, only as part of the general system.

The second shift which is required has three dimensions. First, it entails a revaluation of the ontological significance of finite systems generally, and of human beings and human society in particular, in the light of technological developments which have shown us to be active participants in the creation of new forms of organization. Second, both as a direct result of technologically induced change and as a result of organized revolutionary action it has become increasingly apparent that being is not static but dynamic and in fact (if the arguments of the last section of this chapter are to be believed) progressive in character. A metaphysics which allows only the realization of potentials latent in a certain form of organization, and not the development of qualitatively new forms of organization, is ruled out. Finally, these two dimensions taken together imply a third: namely that human beings have a conscious, leading role in the cosmohistorical evolutionary process. It should be noted that both the technological and the revolutionary-democratic dynamics predate the modern period, reaching back through the medieval guilds and communes to the revolutions of the late-bronze and early iron ages and the brief but important periods of technological innovation which they ushered in.

A recent proposal by Roy Bhaskar (Bhaskar 1993) suggests one way to accommodate these changes. According to Bhaskar, the difficulty with all hitherto existing dialectics, including those of Hegel and, to some extent Marx, has been an insistence on the positivity of being—i.e., on the priority of Being over Non-Being. Even where the category of contradiction is introduced as a determination of being itself, as it is in Hegel and Marx, the priority of the positive leads inevitably to closure of the cosmohistorical process and the collapse of Being into an undifferentiated expressive unity. In the case of Hegel, because of his idealism and spiritual monism, this lead to a reconciliation with the status quo of a still semifeudal Germany. In the case of Marx it led to the claim that history terminates (or, what is the same thing, that prehistory terminates and history begins) with the achievement of communism, a doctrine which was easily mobilized by the Stalinist state to close-off further progress not only beyond, but actually towards communism. Bhaskar proposes instead to give priority to the category of absence which he claims is the condition for the possibility of physical systems of any kind, being implied by spatio-temporal extension, physical interaction, and thus motion, and which is the driving force of human society from the demanding cry of an infant distressed at the absence of the mother, through the most sophisticated demand for the "absenting of constraints on the absenting of constraints" and thus for the full development of human capacities.

It should, first of all, be said of Bhaskar's proposal that it does indeed represent the completion (or at least one possible completion) of the Hegelian-Marxist project. Specifically, it is the completion of a whole line of reasoning within the dialectical tradition (a line of reasoning which goes back to Heraclitus) which gives priority to chaos, change, and contradiction. Historically this trend has scored points by attacking the opposing Parmenidean trend which gives priority to unity and stasis. But this whole way of framing the debate is anachronistic. Long before Hegel and Marx the dialectical tradition transcended this duality. Indeed, the Aristotelian concept of teleological causation is, first and foremost, an attempt to resolve the problem in a way which does justice to both stability and change, unity and difference (Garrigou-Lagrange 1938b). One cannot address the enduring inadequacies in the theories of Aristotle, Hegel, or Marx by attacking Parmenides! More importantly, however, Bhaskar misses the fact that it is not the category of totality by which Hegel legitimates the Prussian or Mitin the Stalinist state. It is, on the contrary, precisely the category of contradiction (ancestor of Bhaskar's "absence") which plays this role. It is the category of contradiction which allows Hegel to represent "the slaughterhouse of history" as rational necessity, and it was by arguing for the priority of the category of contradiction (and negating the negation of the negation) that Mitin legitimated the triumph of the Party over the independent philosophical authority represented by the Bogdanovite and later the Deborinist Academy. Absence, furthermore, implies something which is absent and which is desired, or at least physically required. It implies the teleological attractor. In the final analysis Bhaskar's metaphysics is simply a way for secular Marxists to hide from themselves the invincibly teleological and religious character of their doctrine. Absence, in other words is a "hidden God." And if it is not—if it is merely nothing—then Bhaskar's approach violates the principle of sufficient reason, for nothing, and certainly not a progressive cosmohistorical evolutionary process pregnant with ever richer and more complex forms of organization, can come from Nothing.

The alternative which we propose builds on the insights of Errol Harris (Harris 1965, 1987, 1991, 1992) on the Hegelian side and A. M. Deborin and Alexandr Bogdanov (Bogdanov 1928/1980) on the Marxist side, while insisting with traditional Thomism (Garrigou-Lagrange 1938) that the category of finality be given pride of place. Being, I would like to suggest, is organization. Imagine for a minute something which is stripped of all organization: it has no purpose, no structure, and no relation, either internally or externally. Then the thing, quite simply, does not exist.

In order to illustrate the usefulness of this idea, which is really all we can do in the present context, we begin with some distinctions. First, we should note that both "being" and "organization" are used in a variety of different ways. It is important, on the one hand, to distinguish between mere existence (what Thomas calls possible being) and *Esse* as such, the actual power of Being, which no finite system has in itself. On the other hand, it is important to distinguish between the various dimensions of the concept of organization:

   a. relation,

   b. form, order or structure, and

   c. purpose, end or telos.

To be related is to be, but only in the limited sense of being an element of a larger whole. Any system which has a definite structure, however can be said to have its own distinctive identity, and thus to exist in the much stronger sense of being something of which other things can be predicated. For a system to be organized, however, the structure must be ordered to some end or purpose. "Organization," finally, may mean

   a. being organized, in the sense of being ordered to an end,

   b. having the capacity to organize, and thus create, or

   c. being an end to which things are ordered.

Regrounding and Historicizing Natural Law Ethics

With these distinctions in place, it is easy to show the power of our approach. Relationship implies both unity and difference. Being realized as relationship consists neither in simple, undifferentiated unity nor in pure difference. Without difference there is nothing in particular, but only a One which is at the same time Nothing. Without a prior, underlying unity, difference is mere disintegration: the absence of any capacity to connect, to relate, and therefore potentially to act, have properties, etc. Being consists precisely in the capacity to unite things which differ—in the self-differentiating unity which we call "system." The word "system" comes from the Hellenic roots *sys-* and *histanai* meaning "to put together." At the very simplest level, therefore, system refers to the radical interconnectedness of all things, an interconnectedness so profound that the existence of the tiniest subsystem abstracted from the whole implies the system in its entirety. The most minute alteration at any point in the system affects the system as a whole. The fact that I am sitting here at my computer, thinking and writing, requires and implies, with iron clad logical necessity, everything else in the universe—not only the existence, but the precise disposition of every particular system along every possible world trajectory in the cosmos, from the most intimate thoughts of a young woman on a corner in Bangkok waiting for her lover to the precise disposition of the atoms and molecules in some remote nebula in a galaxy far too distant for its light to ever reach me during my lifetime.

Some important conclusions follow from this analysis. First, it should be clear that it is not really possible, given our scheme, to conceive of being as substance—as something that exists in itself. Finite systems clearly derive their being from each other and from the infinite; the αρχη, on the other hand, while it clearly is the Power of Being, exists precisely in drawing others into being. Because of this both Aristotelian pluralism and Spinozist monism (while each grasping a part of the truth) are fundamentally inadequate. Neither really understands that Being is quite the opposite of self-possession.

Nor should we really think of being as subject. Subjectivity, as a way of being ordered to others and to the infinite, is incipient and emerging in contingent being, but it hardly makes sense to regard merely physical systems as subjective. But clearly such systems exist. Necessary being, on the other hand, while it can be shown to be an unlimited subjectivity and inwardness (a proof which will have to await a later work) does not exist in this subjectivity but rather precisely in its creative power, which is always and only directed outward, as the power of teleological attraction.

Being realized as relationship, on the other hand, has the merit, first of all, of grasping the interconnectedness of being without negating difference. Indeed, it makes it fully possible for us to meet the objection of existentialists and postmodernists who are concerned that any philosophical doctrine of God—or indeed any other totalizing metanarrative which attempts to describe or explain the universe as a whole—inevitably submerges difference into identity. And this is, indeed, a danger for both Spinozist and Hegelian monisms. When being is conceived as substance, and we assert (as we must, once we have taken this first step) that there is only one substance, one system which exists in and through itself, and that that is the whole, we are, in effect, saying that particular systems do not exist and that the rich difference which makes life interesting is, in fact, a mere difference of location in a single system—in effect, an illusion. When being is conceived as subject, similarly, one ends up reducing individuals to mere vanishing moments of the One subject, Absolute Spirit, which develops itself and becomes conscious of itself through them—and then casts them aside. Aristotelian pluralism—and more especially Thomism—avoids this problem only at the price of a certain inconsistency, arguing on the one hand that there are many substances, and that difference is therefore real, while at the same time arguing their dependence on the teleological attraction of the Unmoved Mover (for Aristotle), and on the Single Pure Act of Being which is God (for Aquinas), an argument which is tantamount to admitting that they are not really substances at all. By conceiving being as relationship we unify in a way which not only conserves, but in fact presupposes difference. One cannot, after all, be meaningfully ordered to, in the sense we have defined it, without being different.

At the same time, we avoid the fall into an infinite expanse of difference, without horizon or point of reference, which the "postmodern" philosophy of difference celebrates but which in fact is nothing less than a willful option for death and loss. The difference of being is always and only a difference of relationship, a difference of being ordered to, a difference of sensing and imagining, of knowing and judging, of desiring and hoping and willing, which are never possible for the same, but which nonetheless make difference a principle of unity rather than of division. And this series of differences, even if it is itself infinite in the sense of extending without limit through space and time (and there are good reasons, both scientific and philosophical to believe this) nonetheless terminates in a principle which unifies (because it is the common *telos*) but does so precisely by creating "infinite diversity in infinite combinations."[6]

Thinking of being as relationship has profound implications for the way which we think about essence. It is no longer possible to understand the universe as a composite of immaterial forms and a passive material substrate, or as a set of interacting atoms which sometimes come together to constitute systems. On the one hand *essence*, which Aristotle understood as form imposed on passive matter, and in some places as what gives things their being, must be radically retheorized. At the same time, the atomism dominant since the eighteenth century, for which *what* things are is purely accidental, the product of random interaction and natural selection, must also be rejected. The universe generally, and its various subsystems, *appear* to us as things possessing various properties. The underlying essence or nature of a system or subsystem, however, (what it is), is determined by its internal and external relationships, of which its appearance is merely the expression. *Essence*, in other words, is nothing other than *structure*, both a system's internal structure and its place in the larger structure of the cosmos as a whole, which defines both its own trajectory of development, and its contribution to the development of the cosmos generally.

Now the structures of various subsystems of the cosmos do not merely differ from each other. They are arranged in a kind of hierarchy or dialectical scale. We already know from the results of the special sciences the characteristics of at least several different levels on this scale. Specifically, it is possible to identify physical, biological, and social degrees of organization. Physical systems are not themselves organized in the full sense of possessing differentiated structures of the sort which we find in living organisms which carry out definite functions in the service of some global purpose. They are, however, structured, and in fact structured in just precisely the way necessary to make possible the emergence of complex organization, life, and intelligence. In this sense the physical universe as a whole can be said to be ordered to the higher end of complex organization, life, and intelligence. Even physical laws,

---

6. This phrase is put in quotations because it is a favorite slogan of *Star Trek* fandom. I am unsure of the origin. It does, however, speak of just what sort of popular ontology underlies this uniquely hopeful vision of humanity's future.

such as entropy, which seem to work against the survival of particular complex systems, ultimately serve the cause of progressive cosmohistorical evolution by making room for new forms. Some physical systems are, furthermore, structured in ways which permit them to conserve their form, which constitutes the higher degree of participation in being which Aristotle called the mineral soul. Such systems are also characterized by a chemical holism which means that they have distinctive properties which make them more than the sum of their parts in a way which is not true of mere mechanical ensembles. Biological systems, on the other hand are actually organized, i.e., structured in such a way as to promote an end, namely their own survival and reproduction. In maintaining themselves in hostile environments which would undermine many mineral species, and in reproducing themselves, living organisms achieve a higher degree of participation in being than mere physical or mineral systems. Social systems finally, are not only organized but also have the capacity to organize, i.e., through labor to contribute to the creation of new and more complex forms of organization.

All of these various and sundry forms of organization are ordered to a common end, namely Being, which, however, they pursue in ways appropriate to their structure and under the form of specific goods which are accessible to them. For mineral species, and indeed physical systems in general, this good is the thermodynamic stability which allows them to persist in being. For living organisms the good is nutrition and reproduction—in the case of animals in the form of food and mates actively pursued and enjoyed. In the case of the social form of matter this good is creativity as such, which is known indirectly in the form of ordinary manual and intellectual labor, and directly when the intellect rises by transcendental abstraction or caritative wisdom to the knowledge of God.

This approach to understanding being grasps not only internal relationality, but also the real participation of finite systems in the process of cosmogenesis and does so without violating the principle of sufficient reason. Everything, however humble, which participates in Being is, furthermore, itself a participation in the end or *telos* and thus in a very real sense a natural sacrament in which God is really present, and an authentic way to the divine. In this sense people in tribal and communitarian societies were not wrong to offer worship to animals, plants, and even minerals, even if in the light of philosophy and of the revelation of the divine name *yhwh* we recognize that what is actually to be worshipped is the power of Being in which these finite systems have a share.

Thus, when we say that "something exists" or that "the universe exists," we in fact mean that it is a real participation in Being as such, to the knowledge of which we have already risen, if perhaps without fully realizing it, in traveling the road of the special sciences.

With this said, the outlines of a unified cosmoteleological argument for the existence of God, an argument which simultaneously proves the ultimate meaningfulness of the universe, emerges quite naturally. Not surprisingly, the argument ends up looking quite a bit like a radically historicized version of Aristotle's argument in *Metaphysics* 12.7. What a teleological science shows, even in its present undeveloped form, is an ascending scale of progressively higher forms of organization—higher in the sense that they constitute progressively superior forms of organization. Each of these forms of organization is, in a very real sense, a distinct form of the motion of matter, which is only potential being, towards Being as such (a way of putting things which also connects our formulation back to Engels' language and that of dialectical materialism). Their organization and their motion and their participation in Being are all one and the same. Now in the case of each individual system this organization, motion, and participation in being can be explained proximately in terms of the particular end to which the system is ordered: the possibility of there being any structure at all, varying types and degrees of thermodynamic stability, nutrition, growth and reproduction, sensation, and locomotion, or any of the myriad forms of organization which human beings and human societies labor to bring into being. But each of these particular ends or movers must (and in principle can) be explained in terms of further finite ends or movers at which they, in turn, aim. The whole ordered series, however, even if it is infinite in space and time, must itself be explained. There cannot, in other words, be an infinite logical regress even is there is an infinite physical regress and/or progress in space and time. The series and each of its elements can, furthermore be shown to aim, albeit mediately, through the particular finite movers, at a common end which is *Esse* as such. What each and every form of matter seeks, each in its own way, and except at the highest levels of human development without knowing it, is Being as such. This is the great Unmoved Mover which draws all things to itself.

When we have risen to this point, it furthermore becomes apparent that not only God, but also the universe itself, exists necessarily. That God exists necessarily is apparent. Being as such has within itself the power to be and thus depends on nothing outside itself for its existence. In this sense a sort of *a posteriori* version of the ontological argument becomes possible. The universe, as the ascending scale of different forms of organization which moves towards God, is not to be identified with God and is not a "necessary being." Given that God exists, however, the existence of the universe follows necessarily. This is because it is the attractive power of God which draws the universe into Being. Now God cannot cease to be God, and thus cannot help being attractive and drawing the universe into Being.

This, in turn, imposes definite constraints on physical cosmology. In order for the universe to exist at all, it must in *some sense* always exist, because God brings it into being necessarily. This does not necessarily rule out cosmologies which, like the Big Bang, may imply the finitude of the region of space-time which we now identify with the universe, but it does imply that motion towards God is without beginning and without end and is globally, at least over the long run, progressive in character. In regrounding natural law ethics we have, in other words, also historicized it. Any ethical imperatives we derive will be centered not only on the development of individual systems towards their own particular ends, but also on the development of larger collectivities—civilizations and the universe as a whole—towards God.

PRINCIPLES OF VALUE

Before we move on to derive such imperatives, however, we must make explicit what is so far only implicit in our argument: that Being and God are in fact principles of *value*. If all things seek Being, and if Being is organization, then organization is the principle of value for which we have been searching. Indeed, it is possible to derive a both a qualitative and a quantitative scale of value from this principle. There, are, first of all, qualitative ontological differences between the various grades of being identified above:

   a. being structured in such a way as to make organization possible,

   b. having chemical holism and thus the capacity to retain form,

c. having the capacity for nutrition, growth and reproduction,

d. having the capacity for sensation and locomotion,

e. having the capacity for intellectual knowledge and will and thus ability to organize and create,

f. being the End towards which things are ordered.

Within each of these fundamental ontological grades, the value of a system is determined by its level of organization, or its capacity to unite, under a common structure, a complex diversity of elements. The greater the number and diversity of elements united, and the greater the level of unity, the more organized, and thus the more valuable, the system.

This means that "value" in the ethical sense and value in the economic sense are no different from each other. What human beings do when they labor is to increase the level of organization of their raw material. The "average socially necessary labor time" contained in a product, which both Marx and his classical predecessors regarded as the measure of value, is simply a way of quantifying its level of organization. There are, however, products of nature which are highly organized, and thus exceedingly rare, which possess great value in and of themselves, apart from any human intervention. Our theory, unlike Marx's, allows us to capture this reality while still recognizing that it is *ordinarily* human labor which confers economic value on products.

The concept of value takes on various notes in virtue of the principle of the convertibility of the transcendentals—the Beautiful, the True, the Good, and the One—with Being as such. By convertibility we mean that these terms refer to the same thing as Being, though they add some relation (Thomas, *Summa Theologiae*, I, 5.1, 9.1, 16.3). Consider, for example, the nature of Beauty. By the beauty of a system, we mean simply its level of organization, understood as the object of (sensory or intellectual) perception. The greater the diversity of the elements organized, and the more perfect the harmony in which they are united, the more beautiful the system. This is true throughout the natural world, from the simple harmonies of the night sky, through the more complex forms of the crystalline structures and living organisms, to the rich, lush diversity of complex ecosystems and human societies. And it is true as well of great works of art, which are nothing if not a complex manifold of relations harmoniously arranged. Thus, we find a landscape, natural or painted, beautiful to the extent that it integrates a diversity of elements into a harmonious and purposeful whole. Not too many people are attracted by scenes of pure, undifferentiated gray. Things of great beauty, have, furthermore, the capacity to harmonize and integrate those that perceive them, and thus draw them closer to God. Thus the centrality of beauty in religious experience, in liturgy and so on. Beauty itself, as Albertus Magnus and Thomas Aquinas taught long ago, is the capacity to bring things into being, and is thus convertible with Being itself, or God (Eco 1988).

Now because Beauty integrates diverse elements into a harmonious whole it also possesses *claritas*—it constitutes a window on the Truth. When we are in the process of forming an idea, what we see first is a pattern, a harmonious integration of elements in our experience. The truth value of a statement, a concept or theory, is its capacity to organize large quantities of qualitatively diverse, and therefore highly complex experience. The concept or theory in question does this by explaining the experience in terms of a principle or principles. It is necessary in this connection to focus equal attention on the complexity of the experience organized and on the level of organization of the experience in question. Our experience is most highly organized when we identify highly compact "organizing principles," knowledge of which permits us to derive logically all the rich particularity of the experience on which the principle was based. It is this organizing capacity of theories which leads us to speak analogously of their "power." The most powerful theories are those which comprehend the widest range of experience in unique compact statements which are themselves pregnant with rich experiential content. The Truth itself is, as we have seen, the infinite, necessary and perfect Being which alone completes our explanation of the universe and which grounds all other partial explanations.

The Good, finally, is an end desired or willed or pursued. It is at once the object of our desire or appetite, whether sensual or intellectual, and the actual capacity to organize, to draw things into being. While everything existing is good, in so far as it is capable both of being ordered to the End and of being an (intermediate) end itself, there is a clearly defined hierarchy of goods, measured by the degree to which the system in question is ordered to God and can itself therefore participate in the divine organizing activity. The Good itself is the infinite, necessary and perfect End, which alone has the capacity to draw something out of nothing.

It is interesting to note the intrusion of quantitative language into our account of the transcendentals. This is unavoidable, but it is a bit deceptive. One may attempt to quantify value, by means of a return from transcendental abstraction to formalism, and this move is often quite useful. We have already seen this in the case of Marx's labor theory of value. Charles Bennet's "logical depth" approach to the organization of information systems, which quantifies organization in terms of the number of logical steps necessary to derive a system from its principle (Bennet 1988), is similar in many ways. Other approaches to quantifying organization (and thus value) which focus exclusively on the number of different elements (for example, information content) are more problematic. But no quantification of value actually comprehends the fundamentally teleological character of the concept and thus the radical simplicity of the union effected among the complex elements of organized systems. And no quantification of value can comprehend the fact that the telos, the End itself, far from negating difference when it unites, in fact multiplies it infinitely as it draws ever new and more diverse forms of organization into being.

This is the significance of the fourth and last transcendental: the transcendental One. While the numerical one derives *from* difference (as the "ratio" of "similar differences" and "different similarities" which defines the unit of a formal system) and serves as a principle of identity, the transcendental One, in uniting all things to itself, in fact distinguishes them from the infinite sameness of mere possibility and draws them, in all their individual uniqueness, into the divine light of Being itself. It is, in other words, the transcendental principle of difference.

We are now in a position to derive specifically ethical principles. We should begin by clarifying the nature of the moral question. A certain prejudice has developed in the field of ethics against what, following the analytic philosopher G. E. Moore, is called "ethical naturalism," and "metaphysical ethics," which attempt to reduce the good to some single property accessible either to the natural sciences or to metaphysics, or to both. The result is, devotees of this approach argue, a confusion of fact and value, "is" and "ought." They argue instead that the predicate "good" is simple and un-analyzable, and in fact is applied to many different kinds of things. Clearly it is just precisely the kind of approach to ethics which we are proposing which is the intended object of this attack. The criticism, however, is self-contradictory, for it takes as its canon "ordinary language," the usage of which it claims merely to clarify. But what is this if not to confuse "is" and "ought"? The way people use a certain language, in this case English, is without any further justification made into the standard by which ethics is grounded, and so on.

At the same time, to say that "good" is a simple and un-analyzable predicate is to leave ethical judgment ungrounded and to transform it into nothing more than a peculiar use of language. What transcendental abstraction reveals is not a particular class of things or properties which are good, but rather a transcendental property of everything which *is*, to the extent to which it *is*. The moral imperative is nothing other than the imperative of Being itself understood as that which is desired and aimed for. The Good is what draws finite systems into being in the first place; finite goods are secondary, intermediate ends which possess a participating power to draw into being.

Our analysis of the transcendentals allows us, furthermore, to give this principle some very definite content. We have seen that being is organization. Necessary Being is the End which organizes, contingent being is both that which is organized or "ordered to" and that which, in varying degrees, acts as a secondary ordering end. To be good therefore, is at once to be organized and to participate in the divine creative power of organization. Concretely this means a drive upwards along the ontological hierarchy of being, a drive to grow and develop, to evolve, and to bring into being ever more complex and integrated systems. It means the move from the pure potency of nonbeing to the act of existence, the move from physical to biological and from biological to social organization. It means the development of human creative powers and of humanity's capacity to participate in the self-organizing activity of the universe and thus to share in God's work of creation.

The moral imperative or principle of right can, therefore, be stated, in its most abstract and general form, in the following manner:

> Act in such a manner as to promote the self-organizing activity of the universe, that is, to promote the development of ever more complex forms of organization.

By analyzing the way in which self-organization actually takes place we can, in turn, derive more specific principles of right. In this sense ethics is indeed informed by science not only indirectly, through the mediation of the doctrine of first principles which completes scientific inquiry, but directly, by recourse to investigations which clarify the means to the End. Thus, for example, the fact that organization is indeed a kind of order, and is characterized by at least a relative and temporary stability, allows us to derive the *principle of public order*:

> Act in such a way as to conserve the existing forms of organization unless acting otherwise can reasonably be expected to yield a higher level of organization.

As the same time, however, we know that the universe and its various subsystems grow and develop. This means that one form of organization yields to another, something that by its very nature involves qualitative differentiation, symmetry breaking and an element of instability. This means that the structure of any give system ought not to be so rigid as to undermine these processes and the innovation they make possible. One way to insure this is to have multiple and diverse centers of power, each of which seeks the telos in its own way and on its own terms. Thus the *principle of subsidiarity*:

> Power and decision-making should be as decentralized as is compatible with the ordering of the system generally to the common good.

This can be understood to apply not only within human societies, but in the relationship between human civilizations and the ecosystems they inhabit, as cautioning, for example, against an "industrial" mentality which seeks not only to cultivate higher forms of organization, but to bring the whole evolutionary process under rational human control.

Finally, we know that organization is an ordering to and is, therefore, fundamentally hierarchical in character. The *principle of hierarchy* states that:

> Lower order activities must serve higher order activities and all must serve the telos.

This is *not* an argument for unequal access to resources for consumption. On the contrary, it is precisely the ability to use resources productively, to order them to a higher end and thus bring into being new and more complex forms of organization which marks a system as "higher order." Unproductive consumption (luxury) is a mark of disorganization and disintegration. What it does mean, however, is that the cultivation of sensual goods, while in itself to be recommended, must serve the cultivation of intellectual goods, and the cultivation of lower intellectual goods (e.g., science and technology) the cultivation of higher intellectual goods (e.g., wisdom).

In order to go beyond this, however, and derive more specific moral norms, we will need to consider in greater depth the particular sort of system for which we are deriving norms: i.e., human persons and human societies. Our next step must, therefore, be a consideration of the problem of human nature.

3

The Human Vocation

HAVING DEMONSTRATED THE POSSIBILITY of a rational metaphysics of the sort which traditionally grounded natural law ethics, shown what such a metaphysics might look like, and derived a statement of the moral imperative in its most general form, we need now to address the problem of human nature. This is important because, as we noted in the introduction, the critique of metaphysics has, since the late Middle Ages, been associated with a pessimistic doctrine of human nature, something which persists even among self-described advocates of a natural law or virtue ethics, such as Alisdair MacIntyre. This doctrine has, in effect, served to convince people that they *cannot* be good and *cannot* build a just society and that they therefore need not—indeed had best not—even try. In addition to answering the hegemonic pessimism regarding human nature, we also need to provide a positive understanding of human capacities which is sufficiently detailed to provide the basis for the doctrine of virtue we intend to develop in the next chapter. This will mean, among other things, specifying the principal acts of our cognitive and appetitive faculties. It also means assessing, as far as possible, whether or not the human vocation is limited to this world or perhaps extends beyond it, and if so how.

Our basic thesis is simple. We will show that "strong," doctrines of original sin and radical depravity, whether religious or secular, in fact derive from a univocal metaphysics which, from the very beginning, pits human development against divine sovereignty (or, the case of secular doctrines, against the development of other human beings) and thus quite literally "sets us up for a fall." This will be quite apparent in the case of Augustine and his followers, and we will see that is also behind the pessimism of Nietzsche and Freud. We will also show that such doctrines serve to legitimate wrongdoing and injustice by making them seem inevitable.

But what about Thomas? Does not Thomas also uphold the decision of the Church against Pelagius and for Augustine? And yet his metaphysics is nothing if not analogical. What we hope to show is that Thomas' position on original sin is really rather different from that of the Augustinians and that his assent to their position and his occasional use of rather Augustinian language is not really fully compatible with the larger design of his system. He is, in effect, submitting to the authority of the magisterium while using this doctrine, with which he is less than fully comfortable, in order to account for a general weakness in human nature which seems incompatible with the original goodness of creation and which might otherwise be inexplicable.

We feel no such deference to a magisterium which has bent too often and too long to the oppressor's rod, teaching what the rich demanded, that their sins might be concealed and their power conserved, and which thus now requires teachers of its own. We will attempt to do rigorously and systematically what Thomas and most Catholic thinkers (and indeed most of the Catholic people both before and after Augustine) have done covertly and incoherently. We will offer a doctrine which accounts for human weakness in a way that does not compromise either the essential goodness of human nature or the real and practical possibility of both right action on the part of individuals, regardless of their circumstances and the creation of a just society, while also recognizing the need for a turning towards *Esse* as such, which is always right there in front of us but we rarely recognize, and for institutions which can help point out the presence of *esse* in the world and thus facilitate that turn. Specifically, we will show that human beings are, by nature, ordered to the good. We seek, in other words, the highest good we know. Our understanding of the Good is, however, limited, so that we know the highest Good—God—only dimly and indirectly, while lesser goods present themselves to us more vividly. We seek the Good, furthermore, under conditions of finitude and in the process pursue strategies which not only involve exploitation and oppression, but which bring into being social structures which form us in ways which ultimately degrades our ability to know and do the Good. These structures do not obscure the Good completely, and thus do not actually render right action impossible, and so our responsibility for what we do remains. But they do deform our understanding of the Good, so that we pursue it in a way which leads to failure and frustration. This accounts not only for the fact that human beings have, sometimes and on a very large scale done things which are truly heinous but also for the general difficulty which we all experience in "being all we can be," coupled with the fact that we know that we could have done better and are thus culpable for not having done so. Overcoming this weakness requires not only *self*-discipline and the support of a rightly ordered community but the external discipline of a cosmos which is ordered in such a way as to frustrate our relentless pursuit of lesser goods and show that we are ordered to the pursuit of something higher and also in such a way as to demonstrate the long term unworkability of strategies based on exploitation and violence and the structures to which they give rise. It also requires the manifestation of *Esse* as such in such a way that we can see through lesser goods to the real end to which we are ordered, and thus the presence of institutions which mediate that manifestation. But all this is always and already present in the cosmos precisely because it is a real participation in *Esse* as such and even when degraded serves as a window on the divine.

Whether or not this doctrine is "orthodox" or "Pelagian" is rather a question of semantics. It is Catholic, in the sense of being in accord with the frankly semi-Pelagian *sensus fidelum* of the Catholic people. And, we will show, it provides the most economical way of accounting for both the dignity and weakness of humanity both individually and collectively.

HISTORICAL PERSPECTIVES

Doctrines of Original Sin and Radical Depravity

There are, broadly speaking, two things which conspired to render strong doctrines of original sin and human depravity credible. The first is a simple matter of fact, which even those of us who reject such doctrines will not contest: that human beings sometimes do truly heinous things, resulting in a world full of suffering which, at least on the face of it, appears to be both unnecessary and due to human causes, and that even those who struggle to do what is right often fail miserably. Advocates of the doctrine of original sin and radical depravity have, to be sure, had a rather stronger sense of the latter point than most of us. Romans 7, with its claim that we "cannot do that which we will to do" and its talk of "another law in our members, at war with the law of the mind," does not resonate for me as it did for Augustine and Luther, but I can recognize the reality to which it points. It is hard to be the best we can be.

The second factor, however, is rather more subtle. Reading Paul, Augustine, and Calvin we find a profound sense of our radical culpability for these failures—a sense that each and every wrong act does, in some sense, merit the infinite wrath of an omnipotent God. For them, human failure is not so much a matter falling short—even culpably short—of a difficult goal; it is first and foremost an act of rebellion against God which, if unchecked, threatens the underlying order of the cosmos.

In Paul this sense is, to be sure, just incipient, something which is implied by the logic of his argument in, for example the letter to the Romans. Thus Paul begins by arguing that the Law is accessible to everyone, on the basis of reason (Rom 1:19–20). Human beings have, however, failed to give God the glory he is due (Rom 1:21). The result has been a darkening of the intellect and a progressive descent into knowing and will sin (Rom 1:22–31) which is deserving of death (Rom 1:32). The same is true of the Jews, who have the Law by revelation as well (Rom 2:17—3:6). Paul seems to draw from this the conclusion that it is impossible for people to fulfill the Law, knowledge of which only makes us more conscious of our sinfulness (Rom 3:20). Justification comes only through faith in Jesus Christ (Rom 3:21), or more precisely through baptism into his death and resurrection (Rom 6:3–4), a formulation which probably captures a bit more of the real flavor of Pauline Christianity, which was still dominated by the milieu of the mystery religions.

Paul does not make much of an argument for human inability or radical depravity, beyond suggesting that we do know the Law, and that if we *could* fulfill it we *would have* long ago, and *we have not*. This is seconded by his frustration at his own efforts to do what is right (Rom 7:13–24). The real force behind his moral outrage at humanity's failures, however, seems to come from a sense that sin is an affront to God, who demands that we accord him glory (Rom 1: 21) and submit to His will. Sin is "hostility to God" (Rom 8: 7).

What is the social basis and political valence of this doctrine? We know from the work of Gerd Theissen (Theissen 1982) and Dmitris Kyrtatis (Kyrtatis 1987) that the Pauline communities, like Hellenistic Christian communities generally, were socially quite diverse. They did not, however, include the most oppressed elements in the Roman Empire (agricultural and mining slaves in the West, peasants in the East). And it is clear from Theissen's analysis that Paul stood clearly with the wealthier members of the communities he founded. Thus, when the Corinthians wrote to him about a dispute between the rich and the poor in the community, which came about when the richer members of the community refused to share the fine food they had brought to celebrations of the Lord's Supper, Paul simply advised that the rich show more consideration for the *feelings* of the poor—not for their stomachs—and eat at home (1 Cor 11). Similarly, when the master of an escaped slave complained to him that his slave had claimed that baptism made him a free man, Paul ordered to slave to return to his master (Philemon). Theissen calls this ethic "love patriarchalism." "In these congregations there developed an ethos obviously different from that of the synoptic tradition, the ethos of primitive Christian love-patriarchalism ... This love-patriarchalism takes social differences for granted, but ameliorates them through an obligation of respect and love, an obligation imposed upon those who are socially stronger. From the weaker are required subordination, fidelity and esteem" (Theissen 1982: 107).

Precisely because Paul does not think it is possible to fulfill the Law, he did not require that members of his congregations either act justly or struggle to create a just social order, only that their reign in their most rapacious tendencies. This ethic made Pauline Christianity especially attractive to elements of the Roman ruling classes who were trying to shore up the authority and legitimacy of the Empire in the wake of the serious labor shortage caused by the closing of the *limes* (Anderson 1974). Specifically, Pauline "love patriarchalism" helped the ruling classes make the transition from exploitation of slave labor, which they had habitually worked to death, to the exploitation of settled, dependent peasants who retained enough of what they produced to be able to breed. At the same time, the Pauline theology strictly ruled out any sort of rebellion against the empire (Rom 13).

In Augustine the association of the emerging doctrine of original sin with an implicitly univocal metaphysics becomes all the more clear. We have already seen, in the first chapter, that Augustine's metaphysics is somewhat ambiguous. He inherited from Plato—or rather from the Neo-Platonists—a metaphysics of participation which might have led his theology, as it did that of other Christian Neo-Platonists, in a very different direction, one which emphasized the cultivation of human capacities. His social location and biography, however, lead him to focus more narrowly on the problem of order, both social and spiritual, and this deformed both his metaphysics and anthropology. Thus, Augustine's initial analysis of evil, as simply the privation of the Good, is fully in accord with a Platonic metaphysics of participation: "There is no such entity in nature as 'evil'; 'evil' is merely a name for the privation of good" (Augustine, *City of God*. XI: 22). Sin, furthermore, is simply a turning from the greater, immutable to the lesser, mutable good: "This failure does not consist in defection to things which are evil in themselves; it is the defection in itself which is evil" (Augustine, *City of God*. XII: 8).

Thus far there is nothing in Augustine's analysis which would suggest that human failure either merits eternal damnation or results in a fundamental inability to do good. The turn comes when Augustine asks about the *cause* of sin. The straightforward answer, and the one which would be coherent with the larger Platonic background of his analysis thus far, would be that we sin because of the relative weakness of our knowledge of higher goods, and especially of God, by comparison with our knowledge of lesser goods, which seem more vivid. But Augustine rejects this option, on the basis of a very thin argument, in favor of the view that our "defection" from God to ourselves and other creatures is "without cause." When we sin our activity is "futile" and we has "defective causes": "[W]hen an evil choice happens in any being, then what happens is dependent on the will of that being; the failure is voluntary, not necessary and the punishment is just" (Augustine, *City of God*. XII: 8). The defect, furthermore, consists in disobedience of and rebellion against God. Thus According to Augustine, God "created man's nature as a kind of mean between angels and beasts, so that if he submitted to his Creator, as to his true sovereign Lord, and observed his instructions with dutiful obedience, he should pass over into the fellowship of the angels, attain an immortality of endless felicity, without an intervening death; but if he used his free will in arrogance and disobedience, and thus offended God, his Lord, he should live like the beasts, under sentence of death, should be the slave of his desires, and destined after death for eternal punishment" (Augustine, *City of God* XII: 22). The weakness of human nature, which prevents us from doing what is right, is not so much a direct and natural consequence of original sin, as it is a punishment for our disobedience.

What is the social basis and political valence of this position? It is important to remember that the Augustinian doctrine of original sin was forged in the context of a *double* polemic. On the one hand, Augustine was struggling against the Pelagians, who defended underlying goodness of humanity and more specifically the human capacity to do what is right and to cultivate virtue. At the same time, he was defending the Church against the Donatists, who refused to accept the authority of bishops who had collaborated with the Romans during the last persecution. Now Pelagian concern for questions of social justice have been well documented. Pelagianism was a monastic ideology which found its core of support among a section of the Romanized Celtic aristocracy of Britain, which seems to have believed that the only way to stabilize the empire was to address some of the glaring injustices which characterized its underlying structure. Intensive cultivation of personal virtue, both intellectual and moral, was an integral part of the strategy of reform. The Donatists, for their part, were first and foremost *anti-imperial*. Indeed, Donatus of Casae Nigrae, after whom the movement was named, was himself a *traditore*, i.e., one who had handed the sacred scriptures over to the Roman authorities during the last persecution, but was elected Bishop if Casae Nigrae nonetheless because his reputation for leading raids on the imperial storehouses and distributing free vinegar to the people! The *circumcelliones*, who appear to have been groups of migrant laborers, and who formed the "shock troops" of the Donatist Church, were fond of wandering into the estates of the provincial aristocracy—the social stratum from which Augustine traced his descent—and crushing the skulls of the landowners while shouting *Deo Laudes!* (Frend 1957).

What the Augustinian doctrine does is, in effect, to create an excuse for the rich, by arguing that we cannot, in fact, do what we should, and by arguing that sin and injustice are, in effect, universal, extending more or less equally to everyone. Sure the rich are bad—but so are the poor. At the same time, Augustine provides a basis for the legitimation of authority apart from the wisdom and justice of the ruler. In the case of the temporal power, this authority derives from the need to maintain order in a world dominated by sin and injustice (Augustine, *City of God.* V: 12–22; XIX: 12–16.); in the case of the Church it derives from the institution of apostolic succession, by which the authority which Jesus vested in the apostles is vested in their validly ordained successors, quite apart from their personal merit. The effect was to admit to leadership the vicious and the unjust, while undercutting the claims of the wise and the just by representing their weaknesses as sins meriting eternal damnation, on par with those of the worst oppressors. Augustinian theology, in other words, legitimated the authority of the Germanic warlords who replaced the Empire as stewards of the temporal power, and of a hierarchy closely associated with them, or in some cases with older elites, which was far from distinguishing itself by its wisdom or its justice.

Medieval European civilization was, in fact, quite dynamic and progressive. Feudal land tenure patterns, the division of land into demesne, virgate, and commons, gave the peasantry a stake in increasing productivity. Monasteries, which held an ever larger portion of the land, invested the surplus they extracted not in luxury consumption but in activities which promoted human development—including the development and implementation of new agricultural technologies. Feudal Europe made great strides in the transition from human to animal power, invented the three field system, the alpine plough, etc. The period between collapse of the Roman Empire and the middle of the twelfth century saw agricultural yields increase from 4:1 to 9:1, the first real increase since the agricultural revolution (Anderson 1974). Higher agricultural yields made possible the development of a rich culture centered at first around monasteries and cathedrals, but eventually around universities which absorbed the intellectual wealth of the more advanced Islamic civilization to the south and east.

Under such circumstances the doctrine of original sin, which had emerged during the dark days of the Roman imperium, seemed less and less credible. This was especially true for the rising petty bourgeoisie of the towns and cities, and for the philosophers and theologians who drew on the newly rediscovered works of Aristotle to give voice to their experience and aspirations. We will look in a subsequent section what became of the doctrine of original sin in their hands Thomas, who was their theologian *par excellence.*

There, were, however, those who defended the increasingly untenable rule of the warlords over the creative classes, and it was above all these who also defended the Pauline and Augustinian doctrine of original sin. This is apparent, for example, in Anselm who, like his predecessors, regards both Satan's sin (as we saw in the last chapter) and Adam's, as a matter of disobedience and dishonor towards God:

> Every inclination of the rational creature ought to be subject to the will of God ... Nothing is less tolerable in the order of things than for the creature to take away the honor due the Creator and not repay what he took away." (Anselm, *Cur deus homo* I.13)

> As far as God Himself is concerned, nothing can be added to his honor or subtracted from it ... But when a particular creature, either by nature or reason, keeps the order that belongs to it and is, as it were, assigned to it, it is said to obey God and to honor him ... But when it does not will what it ought, it dishonors God [and] disturbs the order and beauty of the universe. (Anselm, *Cur deus homo* I.15)

Sin, in other words, is first and foremost a violation of the cosmic hierarchy which occurs when a creature aspires to more than is appropriate for him. It should be noted, however, that even for Anselm—one of the most Augustinian thinkers of the high middle ages—the inability engendered by original sin is not so much an inability to do what is right in general as it is an inability to repay God for the dishonor caused by original sin and thus repair the torn fabric of the cosmos (Anselm, *Cur deus homo* I.22–23). It is for this reason, and this reason alone, that the incarnation becomes necessary.

It is only during the Augustinian reaction of the thirteenth and fourteenth centuries, as the warlord elites and their allies within the clergy became increasingly concerned about the threat represented by the petty bourgeoisie and their Aristotelian intelligentsia, that Anselm's doctrine was mobilized in a way which step by step led to a doctrine of inability which would have stunned even Paul and Augustine. A key step in this regard is represented by Duns Scotus, who criticized Aristotelian and Thomistic psychology, which identified the will with the intellectual appetite, on the grounds that such a psychology could not account for the fall of the devil. According to Aristotle vice is fundamentally a result of the fact that, being just barely rational animals still immersed in sensation we see lesser goods more keenly than higher goods and become habituated to their pursuit. But the devil is not an animal at all, and has no sensual passions. If sin is a result of distraction by the passions, he ought never to have fallen. Anselm's doctrine provided the answer, as well as the basis for a new psychology which distinguished between two aspects of the will: the *affectio commodi*, which seeks its own development, and the *affectio justiae*, which seeks what is right. When my development comes into conflict with the rights of another (e.g., God), I am obliged to yield, doing as God commands, loving my neighbor as myself and God above all. The devil, and Adam after him, fell, because they did exactly as Aristotle and Thomas would have counseled: seeking the full development of their capacities, something which could terminate only in divinity.

Catholic Augustinians (especially in the Franciscan tradition) developed this doctrine in conjunction with a spirituality which was still centered on the imitation of Christ, and especially on the cultivation of a radically self-sacrificial love, even if this was understood as being possible only on the basis of divine grace. They retained, in other words, a Catholic spirituality which was focused on the pursuit of spiritual perfection, but defined perfection in such a way as to put it further and further out of reach. It is one thing to ask that people gradually develop towards the pursuit of higher goods and, after a long struggle realize that the universe is ordered not so much to them as to God, when the cultivation of their capacities is regarded as an integral dimension of that ordering. It is quite another thing to demand that as a condition of acceptability to God human beings purge themselves of any self-will whatsoever. As Luther realized, after considerable personal struggle, *that* is impossible. Our only hope is that God will choose freely to overlook our persistent sinfulness and declare us acceptable when in fact we are not.

In Calvin the full implications of the Augustinian approach become explicit. Calvin is quite clear, first of all, that Adam's sin was not sensual intemperance, but rather pride and infidelity: "The prohibition to touch the tree of the knowledge of Good and Evil was a trial of obedience that Adam, by observing it, might prove his willing submission to the command of God. For the very term shows the end of the precept to have been to keep him contented with his lot, and not allow him arrogantly to aspire beyond it" (Calvin, *Institutes of the Christian Religion*, II:1.4). As a result of this transgression, Calvin argues, the whole order of nature has suffered deterioration (Calvin, *Institutes of the Christian Religion*, II:1.5). Humanity, furthermore, had withdrawn from it its original justice and has been punished with a nature prone to every vice (Calvin, *Institutes of the Christian Religion*, II:1.5). This nature, in turn, makes us worthy of eternal damnation.

> Original sin, then, may be defined as a hereditary corruption and depravity of our nature, extending to all parts of the soul, which first makes us obnoxious to the wrath of God, and then produces in us works which in Scripture are termed works of the flesh. This corruption is repeatedly designated by Paul by the term sin (Gal 5:19), while the works which proceed from it are termed sins. The two things, therefore, are to be distinctly observed—viz, that being thus perverted and corrupted in all parts of our nature, we

are, merely on account of such corruption, deservedly condemned by God, to whom nothing is acceptable but righteousness, innocence, and purity ... Next comes the other point—viz, that this perversity in us never ceases, but constantly produces new fruits, in other words, those works of the fleshy which we have formerly described. (Calvin, *Institutes of the Christian Religion*, II:1.8)

The corruption of our nature, Calvin, argues, extends to both the intellect and the will. We retain, to be sure, sufficient intellectual power to excel in the arts and to create and preserve civil order. This is a result of God's indulgence, which prevents sin extending its power so far as to result in the global destruction of humanity. Indeed, we even have a dim knowledge of God's existence. What we cannot know, as a result of our corruption, is God's essential nature and His relations with us, including a true understanding of the divine law (Calvin, *Institutes of the Christian Religion*, II:2.13–22). Calvin explicitly rejects, however, the view that sin is purely a result of this ignorance (Calvin, *Institutes of the Christian Religion*, II:2.25). Even if every sin is not willfully malicious, every sin *does* involve an evil will. Rejecting the scholastic view that original sin consists in a mere weakening of a will which nonetheless aspires to the Good, Calvin argues that this condition of aspiring to the Good but not being able to do it is, rather, the situation of the regenerate. In our fallen state we will ill. "Nevertheless there remains in us a will which both inclines and hastens on with the strongest affection towards sin ... Thus simply to will is the part of man, to will ill the part of corrupt nature, and to will well the part of grace (Calvin, *Institutes of the Christian Religion*, II:3.5).

Once again, the social basis and political valence of this position should be clear. On the one hand, the transition from petty to general commodity production, and especially the brutality involved in the primitive accumulation of capital, which was already in full force in Calvin's time, create a spontaneous experience of human beings as radically depraved. On the other hand, the emerging bourgeoisie, like the feudal warlords before them but more so, *required* a doctrine which makes what they are doing seem, if not just, then at least no worse than what can be expected from sinful humans. It is thus hardly surprising to find Calvinism supported by some of the most rapacious sectors of the emerging bourgeoisie in England and the Netherlands, who were involved in the most brutal aspects of the primitive accumulation of capital. Ernest Mandel notes, for example, that the "Dutch merchants, whose profits depended on their monopoly of spices obtained through conquests in the Indonesian archipelago, went over to mass destruction of cinnamon trees in the small Islands of the Moluccas as soon as prices began to fall in Europe. The 'Hongi voyages' to destroy these trees and massacre the population which for centuries had drawn their livelihood from growing them, set a sinister mark on the history of Dutch colonialism, Admiral J. P. Coen not shrinking from the extermination of all the male inhabitants of the Banda islands" (Mandel 1968: 108). It would not be difficult for people involved in this sort of activity to imagine themselves depraved—and it would be rather a comfort to imagine that everyone else was as well.

It would be unfair, however, to claim that Calvinism did *nothing more* than legitimate the brutal process of primitive capitalist accumulation. Just as Pauline and Augustinian theology had helped civilize and soften the brutality of the Roman ruling classes (Theissen 1982, Kyrtatis 1987, Mansueto 1995, 2002a), Calvinism served to soften the brutality of capital and to turn capitalists away from the most brutal and rapacious forms of exploitation—e.g., the slave trade and plantation agriculture—and towards the development of industry. This is true of both Evangelical Calvinists, who stressed the importance of a personal conversion experience, and Liberals who regarded "usefulness to the community" as a sufficient sign of regeneration. Thus Jonathan Edwards was an ardent defender of Indian land rights in Massachusetts, something which ultimately cost him his pulpit, and Samuel Hopkins, that most radical of Calvinists, was among the first Euro-American abolitionists, and was a sharp critic of the increasingly commercial character of the republic. Thus the pivotal role of the Reformed churches in the social reform movements of the nineteenth century which saved the United States from the fate of becoming and agricultural export economy and made it instead the world's leading industrial power.

In the long run, for precisely this reason, Calvinism proved inadequate as a capitalist ideology. Calvinism still preached regeneration, and something more was expected of the regenerate than of the reprobate. This might still be workable during a period in which capital could represent itself as a progressive force advocating, for example, industrious stewardship of the resources and talents God had given us and struggling, if not always consistently, against the worst forms of social injustice, such as slavery. Things changed, however, when the internal contradictions of capitalism[1] began to require the export of capital to low wage, low technology activities, and thus the division of the world by the principal capitalist powers, something which in turn led to brutal world wars. If capitalism is predicated on a certain pessimism regarding human nature which, however, still allows for regeneration and amelioration, then imperialism is predicated on the conviction that regeneration is, quite simply, impossible.

This is the social basis for the emergence, beginning in the late nineteenth century, of radically pessimistic anthropologies which leave no room for authentic human excellence, temporal or spiritual, whatsoever. The most important of these are, of course, those advanced by Nietzsche and Freud.

The case of Nietzsche is important primarily because it illustrates so well the link between univocal metaphysics and cosmological and anthropological pessimism. For Nietzsche the entire universe is governed by a single principle—the will to power. All talk of the right and good and justice are merely means by which the weak attempt to control the strong and rationalize their own failure. Those who lucidly understand the human condition will boldly pursue their own development even—no especially—at the cost of others knowing that, in the long run they too will be swept away by the forces of decay and disintegration that affect all things.

Nietzsche differs here from Paul and Augustine and Calvin in only one essential respect. These latter thinkers all believed that there was one being of infinite power, whose rule could not in fact be broken and to whom it was, therefore, wise to submit. Being thus secure in his rule, this being could also afford to be generous with his rebellious subjects and provide for those who had rebelled some means of redemption, though this was a free gift which he was by no means obliged to bestow on them. Nietzsche, on the other hand, regards all power as finite. There is no one to whom we know in advance we must submit and there is none who can redeem us from the fate which ultimately awaits us (Nietzsche 1889/1968). The universe is a zero-sum game in which everyone ultimately loses.

---

1. I am referring here to the tendency, noted by Marx (Marx 1867/1976) and further explained by Lenin (Lenin 1916.1971), for the rate of profit to fall as the economy becomes technologically more advanced, so long as emerging technologies do not enjoy a monopoly rent on innovation and so long as wages cannot be reduced to compensate.

Freud takes Nietzsche's basic insight and transforms it into the basis for a fully developed psychology. Human beings are endowed with two primary drives: *eros*, or desire (especially sexual desire) and *thanatos*—aggression or the death instinct. Unlike other animals, however, we have large brains and opposable thumbs rather than large claws or stomachs which can digest grass. We can survive only by transforming our environment through work, something which requires discipline and cooperation. This, in turn, requires the sublimation of our drives through a long process of socialization. The key link in this process is the famous Oedipal crisis. The child, seeking to phallically possess the mother, is frustrated and forced to repress this desire. In the case of the male child this comes about through fear of castration by the father. The resulting trauma results in anger and frustration which the child eventually turns against himself, effectively breaking off a piece of the death instinct and constructing what Freud calls the super-ego. In the case of the female child the process is less traumatic. She merely recognizes that she is already castrated and experiences herself as inadequate and in need of a man. Because of this her super-ego is less well developed and women are more instinctual and less moral. In either case human beings are condemned to a life of frustration. What we *really* want is to rape our mothers and eat them for a snack. Instead we must work what we eat and confine our sexual passions to context of a monogamous marriage.

The political implications of this analysis are clear. The principal causes of human frustration lie not in one or another social structure, but in human nature itself which wants something (the opportunity for unfettered aggression and sexual conquest) which it cannot have. There is little point in trying to build a more just social order. It will merely result in further frustration by requiring of human beings even more sublimation, something which is hardly possible on a large scale. Freud, in fact, regards religious experience, when it is not simply the result of an infantile neurosis based on fear of the father, as a result of just precisely this sort of excessive sublimation, which drains human energy form the business of work and monogamous marriage to the cultivation of an "oceanic feeling" of identification with all things (Freud 1927/1928, 1930).

In the case of all these thinkers it is an underlying univocal metaphysics, which makes the difference between God and the universe purely quantitative, and thus sets up an opposition between divine sovereignty and human development, or else eliminates God from the picture entirely, which leads to pessimism regarding human nature. It is a univocal metaphysics which makes it impossible to understand how our pursuit of divinity might actually do honor to God and it is univocal metaphysics which makes our drive to grow and develop a threat to the similar growth and development of other creatures, rather than a participation in an undivided power of Being which excludes all zero-sum games.

We need now to turn to Thomas' approach to this problem, and see what difference an authentic metaphysics of *esse* makes for our understanding of human nature.

THE THOMISTIC ALTERNATIVE

If one wanted to make Thomas look as if he assented to the Augustinian doctrine of original sin, this would not be difficult to do. Thus, in his consideration of the *casu diaboli*, Thomas says that Satan's sin consists in a failure to be subject to God as he should have been (Thomas, *Summa Theologiae* I:1:63:1), and that he desired to be like God in a disordered way, seeking to have by his own power what he could have obtained by divine grace, and that he furthermore sought dominion over others (Thomas, *Summa Theologiae* I:1:63:3). This is fully in accord with Augustine's position. The same is true of Thomas' treatment of original sin, which he treats as deriving from a failure to remain subject to God.

> Now the whole order of original justice consists in man's will being subject to God, which subjection, first and chiefly, was in the will, whose function it is to move all other parts to the end, as stated above, so that the will being turned away from God, all other powers of the soul became disordered. Accordingly, the privation of original justice, by which the will was made subject to God, is the formal element in original sin, while every other disorder of the soul's powers is a kind of material element in respect of original sin. Now the lack or order of the other powers of the soul consists chiefly in their turning inordinately to changeable good, which lack of order may be called by the general name of concupiscence. (Thomas, *Summa Theologiae* I–II:82:3)

This all sounds like traditional Augustinian doctrine.

If we look more closely at Thomas' analysis, however, we find something very different. First, as if to let us know that he is actually rather uncomfortable with the whole doctrine, Thomas prefaces his discussion with a statement which suggests that he upholds the doctrine of original sin only because it is a defined dogma: "According to the Catholic Faith we are bound to hold that the first sin of the first man is transmitted to his descendants by way of origin" (Thomas, *Summa Theologiae* I–II:81:1). This is not something that Thomas does every time he addresses a defined dogma, and thus cannot be dismissed as a mere convention or an attempt to ensure that his students know which doctrines are definitively taught and which are not.

Second, and more important, however, is the fact that his understanding of the whole logic of sin, original or otherwise, is very different from that of the Augustinians. Sin, for Thomas, is always and only a result of intellectual failure. This is the full text of his analysis of how Satan, who was free from sensual passion, could have sinned.

> Mortal sin occurs in two ways in the act of free choice. First, when something evil is chosen, as man sins by choosing adultery, which is evil of itself. Such sin always comes of ignorance or error. Otherwise what is evil would never be chosen as good. The adulterer errs in this particular, choosing this delight of a disordered act as something good to be performed now, from the inclination of passion or habit, even if he does not err in his universal judgment, but retains a right opinion in this respect. In this way there can be no sin in the angel, because there are no passions in the angels to fetter reason or intellect, as is manifest from what has been said above [Thomas. *Summa Theologiae*. I:59:4]; nor again could any habit inclining to sin precede their first sin. In another way sin comes of free choice by choosing something good in itself, but not according to the order of due measure or rule, so that the defect which induces sin is only on the part of the choice which does not have its due order (except on the part of the thing chosen); as if one were to pray without heeding the order established by the Church. Such a sin does not presuppose ignorance, but merely absence of consideration of the things which ought to be considered. In this way the angel sinned, by seeking his own good, from his own free choice, without being ordered to the rule of the Divine Will. (Thomas, *Summa Theologiae* I:63:1)

While Thomas is careful here to avoid saying that Satan's sin is the result of ignorance, a position rejected by the Augustinians and thus theologically suspect, he effectively attributes the sin to an intellectual failure of another sort—a failure to understand correctly *how things work*. The reference to praying in a way contrary to the order established by the

Church makes it sound as if the failure is almost technical in character. Thomas does not, to be sure, spell out the precise nature of Satan's technical error, but it is apparent when we set the passage in the context of the *Summa* as a whole. Satan sins because he seeks to become divine by means of his own power, something which is quite simply impossible. A contingent being cannot become divine by its own power, and any attempt to do so will result in disorder, both in the being that sins and in the universe as a whole. Sin, angelic or human, original or actual, always originates in an intellectual failure, something which is ultimately a result of *finitude*.

What about the question of inability? For the Augustinians our inability to do what is right is punishment imposed by God. Having refused to subject our will to His, He makes our passions rebel against our will. For Thomas, on the other hand, inability is a natural consequence of sin itself. It is, furthermore, not connected specifically with original sin, but is rather a result of *mortal* sin generally. For Thomas, the principal effect of sin is a disturbance in the order of the soul, which inhibits our ability to grow and develop and thus reach our natural end.

> Now the disturbance of an order is sometimes reparable, sometimes irreparable. For a defect which destroys the principle is always irreparable, although if the principle be saved, defects can be repaired by virtue of that principle ... Now in every order there is a principle by which one takes part in that order. Consequently if a sin destroys the principle of the order by which man's will is subject to God, the disorder will be such as to be considered in itself irreparable, although it is possible to repair it by the power of God. Now the principle of this order is the last end, to which man adheres by charity. Therefore, whatever sins turn man away from God, so as to destroy charity, considered in themselves, incur a debt of eternal punishment. (Thomas, *Summa Theologiae* I–II:87:3)

This punishment is not externally imposed, but rather a natural result of our turning away from God. Now the question, of course, is just what sort of action could actually *destroy charity*. Thomas regards as mortal any sin which puts something else above the love of God, or even above love of neighbor, but then seems to qualify this by saying that it is enough to avoid mortal sin that our lives be ordered *habitually* to the last end, even if they are not actually so ordered in each and every particular (Thomas, *Summa Theologiae* I–II:88:1:a2). What makes a sin mortal, for Thomas, in other words, is not so much the fact that it is an offense to God, but rather the fact that it involves such a profound disruption in the order of the soul that we actually stop pursuing Being as such. And what we do not seek we will not find, unless it is once again shown to us by One who intervenes to help us once again find our way.

The underlying logic of the Thomistic position is thus quite different from that of the Augustinians. Sin is a result, first and foremost of our finitude which leads to intellectual failure. These intellectual failures can be of two sorts. On the one hand, we may misunderstand the nature of the highest Good and thus seek it in a way which dooms us to failure—or rather think we are seeking the highest Good when in fact we are seeking something quite different—e.g., quantitatively infinite power rather than the undivided power of Being as such, which belongs to no one, but simply Is. On the other hand, because of the limits of our intellectual powers, the highest Good is known only dimly, and we may be distracted by lesser goods which appear to us more vividly, and eventually become so absorbed in the pursuit of these goods that we forget God entirely. In either case, when the disorder becomes habitual, we can so radically lose our way that only divine intervention can help us find it.

In Thomas, to be sure, this logic is rather concealed—perhaps intentionally—by a concern not to appear to contradict defined dogma. There are, furthermore, aspects of his doctrine that need further development. What is the relationship between habituation and social structure? What does it mean for Necessary Being, which is always present in everything that exists, to "intervene" to help us find our way? What we will attempt to do in the remainder of this chapter is to spell out a complete and consistent Thomistic doctrine which answers these questions and offers a credible account of human weakness without concession to the Augustinian doctrine of original sin.

ELEMENTS OF HUMAN PSYCHOLOGY

We have already shown that all human action begins with cognition. We have also already analyzed briefly the nature and dynamics of human knowledge. What we need to do here is simply to set what we said earlier within the context of our larger argument. The material basis of the intellect lies in the human nervous system. Two factors are of particular importance here. First, like other higher animals, human beings are capable of complex sensation. Data which is gathered by the internal senses is formed into images and stored in the nervous system in what neuropsychologists call "dispositional representations" (Damasio 1995). With appropriate stimuli, these areas of the nervous system become excited and recreate the experience which gave rise to them. While it is difficult to show the existence of an "onto-" relationship between image and objective reality, research does show that the patterns of neurons which fire when monkeys are shown a triangle actually resembles the object they have been shown. It is, furthermore, difficult to understand how animals could survive were there not some sort of similarity between image and object. Second, the complexity of the human nervous system makes it possible for us to form links between images. It is this linking of images with each other into complex patterns which constitutes the material basis for properly intellectual knowledge.

Which ideas we actually develop, however, depends on the operation of structural factors, and specifically on the operation of the Agent Intellect, which we have identified with human society itself. Living in a given society we actually *live* its structure and become connatural with it. The images we garner from the senses are then illuminated by these structures, revealing certain aspects of the real nature of things while leaving others concealed or obscure. Thus Durkheim demonstrated that participation in simple band societies provide a basis in experience for the idea of whole and part, relationship, and a rudimentary idea of the connectedness of things (Durkheim 1911/1965). Participation in a tribe, with a complex kinship system, provides a basis for the development of more complex schemes of classification, and thus a rudimentary sense of structure. Later the Soviet philosopher Bogdanov (Bogdanov 1928/1980) pointed out the role of the village community, in which each individual has a definite function in the context of a complex division of labor directed towards a common end, for the emergence of the idea of organization, and of the universe as an organized, meaningful system. The Soviet neuropsychologist Luria, in the 1920s and 1930s, showed that certain more complex intellectual operations, especially higher abstraction, presuppose involvement in more complex social interactions (Luria 1974/1976).

As we noted earlier, this approach provides a solution to the old debate regarding the unity or plurality of the Agent Intellect (von Steenberghen 1980). The social system is both one and many. It is "one" in the sense that it is ultimately a single interconnected system, prior to the individual, which informs his/her particular intellect from the outside. It is many both in its internal diversity and in the sense that it is internalized, and internalized differently by different individuals, so that however dependent we are on our social context for the basic forms of our thought, there is no group mind which is doing our thinking for us.

We have also noted that this approach, far from leading to an irreducible relativism, effectively reconciles epistemological and metaphysical realism with the sociology of knowledge. There can, on the one hand, be no doubt that human societies, like the sensory systems of various animal species, are finite and can reveal only part of the systems which they perceive. There is, furthermore, no doubt that the part of reality which is revealed by these structures is selected by the needs of the social systems in question, just as animals develop those senses which serve their adaptive strategies. But abstractions which help a society to survive and flourish must disclose something important about the way the universe really works, just as well adapted sensory systems disclose something important about an animal's environment. Ideas and systems of ideas which lead to stagnation and decline are probably flawed in some way. And this is all we really need in order to show that abstractions are not *merely* social products which have no relationship whatsoever with the organization of the universe, but rather products of an interaction between human beings and the world which discloses real if limited truths, truths which can be tested in practice and then serve as the basis for further development.

This, in turn, points us towards the teleological principle of intellectual knowledge: i.e., immediately the intelligible object itself, which we always and only grasp only partially, and ultimately the Truth as such, the principle which, to the extent that are able to comprehend it, at once explains and orders all things. All knowing, however limited by the material constraints of the human nervous system and the structure of the society in which it takes place, is always and only a search for the Truth. As the inadequacies of our ideas come to light we cannot help but struggle for a higher synthesis which stretches the limits not only of existing ideologies by also of the social structures in which they are grounded, and ultimately, perhaps, even of the bodies which are the present condition and instrument of our knowing.

Once we know something, our appetites respond either by seeking it or by seeking to avoid it, depending on whether or not it is good for us. Appetite, like cognition, operates at both a sensual and an intellectual level. The sensual appetites are those that depend only on sensory knowledge. We see a beautiful woman and are drawn towards her; we catch the scent of a simmering *tangine* and seek its source. In either case the pursuit may be more or less arduous, inspiring not only desire for the object, joy in possessing it, and a loving concern that it continue to be there for us, but also hope that we will actually attain our goal and a certain daring in the pursuit. Or perhaps it is the foul order of death that we smell, and respond with aversion to the sensation, sadness at what caused it, and hatred for the loss, as well as despair at the fact that we too will someday die, fear that that day might come sooner rather than later, and anger at the bare fact of this limitation.

This is, of course, nothing other than the traditional Aristotelian account of the passions. It is, furthermore, like the Aristotelian theory of knowledge, increasingly well substantiated by recent developments in neuropsychology. Images, as Damasio (Damasio 1995) points out, are always associated with definite body states—a pounding heart, a tightening in the chest—which we experience as passions, and which are simply our body's response to what it knows to be goods or evils.

I insist here on the Aristotelian *passion* rather than the term *emotion* which is more usual in our day out of concern to emphasize the point first made by Mary Daly in *Pure Lust* (Daly 1984), namely that the term *emotion* is often used in modern psychology as though it were something which has no relationship to the outside world. Passions on the other hand are real responses to real goods or real evils—responses which may be limited, and which might sometimes prompt us to act rashly, imprudently, or without considering the bigger picture, but which are, in themselves, quite valid. Thus the emotion of *anxiety* is simply a state of mind without aim or purpose; fear on the other hand is the state of a body responding to a perceived threat. It serves the purpose of making us avoid unnecessary danger.

Note that the good being sought here, or the evil to be avoided, is simply that of the individual organism. Without intellect we can be aware of no higher good. And note that our appetites may well have evolved under conditions rather different from those in which we now live. Thus our desire for more fat and more salt and more sugar than is really good for us now that we can be assured of a steady supply. But the fact that the goods to which our senses and passions order us may be limited and that there may be some lag in adapting our appetites to new ecological conditions, does not mean that they are not goods. There is nothing wrong with wanting what our bodies are naturally disposed to seek, in order to realize the ends for which they evolved: nutrition growth and reproduction, and the sheer enjoyment of sensation and locomotion.

The intellectual appetite or *will* forms the sensual appetites or passions just as the intellect forms our sensory cognition. The complexity of the human nervous system allows links to be formed between images which are the biological basis for abstract concepts. And just as individual images are linked with body states, so too are these complexes of images linked with complexes of body states which are more nuanced and multi-dimensional than any individual passion, but which nonetheless presuppose passion and build on it.

In order to illustrate just how this works, let us return to the beautiful woman we mentioned above, but let us assume that being human beings rather than mere animals we not only see her and desire her and seek to possess her, but that we engage her in conversation and find that she is even more wise and loving than she is beautiful. Now, growing within our desire and joy and sensual love, there will be a higher love which values her wisdom and her other virtues as something valuable in their own right. Much as we might desire to hold her in our arms and caress her and perhaps do more, our highest aim will be to enjoy conversation with her and to ensure that her wisdom is shared as widely as possible. This will temper the ardor of our pursuit, so that if and when we hold and touch her it will serve to enrich our intellectual relationship, and so that we will be able to take into account something else of which our intellect also informs us: namely her will and her desires, as well as any other commitments that we or she may have. Any daring we show in pursuing her will be refined into real courage. We will, for example, not hesitate to risk losing her by being honest about faults we have or faults we see when doing so will help one or the other of us to grow. We will, in short, make the right choices, and act with justice, giving all things their due.

Or consider the *tangine*. As rational animals we will respond to its scent not only as the promise of a tasty meal, but as an opportunity for intelligent conversation. And knowing that all human beings need meals and enjoy tasty ones, and that all human beings have something to bring to the common table of our discourse, we will will that everyone partake of this meal and not only ourselves, and will be willing to eat less if that is the only way to ensure that all are fed, both physically and intellectually.

And we will make our shared meal an occasion for building community and deliberating regarding the common good.

Our ability to love in the higher sense, or to will justice, depends on our sensual passions just as our capacity for abstraction depends on our capacity for sensation. Without images from which to abstract, there is no knowledge of intelligibles; without passion there can be no justice, which is after all simply a complex of passions joined together and ordered to a higher end.

It should be clear at this point that our level of moral development depends, in general, on our level of intellectual development which, given what we have said thus far, it follows more or less directly and necessarily. The clearer our vision of higher goods, the greater the degree to which our sensual appetites will be formed by the will and ordered to the pursuit of these higher ends. This formulation does, however, require some clarification.

First, it is important to be clear just what sort of intellectual development leads to moral development. We have distinguished (Mansueto 2002b), following the Thomistic tradition, between three different degrees of abstraction. The first, *totalization*, involves abstracting from concrete particulars to the class or category to which they belong: e.g., from Fido and Fifi to the category of *dog*. This sort of abstraction is effectively universal and everyone who possesses language is capable of it. The second degree of abstraction, *formalization*, involves abstracting from matter entirely to the form or structure of a thing. This is what mathematicians do, and it is the basis of what passes for science in the modern era. We have shown that formalization emerges only in societies in which market forces play a significant role and becomes the "ideal of knowledge," i.e., the standard by which other forms of knowledge are judged only in societies organized by generalized commodity production. While both of these two degrees of abstraction might contribute to the development of various intellectual virtues, including prudence, neither directly bears on our ability to see higher goods. This is a function of transcendental abstraction, which abstracts from things to the ends to which they are ordered, and ultimately, by way of either a mythological or scientific cosmology to the Good which draws all things to itself. We have shown that the capacity for transcendental abstraction is rooted in the experience of belonging to communities which are ordered to definite ends clans, villages, community organizations, trade unions, political parties, religious communities, etc. and is eroded by the development of generalized commodity production. This is because people experience a market society as a system of only externally related atoms (individuals) or quantities (prices) without any global purpose.

It is important to be clear that the while transcendental abstraction can be joined to formalization—this is what we philosophers do when we rise to first principles by means of the dialectic—and that while this specific type way to knowledge of the Good is ordinarily cultivated by formal education of some sort, the capacity for transcendental abstraction as such does not depend on formal education but rather on actually doing the Good and thus being connatural with it. While learning is one path to wisdom, the wise are by no means found only or even primarily among the learned.

This brings us to our second point. In order to do the Good we must know the Good. But our ability to know the Good depends in significant measure on the structure of the society in which we live. The effect of social structure is, furthermore, both global and local. It is global in the sense that it is by living certain structures and becoming connatural with them that the images we garner from the senses are illuminated and their intelligible content reveal. What we can know is thus dependent on the social structure. It is local in the sense that social structures which cultivate right action will cultivate people who are connatural with the Good and will know it. Another way of putting this is to say that the choices we make, while informed first and foremost by our knowledge of the Good, are also influenced by past choices, which have habituated us to certain patterns of action. And it is not only our own past choices to which we become habituated, but those of the many millions of human beings who have come before us and who by their choices have crafted the structure of the society in which we live. This structure affects us not only by providing rewards for some types of action, which may not always be the most virtuous, and by punishing other types of action, which may not always be vicious, but also because it informs and constrains the whole way in which we think about the Good.

It is in this way precisely that we can explain how human beings, who are by nature ordered to the Good, in fact fall so far short of their potential and often commit acts which are quite vicious. Let us trace out this process in some detail.

Realization of our appetites, intellectual or sensible, requires action. Human cognition, like any conceivable material cognition, is thus not only theoretical but also practical. We do not simply enjoy directly the object of our knowledge. Rather, in understanding it, we discover ways to make such enjoyment possible. While this may involve something as simple as picking a piece of fruit off a tree, the specifically human way of securing the objects of our enjoyment is by actually bringing these objects into being through labor. This means reorganizing physical, biological, or social relationships in order to create a more complex, highly organized system than previously existed. While at the simplest levels this labor may appear simply as a means to an end quite distinct from itself, it soon becomes an end in itself, the unique means by which we participate in the self-organizing activity of the universe and the drive of matter towards ever higher levels of organization. Cultivating fruit trees or vines, or tending sheep, initially just a means of securing a more reliable supply of certain foods under particular ecological and technological conditions, soon become enjoyable activities in their own right, as we strive to produce the best wine and the finest cheese we can. This is even more true where the object of labor is itself the social form of matter. Building relationships and enjoying them are one and the same act. The same thing is true for the arts and sciences, for philosophy, and for religion.

But human beings engage in all of these actions under conditions of finitude. Imagine a cluster of village communities developing in a fertile river valley. Initially, perhaps, when the population is very small, they can survive by means of a haphazard horticulture, planting when it gets warm, or just as the river recedes and harvesting when the crops are ripe. As population increases and they begin to strain the carrying capacity of the land they have less margin for error in deciding when to plant and they need to make more systematic use of river, planning ahead for floods and using the water to irrigate drier land further from its banks. This in turn requires cooperation between the villages. Perhaps there is already a shrine or temple of some sort where the peasants from one or more of the villages come together to celebrate certain feasts. The priests associated with this temple must already have a way of knowing when the feast should be celebrated—probably because they pay attention to the motions of the heavenly bodies. Gradually these priests begin to devote more and more of their time to astronomy and develop a reliable calendar. They may also plan and coordinate the construction of irrigation systems.

Grateful for the way in which these innovations improve their productive capacity, the peasants shower their priests with gifts, allowing them to devote full time to their intellectual pursuits. Population grows, the arts and sciences flourish, and the cluster of villages becomes a city. Note here that finitude and scarcity were actually catalysts for development, by requiring the society to develop new knowledge and new technologies.

Imagine now that this fertile valley is relatively small and that beyond it lie great steppes which are far less hospitable. The land is either too dry to cultivate or yields so little that the people must spend all their time cultivating vast fields just in order to survive, leaving no time for the arts and sciences. Or perhaps it is more effective for them simply to herd domesticated animals. Naturally they desire the same goods enjoyed by their neighbors in the river valley. One day, while selling animals in the market, one of their shepherds notices a new sort of tool for sale, a metal plowshare with a sharp edge. The edge is so sharp, in fact, that he cuts himself.

The rest, of course, is (quite literally) History. Plowshares are beaten into swords and pruning hooks into spears and our flourishing temple city is soon paying tribute to conquering warlords from the steppes. Or perhaps they fight off the invaders only to become conquerors and exploiters themselves. Soon the cultivation of the intellectual virtues and an ethic of service to the community gives way to ruthless violence and a craving for luxuries. The beautiful objects which once graced the temples are now part of the booty of the conqueror. Gradually it begins to seem to members of both societies that the conditions of life and thus life itself are the result of violence and conflict. Generous offerings to the gods and their priests give way to bloody sacrifices, perhaps even of human beings. The peasants are drained of more and more surplus and get less and less in return, either individually in terms of increased productive capacity, or collectively, in terms of their contribution to human civilizational progress.

Or perhaps there are no roving tribes on those steppes. As our city becomes more developed some of its more enterprising priests or craftsmen or peasants realize that there must be other cities like it elsewhere in the world. They begin to explore, bringing with them the best their city has to offer, hoping to trade for goods as yet unimagined. Eventually complex trade networks emerge building links between cities and civilizations. But some members of each of these cities are better situated to take advantage of the possibilities of trade than others, and prosper, while others decline, going into debt and eventually losing their land rights and being forced into servitude. Those involved in trade, meanwhile, forget the curiosity which first motivated them and become obsessed with the pursuit of wealth, which they are now accumulating at such a rate that they soon displace the old priestly families associated with the sanctuaries, or else corrupt them and turn them into moneygrubbers as well. Parents no longer raise their children to pursue wisdom, but rather to seek wealth, actually instilling greed and avarice as if they were virtues.

Note that in both cases the chain of events we are describing was set in motion not by some underlying human depravity and not by some free and clear choice for a lesser good. It was, rather, set in motion by a desire for civilizational progress. Our nomadic tribe had no road open to it but conquest if it was to develop; our merchants were only taking the next step in the exploration of the world, a step which was essential if their society was not eventually to stagnate. But both choices led to the development of exploitative social structures, and together set the world on the road to capitalism, which makes the cultivation of authentic virtue difficult at best and perhaps impossible for those who are embedded exclusively in capitalist social relationships.

It is in this context that it becomes possible to understand just how human beings would not only be distracted from the pursuit of God by lesser goods, but also how we might *misunderstand* the highest Good in a way which leads us to pursue something else under its name. Societies which survive, grow, and develop by means of conquest and exploitation, whether military or commercial, survive, grow, and develop by means of the quantitative extension of their wealth and power, rather than the qualitative deepening of their creativity. If we live in such a society, then (given the theory of knowledge we have outlined above) we will inevitably come to understand the first principle in a way which reflects this way of life: as quantitatively rather than qualitatively different from the phenomena of our day to day experience. And when we seek God, we will seek not Being as such, but rather the infinite extension of our control over the labor and resources of others—and we will fail. This radical misunderstanding of the first principle will, furthermore, not only serve to legitimate oppression; it will color the way in which we resist oppression, so that even struggles for liberation become deformed by it and ultimately fail.

And yet as difficult as the actual course of human history, set in motion by the two choices we describe above, has made the path of virtue, it has not made human beings incapable of either individual or collective salvation. This is true for three reasons. First, exploitative social structures simply do not work in the long run. Thus the civilizational collapse at the end of the Bronze Age, as the exactions of the warlord state undermined innovation and social progress; thus the perpetual crises of the new wave of empires which developed after 200 BCE to capture as much as possible for the Silk Road trade for exploitative elites; thus the current crisis of capitalism. Second, and more important, while life in an unjust society may deform our character, it does not and cannot destroy our natural ordering to the good. Given the *capacity* for wisdom and love, we human beings are never really satisfied with anything less. That is why people in every society, no matter how unjust, have challenged the hegemony of the warlords and moneymakers, whether politically, by struggling to build a more just social order, spiritually by reminding people of their ordering to higher ends, or both. Third, God is always there, right before our eyes, and Her incredible beauty as a lure which even the hardest heart cannot resist forever. This is the real meaning of divine grace, that even after we have turned away from God and are pursuing Nothing rather than What Is, Death rather than Life, God is right there in the simplest things waiting for us to rediscover Her.

There are, furthermore, virtues humanity would never have known—least not fully—were it not for the regimes of conquest and trade. The experience of warfare has forced us to cultivate fortitude in a way which would not otherwise have been possible, and it is due to trade that we have been forced to learn new languages, both literally and figuratively, to understand visions of the Good different from our own, to learn from them, and to defend our views by means of an appeal to a reason which at least aspires to universality, rather than to experiences those in other cultures do not and cannot share.

It might be possible to dress this doctrine in Augustinian clothing and claim that it is in fact an interpretation of the doctrines of original sin on the one hand and divine grace on the other. Structural sin binds us fast; God's grace, in the form of Her own attractive power and the internal contradictions of unjust social structures, sets us free. But this would not really be true to the spirit of either the doctrine I have proposed or of Augustine. My analysis of the constraints imposed by social injustice on the cultivation of virtue involves no real doctrine of inability and is thus Aristotelian and Pelagian in spirit rather than Augustinian. And while I have no difficulty using the term grace to describe either the incredible beauty of God, which leaves us dissatisfied with all finite goods, or the stern discipline by which She frustrates our injustice and leads us back to the path of knowledge, the grace in question is not really Christian, at least in the Augustinian sense. One thinks instead of YHWH at once correcting and comforting the people of Israel, or even of the Hellenic Athena, drawing people into conflict in part at least to force them to come to terms with their own limitations, while all the while standing at their side counseling them on the ways of wisdom.

THE TRANSHISTORICAL VOCATION OF HUMANITY

This difference becomes clearer when we consider the implications of our analysis for what Christians have historically called eschatology or the doctrine of last things. It should be clear from the analysis of human nature which we have elaborated thus far that human beings are structured in such a way as to endow us with a dual vocation. By means of abstraction from the images we garner from the senses, we rise to knowledge of the categories to which things belong (totalization), of their underlying structures or essential natures (formalization), and to the End to which they are ordered (transcendental abstraction). The very physical constitution of our bodies then disposes us to *do* something with that knowledge. Unlike other animals which either have or may be in the process of developing intelligence and sapience, such as the parrots and dolphins, we are structured in such a way as to be able to transform our environments. We do this first of all by making tools, which allow us to survive in ecological niches which we would otherwise find inhospitable. These tools then dispose us to specific forms of cooperation—group hunting, village communities cultivating common lands, temple complexes managing complex hydraulic systems—which in turn, by the mechanisms we have outlined above, dispose us to understand the End to which we are ordered in a specific way. Social structures and ideologies which facilitate the authentic development of human capacities survive; those which do not lead eventually, depending on how destructive they are, either to civilizational collapse or to social revolution, and are replaced by forms more adequate to both the material conditions of human development and to its ultimate End.

From this point of view it would seem that that End is nothing other than the cultivation of virtue and the progress of human civilization itself, where progress is understood as the creation of structures which encourage the cultivation of virtue. And in so far as civilizations can achieve what no individual can, there can be little doubt that in a certain sense at least the goal of civilizational progress is a higher one than that of individual virtue. The development of new technologies, the creation of wealth, the establishment of political communities which encourage creativity and justice, and the progress of the arts, the sciences, philosophy, and religion: this is what human beings can do that no other species, at least on this planet, can. Indeed, it is something even Thomistic angels cannot do, elevated as they are above the material and thus above the possibility of progress and change. Clearly civilization building is, if not our only task as human beings, perhaps our most unique one.

But what about the fate of the individual human person? We do not need philosophy to tell us that human beings, in general, believe that death imposes a tragic limit on their development and frustrates the desire for *Esse* which seems constitutive of our being. There have, historically been four different approaches to this question. The first, shared by most nihilists and materialists, is that much as we may want to live for ever, there simply is not any good reason to believe that we will. Our senses tell us that when the bodies dies so too does the soul. Memories of past lives and reports of intercourse with the dead are dismissed as the products of wishful thinking which have never been confirmed in a way which is public and reproducible. Progressive (e.g., dialectical) materialists allow that we live on in our contributions to the human civilizational project and the cosmohistorical evolutionary progress, but to believe in anything more than this is, once again, merely wishful thinking.

This view is unassailable from the standpoint of a science which stops short at formalization. In order to make this point we need only make reference to Frank Tipler's baroque fantasy in which human beings re-engineer the entire universe in such a way as to make it into a giant supercomputer capable of running perfect emulations of all that have ever lived—and all who have not—for what will *seem* like forever (Tipler 1994). The effort required to imagine how eternal life might be possible within the context of the world view of modern science makes it clear why so many who are informed by this view regard the idea as ludicrous.

From the standpoint of a science informed by transcendental abstraction, however, matters are not so simple. We must ask not only how things are structured but to what End that structure is ordered. And it is not entirely clear why, if our end was finite, our desire would be for the infinite. This is why Thomas believed that it is possible to demonstrate *philosophically* the immortality of the human soul. Against the hermeneutic of suspicion advanced by the party of nihilism and despair, the true dialectician advances a hermeneutic of hope.

The question is just what eternal life for human beings might look like. And here philosophy begins to run up against its limits. The answer historically suggested by most Aristotelians is that as we develop intellectually we gradually become identified with the agent intellect. That part of us which is so identified endures; that part of us which is not dies with the body. For those who, like ibn Sina, maintained the plurality of the potential intellect, this immortality might look something like a mystical union with the lowest member of the angelic hierarchy. For those who, like ibn Rusd, maintain the unity of the potential as well as the agent intellect, it seems rather like saying that our ideas live on—but we do not (Avicenna 1025/1981, Averroes 1175/1978)).

Even ibn Sina's view is, however, unsatisfactory from the standpoint both of our analysis of human nature and our metaphysics. First, our analysis of the nature of the agent intellect is rather different than ibn Sina's. For him the agent intellect was, in effect, an angelic intelligence, the least of a whole hierarchy which emanated necessarily from the Necessary Existent. For us the agent intellect is simply human society. While it might be possible to argue that human society possesses consciousness and will, we have not done so and so mystical union with human society is, in any case, hardly a satisfying vision of the eternal life. More important, however, is the fact that what we humans aim at is not simply knowledge of what is possible for human civilization, but rather at knowledge of God. And the God we aim to know is not simply Knowledge but *Esse* as such—the very power to create. Coupled with the fact that we humans are structured not simply to know but also to create, this means that a purely contemplative eternity does not seem particularly satisfying and is not, in any case, really in accord with human nature.

This is why many philosophers have found themselves attracted by visions of human destiny which transcend what philosophy can demonstrate: the Jewish, Christian, and Muslim visions of resurrection and paradise and the Platonic, Neo-Platonist, Buddhist, and Hindu visions of rebirth and reincarnation. While none of the many variants of these visions admit of definitive demonstration, what philosophy can do is to determine whether or not any of them are contrary to reason or to what we already know about the world, and to assess the extent to which they fit with what we can demonstrate about God and the universe. From this point of view a whole class of doctrines regarding resurrection and paradise can be ruled out, as contrary to philosophical theology and anthropology. This is the case with any doctrine which makes eternal life the free gift of a sovereign God who bestows it either on everyone or on a body of the elect without respect to their actual level of development. Such an eternity is either impossible, because humans have not developed to the point of being capable of it, or it is the result of a sort of spiritual rape, in we are made capable of it in spite of ourselves. It also contradicts everything we have discovered about the nature of God, who acts first and foremost as final cause, drawing all things to Herself by teleological attraction, and whose infinite power is thus fully compatible with the finite but real freedom of Her creatures.

Rather more attractive and reasonable is the Catholic variant of this doctrine, according to which God infuses the *capacity* for eternal life, namely the potential for caritative wisdom, and *aids* us in cultivating that capacity, so that eventually we actually merit and are capable of the eternity we actually desire. Two points are, however, in order. First, we should note that there is a real ambiguity in the Catholic understanding eternal life, in that the doctrines of the Beatific Vision and of the resurrection of the body are not fully integrated with each other. Thomistic anthropology and metaphysics explains just how the Beatific Vision—an eternal vision of God in Her essence as a disembodied soul—is possible. But Thomas also acknowledges that we are not complete human beings without our bodies (Thomas, *Summa Theologiae*, 1: 76), and the idea of a body which is not also a limit is logically incoherent. Second, Catholic doctrine requires, in effect, that all but the most developed human beings have a second life after this one in a sort of painful utopia called Purgatory where we complete the hard work of spiritual development which, through lack of time or effort we have left undone. But is this not just a way of importing into Catholicism something like a doctrine of reincarnation?

There are, furthermore, grave problems with traditional Catholic eschatology from the standpoint of the problem of personal identity—

the question of what makes us the specific individuals we are and the same people from one moment to the next. It is not possible or appropriate in this context to discuss comprehensively what has become one of the most controversial problems in philosophy. Suffice it to say that personal identity cannot be ascribed either to our matter, as most Aristotelians would have, since evidence suggests that all of the atoms in our bodies change out every seven years. Nor can personal identity be identified with our structure or form (i.e., our physical, biological, and psychological constitution), since that changes over time. And a resurrected human being would furthermore, have both different matter and a different (i.e., "glorified") form than s/he had before death.

The metaphysics which we outlined in the previous chapter may be helpful in this regard. Being, we said, is fundamentally organization. To exist contingently, as we do, means first and foremost to be related—it means to seek Being. And what we are—our essence—is determined by our structure. What we *are* is first and foremost a specific way of seeking Being, a way which, however, is constantly changing, constantly growing and developing. And this growth and development, by its very nature, implies loss and letting go—it implies dying to what we were before in order to become what we seek to Be. Now this is true even within the scope of a single lifetime. Our bodies mature and then age and our personalities change—hopefully for the better. I am, thankfully, no longer the same person that I was when I was four. I have less hair and more wisdom. Those who resist this sort of radical change—who cling to outmoded and immature identities—are precisely those who have the most difficulty growing. The continuity of our existence is that of a trajectory of change, not that of a stable self.

Now what is true within one lifetime must be even more true of the transition between this life and any possible future existence. There is, on the one hand, nothing in our cosmology or metaphysics which rules out life beyond death. On the contrary, the drive towards being and the complex of relationships which we helped to shape and which in turn made us what we are at least partly independent of this or that particular body. To be more specific, we are born with certain potentials, we cultivate that potential, and when we die we leave behind a new set of potencies. And since God acts as final cause, drawing potency into act, we have every reason to believe that those potencies will in time once again be activated. Death is, on the other hand, a far greater crisis than any we undergo within this life, and we should thus expect that the change which results will be much greater. As with the "little deaths" we undergo while living but more so, we will slough off what has not been working to concentrate either on developing existing strengths or cultivating new ones. We will be different, albeit for reasons which can be understood adequately only in the context of our pasts. Perhaps the best analogy is that of a society which undergoes a revolution. It is different—no longer an absolute monarchy but rather a democracy, no longer a capitalist society but rather socialist. But *its* democracy and *its* socialism bear the stamp of the past. They are part of an ongoing tradition.

For all these reasons it is the doctrine of rebirth or reincarnation, now associated most especially with Buddhism and Hinduism, but once quite widespread in the West as well, which seems most adequate. We humans aspire to a degree of development which no one life—indeed no finite number of lives—can give us. And yet we know that nothing in the universe is without purpose. And so we hope reasonably in a series of lives which will allow us, perhaps over an infinite expanse of time, to realize our End. And yet realizing that End also means letting go of who we are now—it means overcoming, as the Buddhists teach—that attachment to a self which, ultimately, simply does not exist. Nothing has inherent existence except Being itself and Being is, as we saw in the last chapter, not Substance or Self but rather a radical generativity which lives by creating.

Our approach to this doctrine will, to be sure, bear a distinctive stamp. There is nothing in our analysis to support the contention, central to earliest Buddhism, that life is essentially suffering. Life is, rather, desire, a desire which is initially misguided and believes itself to be a desire to *have* when in fact it is a desire to *create*. Suffering disciplines us by helping us to overcome this illusion. Human development, furthermore, does not consist exclusively or even primarily in overcoming the illusion of self, but rather in the cultivation of our creative capacities. It is just that the full development of these capacities requires that we transcend the illusion of self and learn how to tap into the power of Being as such. Our $\tau\varepsilon\lambda o\varsigma$, furthermore, is not to pass over into *paranirvana* understood as extinction or even as a kind of refined bliss, but rather to continue to grow towards God, becoming more than merely human. Here the imagery, if not the specific doctrine, of the *Dasabhumika Sutra* (The Sutra on the Ten Stages) and the *Bodhisattvabhumi* is especially compelling. As we grow and develop, both within this lifetime and from life to life, we grow in creative power, eventually becoming capable of emanating a *Buddhaksetra* and ripening to maturity myriad sentient beings. We become, in other words, creators and teachers in ways that we cannot now even imagine.

The human vocation is, in other words, at once to realize the full potential of our humanity, both individually and collectively *and* to transcend humanity by developing our creative powers in a ways and to degrees which mere humanity does not make possible. This process of growth and development is always also a letting go, not because anything in the universe is intrinsically unworthy of our love, but because what we really love is not having but creating and this means, in the end, not even having ourselves.

In this progress we are at once called and driven forward by the incredible beauty of God who incites in us a desire for something which is beyond imagination and beyond understanding, but which we imagine and struggle to understand nonetheless, and by the hard discipline of matter, which simply will not allow us to do (at least not for long) things which do not promote our own development and the authentic progress of human civilization. Even death and civilizational collapse, which put an end to bad experiments and remind us that even good ones are not absolute, serve to point us towards higher Goods and refine the precision with which we aim at the divine τελος.

We need now to turn to a consideration of the precise character of human excellence and learn how to cultivate it.

4

Human Excellence

Having defined the specific nature of the human vocation, it is now necessary to explore just what it means for a human being to excel in the exercise of that vocation. This is the question which natural law theory has traditionally considered under the heading of virtue. We will begin by analyzing the nature of virtue in general, paying particular attention to the question of just how our doctrine, which forms part of an historicized natural law ethics, differs from traditional virtue theory. We then go on to explore the particular virtues, including the intellectual virtues, the moral virtues, and the theological virtues.

VIRTUE IN GENERAL

We have already seen in the last chapter that human beings are defined by certain definite capacities or potentials. In addition to the capacity to retain form, which we share with the minerals, the capacities for nutrition, growth, and reproduction, which we share with the plants, and the capacities for sensation and locomotion, which we share with the animals, we have the capacity to abstract from the images we garner from sensation their intelligible content, knowing what things are, how they work, and where they—and we—fit in the larger economy of the universe. Ultimately this capacity allows us to rise to knowledge of a first principle in terms of which the universe can be explained and human action ordered. Having this knowledge we become the conscious partners of God in the work of cosmogenesis. This means, on the one hand, that human beings are by nature world-builders. It is our nature to make things, to create ever more complex forms of organization. Lesser animals merely reproduce themselves, or at most expand the scope of their experiences; we are actually capable of understanding and advancing the drive towards divinization immanent in matter itself. At the same time we approach this process, at least initially, as a pursuit of finite goods. Seeking food, and lacking the natural equipment of a lion or a goat, we make arrowheads and plowshares and hunt or till the soil. Needing to cooperate in the pursuit of these activities we form bands and tribes and villages and cities. Gradually, our hunger at least temporarily satisfied, the building of cities itself becomes a good. And throughout this whole process we are constantly engage in reflection on the *meaning* of our activity—on just where it fits in the larger scheme of things. We make myths and compose epics and lyrics and tragedies and comedies. We write dialogues and compose philosophical and theological systems. And in each of these activities we at once advance God's work in the world and hope to find our end and fulfillment.

As we develop so too do our appetites. No finite good can satisfy us. Because of this the process of world-building is also, at the same time, a process of spiritualization. Matter and finitude become teachers of the spirit which gradually raise the intellect and the will towards higher ends, and ultimately towards God. Our understanding of God, furthermore, becomes ever deeper, so that we gradually understand that the first principle to which our senses and reason lead us, and which our will naturally desires, is profound and inexhaustible, incapable of full comprehension and a catalyst for ever deeper desire. This does not, to be sure, mean that we lose our taste for worldly goods. Rather, we just come to understand that they cannot satisfy us, and so we do not become bound by pursuing them or lost in grief when they pass. We come, rather, to see them as participations in the Good we do seek, in Being as such, and thus as natural sacraments which order us ever more profoundly towards God.

Virtue in general is nothing more or less than progress along this path. It means, on the one hand, developing the capacities we need to carry out our specifically human vocation of world-building, while at the same time coming to terms with the limited nature of all our creations, gradually turning our eyes ever higher, towards God. We are like trees which grow ever upwards, towards the heavens, but which grow better and bear sweeter fruit when pruned back, or like a forest which can realize its potential for biological diversity only if fire occasionally burns back some of the trees.

To put the matter more formally and rigorously, the capacities which define us constitute what Aristotle and Thomas called the first degree of actuality of the body. Given our historicized, evolutionary perspective, we prefer to say that they constitute the minimum degree of actuality of the body of a rational animal, won after many lifetimes in the mineral and vegetable and animal worlds. We are millions—no, billions—of years in the making. The exercise of these capacities represents a higher degree of actuality, and habits, which form as particular activities become second nature, higher degrees still. We are, in other words, born with the latent potential for cooking or chemistry or choice. As we exercise these capacities we become more than we were, and gradually become cooks or chemists or active human beings. When we learn to do these things well, we gain the virtue of τεχνη or science or justice and become excellent human beings.

The result is, however, is a tendency to become overly attached to our achievements—or worse still to ourselves. This attachment is, at a certain stage of development, necessary in order to defend emergent forms which might be vulnerable to attack. But if inordinate attachment persists, it becomes an obstacle to further development—a kind of hard shell which prevents further growth (Bogdanov 1928/1980). It is here that matter saves us. In the course of our activities we also experience inevitable frustrations. Some of these frustrations can be attributed immediately to the wrong actions or limited capacities of ourselves or of other people, or to the existence of unjust social structures. All, however, as we demonstrated in the last chapter, ultimately derive from the condition of finitude and there is no set of social conditions which can eliminate frustration entirely. Indeed, as social conditions improve, the intellect and will develop further and aspire to still higher goods, so that the experience of limitation is definitive of the human condition. And if nothing else intervenes death does, and death is always the companion of the wise. These frustrations and the knowledge of our finitude and mortality prune back the deformations which come naturally with human development and break the protective shell of pride and attachment, allowing us to once again set our sights ever upward.

Within this conception of virtue there can be no hard line draw between the sacred and the secular or the profane. World-building—and the cultivation of the human person which at once makes it possible and which it promotes—are themselves sacred tasks, a real participation in the creative life of God. And the experience of finitude and limitation, which help to turn our eyes upward towards God, is often quite mundane.

Indeed, one might even say it is definitive of the mundane. Rather, the positive and negative movements of the spirit, the moments of illumination and partial fulfillment and the long, dark nights which drag on without end are all part of a unified process of spiritual development in which we experience the simplicity of the divine through a prism, as it were, feeling now the warm of the Sun, now the rich moisture of the Moon, now the harshness of battle, and now the cold winter of finitude and death.

We are now in a position to state with some specificity just how our historicized approach to the problem of virtue makes a difference. Traditional natural law theory—and the same thing might be said of much Hindu, Buddhist, Confucian, and Taoist ethics—faced a fundamental dilemma. It is, on the one hand, quite apparent that human beings are capable of extraordinary things. At the same time, we are also capable of *knowing* a higher good than we can realize, either individually or collectively. The soul is, as Aristotle put it, in a sense, all things—but only in a sense. Natural law ethics has thus been faced with a choice. One possibility is to emphasize the essential goodness and latent potential of innerworldly human activity, and to underplay both the very real disappointment of death and the very real dangers of pride and attachment. This is the way of the Jews and Muslims, the Radical Aristotelians and the less metaphysically inclined Confucians and in its most radical form leads towards Marxism, in which the transcendental nature of human aspirations is eclipsed entirely in favor of an exclusive emphasis on civilization building. The other possibility is to treat the *via dialectica* as an ascent, pure and simple, from the material to the spiritual. This is the way of Neo-Platonism, of Buddhism, and of much Hinduism, and Taoism. A few, of course, attempt a middle path, acknowledging the real but limited value of secular, worldly goods while affirming the need for human beings to grow beyond them. This solution, which is that of traditional Thomism, has tended to be unstable, with worldly activity relegated to a lesser "lay" realm and mystical theology taking on increasingly Augustinian overtones, with matter being treated less as a teacher than as a sort of positive evil.[1]

What our approach does is to comprehend the process of spiritual development as a dynamic whole in which the activity of world-building and the cultivation of human capacities are valued as themselves fully

---

1. This is characteristic, for example, of Garrigou-Lagrange, whose otherwise quite subtle and developed account of the spiritual life shows real tendencies towards Augustinianism (Garrigou-Lagrange 1938).

sacred—but also as fraught with dangers and pitfalls. Matter and finitude are understood not as evils but as teachers which at once catalyze new forms of civilizational activity and remind us that nothing finite can satisfy us, while breaking down structures which, while once progressive, now hold back growth and development. As we will see, this allows us to affirm the full range of traditional Jewish, Muslim, Aristotelian, and Confucian virtues, with all their concern for worldly activity, while still learning from the Buddhists and the Taoists the lessons of detachment and "attacking by yielding." Neither way is higher; both form and integral part of matter's long march towards God. Along the way the twin images of the *tzadik* and the *bodhisattva* are there to guide us.

THE SPECIFIC VIRTUES

The Intellectual Virtues

We demonstrated in the first chapter that the moral imperative consists in promoting the progress of matter towards God, i.e., in promoting the development of increasingly complex forms of organization which have an ever greater share in Being. This conclusion has profound implications for the way in which we understand the relationships between the virtues. Specifically, it means that intellectual virtue is always prior to and the condition for moral virtue. This is because in order to promote the progress of matter towards God we must first *know* God, at least in some preliminary and rudimentary way. We must also understand the latent potential of the various forms and grades of matter and the most effective means of promoting their growth and development. We must, in other words, have wisdom and science, which in turn presuppose the virtue of understanding, and the virtues of practical intellect, tecnh, and prudence. Of these the virtues of the theoretical intellect are prior, because they provide us with our end or teloV and help us to understand the natural dispositions of the matter on which we are working. We thus consider them first, and then turn to the virtues of the practical intellect.

THE VIRTUES OF THE THEORETICAL INTELLECT

Theoretical intellect is the capacity to understand the organizing principle of things, and then use that principle to explain them, demonstrating just how they fit into larger global system, and ultimately into the kosmoV as a whole. It is first and foremost about the search for *meaning* and is ordered to meaningful action—i.e., action which, in one way or another, promotes the progress of matter towards God.

We have already considered the larger conditions for the development of the theoretical intellect in the previous chapter: i.e., on the one hand, the existence in human beings (and any other intelligent species) of a nervous system capable of forming, remembering, and transforming not only individual images, but complex systems of relationships between images, which are the material forms of concepts, and on the other hand, participation in social structures which provide the basis in experience for the various grades or degrees of abstraction: systems of classification, mathematical formalizations, and teleological explanations. Here we need to consider the actual exercise of the theoretical intellect and to specify in just what, precisely, theoretical excellence consists.

Now there are two distinct elements in any act of the theoretical intellect. The intellect begins by apprehending a universal. Only once the idea has been understood is it possible to pass judgment on it, either by evaluating its internal coherence or by trying to use it to explain some particular body of data and thus to test its explanatory power. The two operations of the theoretical intellect are thus *apprehension* and *judgment*. Let us consider each in turn.

The act of apprehension involves the formation of a complex series of links between the images we garner from experience which allows us to *understand* the things to which these images refer as

- members of the same class or category, in which case the act of apprehension takes place at the level of totalization,

- the elements of a set defined by a definite mathematical (or other formal) relation, in which case the act of apprehension takes place at the level of formalization, or

- aspects of a larger organized system all ordered to a common end, in which the act of apprehension takes place at the level of transcendental abstraction.

Regardless of the level at which it takes place, apprehension is fundamentally a type of intellectual vision or intuition—it is the ability to *see* the connections between things. Excellence in seeing connections is what we call the virtue of *understanding*.

Built on and layered over the acquired virtue of understanding, Thomists have traditionally identified two additional habits: the theological virtue of faith and the gift of understanding. Faith is simply an intellectual assent, a willingness to believe truths which transcend the natural powers of the human intellect, and to take those truths as the basis for future action. Acting on those truths we eventually enter into the dark night of the soul and come to understand them. Thus one begins by simply *believing* in the doctrine of the Trinity, of the Incarnation, Crucifixion, the Resurrection, perhaps finding some comfort in the idea that there is meaning present in the universe which did not naturally and spontaneously (and does not yet even supernaturally) "meet the eye," and that most especially that there is meaning in the mystery of suffering and loss. By living our faith, however, we are lead to act in a way which often brings more pain than comfort—loving others, and God, for their own sake and not merely because of their usefulness to us. Gradually the idea of giving our life and receiving it back, miraculously as it were and at a higher level, of the indwelling of the infinite God within a finite world, and of the irreducibly social nature of a God who is nonetheless also and only One gradually seem to make sense. We have received the gift of understanding.

Just how does one cultivate the virtue of understanding? For anyone who has spent time teaching this is at once a vitally important and terribly difficult question. Once students understand an idea it is easy enough to help them test its explanatory power and form judgments regarding its value. But the ability to see and understand often seems as if it is merely a given—a raw talent rather than a cultivated capacity.

Now there is an element of truth to this claim. It is at the level of apprehension and understanding that the material and formal conditions seen to matter most. Undoubtedly some are born with a better capacity to form neural networks than others, just as some are born with better eyesight or hearing or physical strength. The nature and complexity of the social structure and the individual's location therein, furthermore, determine whether or not they have any basis in experience for the ideas they are being asked to understand. People immersed in market relations naturally think in terms of formal abstractions, members of nonmarket village communities do not (Luria 1976, Mansueto 2002), but do tend to think spontaneously in terms of ends or purposes, and thus have a "knack" for teleological reasoning and thus for transcendental abstraction.

This does not, however, mean that understanding cannot be cultivated. And here what we have said about the theological virtue of faith and the gift of understanding are particularly helpful. Understanding always begins with faith—with a willingness to believe, or at least "try on" ideas and live them. If we don not have this willingness we do not learn. This is apparent when we consider how we come to apprehend things at the first degree of abstraction, i.e., totalization, and at the highest degree, i.e., transcendental abstraction. As we are learning language, we simply *accept* the nomenclature and the system of classification embedded in the language. Only gradually, by using it on a day to day basis do we actually understand the paradigmatic system behind it. One way to help students take this step is by actually teaching them the paradigmatic or semantic as well as the syntactic or grammatical structure of languages. By this I mean actually pointing out the complexes of words derived from a common root and thus sharing a common root meaning. Similarly, we simply *accept* the fact that paper is meant to written on and that walls, however much they may look like paper, are not, and if we do not accept this we receive a bit of subtle or not so subtle guidance on the matter. Only after working with walls and paper and other things for a while do we really come to see why this is the case. But a good parent, while insisting that the child accept that walls should not be written on, will also point out why this is not a good thing.

In at both the natural and supernatural levels, we should note, accepting ideas on faith is inextricably bound up with membership in a community. By learning a language and learning what things are for and how they are done we enter a whole social world with which we gradually become connatural—just as by learning and living religious doctrines we enter a community of faith and a world of meanings which gradually becomes as much a part of who we are as we are of it. This is why the act of faith has, in the Catholic tradition, historically been bound up with the sacrament of baptism and with a decision, whether made by us or by someone else on our behalf, to enter into and share the life of the Church.

It is specifically with regard to teaching formalization that we tend to miss the importance of faith. Some students just seem to make the leap from concrete to abstract mathematics, i.e., from arithmetic to algebra quite naturally, while others do not. Whether or not they are able to make this leap in turn *determines* whether or not mathematical physics and its derivatives (i.e., the whole of what is usually called modern science) is going to make sense to them or not. Similarly, some students seem quite naturally to make the leap from an ordinary use of language to the more formal terminologies and grammars which are the stuff out of which the social sciences and the hermeneutic disciplines are made. Others act as if you were speaking to them in another language. I would like to suggest that those who succeed in making the leap to formal abstraction do so because they are able to take on faith the rules of arithmetic which govern basic algebraic relations long enough to *see* that they actually work, or to take on faith social scientific or philosophical concepts long enough to *see* their value.

The question, of course, is why? It is tempting simply to say that some have the neurological equipment and others do not, and this is undoubtedly sometimes the case. But teachers who are attentive to what is actually happening in their classrooms know that students who cannot understand meet them with not only incomprehension but also with (a more or less thinly disguised) resistance. It is as if we were asking them to do something they do not want to do, or become something they not want to become. And this is just precisely what is happening. We are asking them to take on faith certain relations which are foreign to them and thus to enter into a community, or rather a social structure, which is alien and perhaps more than a little frightening.

The difference between students who understand and those who do not is not simply biological. It is social. They inhabit subtly different social worlds. Specifically, those who understand formal reasoning inhabit a world where individuals (things and persons) are treated as formally equivalent even though they are obviously in many ways both quantitatively and qualitatively different. Those who do not understand inhabit worlds where this is not the case. Generally speaking this difference is reflected for younger students in the form of discourse and social relations within the family and peer groups and for older students in the nature of the work they do and the way the workplace is organized. Are social relations governed by abstract principles or by specific, concrete norms?[2]

---

2. I taught philosophy for the past two years at the University of New Mexico—Gallup, which has a student body which is roughly 70 percent Diné (Navajo). I assumed that it would be best to begin with a course in ethics, since ethical issues are usually more accessible to students than the highly abstract problems of epistemology and metaphysics. I soon found, however, that this was not the case with the Diné. Ethics left them cold; arguments for the existence of God, even though the philosophical concept of God is rather foreign to their culture, excited considerable interest. Indeed, it soon became ap-

What this means is that if we are to cultivate understanding at the level of formal abstraction we need to be up front about the fact that we are actually asking our students to enter a new part of the social structure and involve them in activities which provide a basis in experience for the ideas we are trying to convey. We are asking them to become decision makers, whose judgments will have broad implications for whole classes of things and people essentially none of whom they will know directly and personally, and we need to give them experience making those kinds of judgments. Only by living formal abstractions will they every have any hope of understanding them. At the same time, we need to respect their right to choose not to cultivate this particular capacity, and not force on them a way of being they regard as inimical to their traditions and values. It is just that they cannot simultaneously make the choice not to live the social structures which make formal abstraction possible and still expect to master the skills necessary to prosper in a society governed by those structures. Formalization and the disciplines based on it are not culturally neutral tools; they are—every bit as much as the religious traditions of preliterate peoples—an integral part of a cultural complex which must be lived in order to be understood.

This brings us to the question of to what extent the virtue of *understanding* is actually necessary for human excellence in general, and to what extent it is a virtue appropriate to specific callings, like chemistry or political prudence. We began by saying that one must know God before one can help matter grow towards God, and this seemed to imply that the virtue of understanding is a precondition for moral excellence. Our analysis has, however, introduced some distinctions. First, it has become apparent that the virtue of understanding always develops on the basis of faith, whether it is faith in the validity of the semantic structure of the language one uses, faith in the rules of arithmetic, faith that paper is for

---

parent to me that the Diné have a remarkable facility for certain types of formal abstraction, something which is not generally found among people not fully embedded in the market system. I eventually discovered that the Diné kinship system involves the idea of relations of parenthood, grandparenthood, etc., among clans, so that it is possible for a four-year-old girl to be "grandmother" to an eighty-year-old man. This creates a basis in experience for understanding purely formal relations which helps to explain the facility of my Diné students for epistemology and metaphysics. At the same time, traditional Diné social structure is very loose and puts little emphasis on complex forms of social cooperation. This helps explain why the whole problem of ethics and the idea of ethical norms is foreign to them.

writing and walls are not—or faith in the ultimate meaningfulness of the universe as it is understood by various religious traditions. Second, it is apparent that understanding at the levels of totalization and transcendental abstraction is more universally necessary than understanding at the second, formal degree of abstraction. Life in human society is impossible without mastery of the basic semantic structure of at least one language. And *moral* action is impossible without an ability to know ends or purposes—both the natural end of the full development of human capacities and those higher, supernatural ends which call us beyond the merely human. Furthermore, it seems that while one begins with faith, that everyone who lives the faith gradually develops at least some degree of understanding.

It seems proper to conclude, therefore, that it is faith which is necessary for human excellence in general, but that understanding naturally grows up on the basis of faith, and that the excellent human being will be one who understands what things are and what they are for, both immediately, in a way which allows them to be active participants in the life of a community, and ultimately, in a way which allows them to develop real spiritual depth. Understanding at the level of formalization, on the other hand, is necessary chiefly for those who are called to the sciences or to scientifically formed tecnh, or who are called to leadership in complex societies.

The second operation of the theoretical intellect is *judgment*. By judgment we mean the act of bringing the particular under the universal and thus *explaining* it, or else, beginning with a universal, deriving particulars from it, be they lower level principles or particular facts. When we find that we can in fact explain particulars using the principle in question, we make a judgment that the principle is, in fact, at least relatively true. Judgment in this sense pertains equally to explaining the universe and to ordering action. Having arrived at a principle we can then either use that principle to explain the world around us, or we can use it derive principles to govern human action.

Apprehension and judgment clearly work hand in hand. Surveying a body of data we *see* a pattern, or at least think we do. We then attempt to use that pattern to *explain* the data and arrive at certain anomalies. From here we go back and examine our reasoning and ask what in our explanation would have to change in order for it to work. The dialectic is, in fact, nothing other than this back and forth movement between these two acts of the intellect.

Excellence in judgment has historically been regarded as taking two distinct forms: the virtue of *science* and the virtue of *wisdom*. Science is excellence in making judgments regarding particular *genera* of things; wisdom is excellence in making judgments regarding all things, i.e., in explaining and ordering things in terms of the first principle.

Let us consider science first. The nature of science is of vital importance for our argument, and we have already visited it, at some length, in earlier volumes of this work. Historically, science was regarded as excellence in demonstration or explanation. This meant that science, while distinct from wisdom, was closely joined to it. The scientist began the work of explaining the universe: engaging in observation, identifying patterns, looking for principles which could explain them, and then testing those principles for their explanatory power. The metaphysician (who was always also a scientist) completed this work by looking for a global principle in terms of which the diverse forms of organization which make up the physical, biological, and social world might themselves be explained, and which could render intelligible the fact that there is, after all, something rather than nothing. Science, in other words, terminated in metaphysics. The two virtues were treated as distinct largely because the skills involved in explaining particular physical or biological or social phenomena are so different from those involved in developing a synoptic view of the whole that it would be quite possible to excel at the one and not at the other. Science is cultivated in intense interaction with specific forms of material organization. Wisdom, on the other hand, uses the special sciences themselves as its raw material.[3] But science was always understood as an integral, indeed constitutive dimension of the *via dialectica*, of the mind's road to God, and was formed by the superior disciplines of metaphysics and ethics to which it contributed. Specifically, since the end of science was explanation, and since any complete explanation must terminate in a principle which itself needs no further explanation—which has the power

---

3. There are, to be sure, types of science which use the results of other scientific researches as their raw material. Comparative historical sociology, for example, uses the results of historical studies as a raw material in developing and testing broad claims regarding human society and human history as a whole. These disciplines are, however, by nature very close to metaphysics and are often driven by metaphysical or ethical interests.

of Being in itself—science was formed in a way which favored teleological strategies. This is because the only way any principle can cause other things to be moved without itself moving is to move by teleological attraction. Any sort of scientifically informed tecnh was, furthermore, regarded as posterior to wisdom and ethics. One was not admitted to the study of astrology or alchemy or medicine, for example, without first demonstrating both a theoretical understanding of metaphysics and ethics and a character formed by that study (Eamon 1994). This was to ensure that the powers conferred by technical knowledge were, in fact, used in service to the Common Good.

As we saw in the first chapter this view came increasingly under attack after the middle of the thirteenth century. The attack was initiated by clerical intellectuals allied with the emerging monarchies and bourgeoisies. The monarchies and the bourgeoisie were anxious to undercut the rational metaphysics on which natural law ethics depended and thus "liberate" themselves from its constraints. Since this rational metaphysics in turn depended on a teleological understanding of the universe, any attack on that science helped advance their agenda. This concern was layered over by the interests of the clerical intellectuals themselves, who regarded the progress of Aristotelian science, which seemed on the verge of developing a complete, and in their minds deterministic, explanation of the universe, as a threat to the revealed wisdom of which they were the carriers and thus to their status as the intellectual leadership of Europe. The scientific revolution of the seventeenth century represented simply the culmination of a long process in which teleological explanation increasingly gave way to formal description and "science," as it continued to be called, was emancipated from its service to wisdom and in turn came to serve tecnh and through tecnh to serve Capital.

The "science" which has today become dominant is the product of these developments and bears their mark. While it would be excessive to say that nothing that working scientists do bears on their proper vocation, i.e., on explaining the universe, they have been formed in a way which prevents them from taking anything more than the first step in this process. Specifically, "modern science," is little more than mathematical model building. This does, sometimes, permit the development of partial explanations. The properties and behavior of the various chemical elements, for example, can be explained using a combination of quantum theory and thermodynamics. Such successes, however, are largely accidental and are ignored by scientists themselves. To the extent that there is any effort to arrive at a synoptic view of the universe, furthermore, it consists in the search for a unified theory, i.e., a single mathematical formalism, from which all other formalisms can be derived. Such an "explanation" of the organization of the universe as somehow mathematically necessary is both radically inadequate—it fails to explain why the universe is organized in a mathematically intelligible way in the first place—and has the specific quality which makes it acceptable to the bourgeoisie: it yields no obvious moral imperative.

Authentic science is first and foremost a search for meaning in the material universe. It begins with an appreciation of the *beauty* of the material world and with a simple desire to know why things are the way they are. It is that appreciation for beauty that insures that the scientist will continue to be ordered to first principles. Science depends on empirical investigation. In this regard experiment, the idol of modern science, is vastly over-rated by comparison with observation of things in their natural state. Experiments are artificial situations in which an attempt is made to isolate unique causal factors, something which at once presupposes that we understand the true nature of causality, and which excludes in advance the possibility that the universe is a single interconnected system which can always and only be understood as a whole. Science looks for patterns and then for principles which can explain patterns. And science tests those patterns by assessing their explanatory power. In this regard it is vitally important to keep in mind two principles: Occam's Razor, which holds that other things being equal the simplest or most economic explanation (the one which involves the fewest unproven assumptions) is generally to be preferred, and Mansueto's Switchblade, which reminds us that the simplest, most economic explanation is not always the most reductive. Finally, even if the scientist does not go on to become a metaphysician, it is vitally important that s/he be involved in debates regarding the metaphysical implications of his or her work. This is necessary both to ensure that the results are interpreted properly and because it is the metaphysician who ultimately sets the scientist's research agenda. The scientist excels at a special science, but only the metaphysician actually understands what science is and where it fits in a larger strategy for human development.

What this means, of course, is that if we are interested in cultivating true science we must radically alter the way in which scientists are selected and trained. A broad education in the liberal arts is no less important for the scientist than for the metaphysician, the pastor, or the lawyer. This must include significant work in philosophy, including, early in the career, significant reflection on the nature and tasks of science. While science consists in excellence in judgment, and while this certainly requires a willingness to reject attractive but unsupportable hypotheses, we must put an end to the practice of treating a scientific education as consisting purely and simply of disillusionment. It is, rather, a question of learning to distinguish the real meaning from the apparent. Scientists, finally, must always work in the closest possible relationship with metaphysicians. On the one hand, they provide to the metaphysician the raw material of his/her discipline. They must, therefore, have the freedom to conduct their research freely and without fear of reprisal for presenting unwanted results. At the same time, they must understand that their work ultimately serves that of the metaphysician, who sets the agenda for the sciences and thus forms the work of the scientist in every detail.

This has profound implications for our understanding of any possible supernatural degree of science. A supernatural excellence in explaining things would mean, first and foremost, looking beyond their more immediate causes to the first principle and showing why they must be as they are. This is, of course, just precisely what wisdom does and it is why wisdom perfects and completes science. In addition to giving us knowledge of the first principle in itself, wisdom will allow us to complete our explanation of specific classes of phenomena by situating them in the context of a larger philosophical or theological cosmology. For this reason, the acquired virtue of science does not have a specific theological virtue or gift of the Holy Spirit associated with it. It is perfected first by acquired and then by supernatural or caritative wisdom.

This brings us, of course, the virtue of wisdom. And here we face a special epistemological problem. We have demonstrated elsewhere (Mansueto 2002b) that it is, in fact, connaturality with various principles that makes knowledge of them possible. And we are, of course, connatural with physical, biological, and social forms of organization, in which we participate, making possible the development of the special sciences. Wisdom, however, involves knowledge of the first principle, i.e., God, with whom we are not *essentially* connatural. Our essence, in other words, is not the same as God's, which is *esse* as such, nor does it include the divine essence in its definition, in the way being human includes being animal, being alive, retaining form, etc.

What this means is that the cultivation of wisdom requires that something more than merely the exercise of our latent human capacities. It requires at least some degree of connaturality with the divine. It is for this reason that both the dialectical tradition and the religions flowing out of Ancient Israel have regarded the just act as the foundation of wisdom. Thus Plato required that his philosopher kings, as a precondition for even entering on the study of philosophy, undergo a long moral training and spend fifteen years in subaltern political posts which would give them the experience of right action. Similarly, in the Hebrew scriptures, wisdom or knowledge of God (*da'ath 'elohim*) is always presented in parallelism with right action, and especially with action on behalf of justice. The confluence of these two ideas is reflected in the Thomistic concept of "caritative wisdom," in which, loving God for Her own sake we in effect love God with divine love and, thus becoming connatural with God have direct, nonconceptual and experiential knowledge of Her.

Now not all wisdom is caritative, but it *is* all based on right action which gives us one or another degree of connaturality with God and makes knowledge of Her possible. This is the second reason for dividing science from wisdom. Science terminates quite naturally in wisdom and can show that there must be a first principle in terms of which the universe can be explained. But it is incapable of knowing what this principle is—even at the level which Jewish, Christian, and Islamic thought have traditionally ascribed to philosophy as opposed to revelation. For this it is necessary to actually share in the divine nature. This is the difference, for example, between Aristotle's argument for the unmoved mover in the *Physics*, which operates purely at the level of science and which says nothing regarding the nature of the unmoved mover, and the argument in *Metaphysics* XII.7, which (albeit incompletely and rather incoherently) identifies the unmoved mover with what would later be called the transcendentals (Being, the Beautiful, the Good, the True, and the One), and ascribes to Her intellect and will and thus personality.

What this means, of course, is that while science terminates in wisdom, it is possible to have science without wisdom *and* wisdom without science. Indeed, while science is a virtue appropriate to certain specific vocations, wisdom of *some* sort is at once the precondition for moral excellence generally (one cannot do the Good without knowing it) and the end to which human beings generally are ordered. It is thus useful to distinguish between different types of wisdom, based on their relationship with other virtues. There is, first of all, wisdom which is simply connatural, based on right action, and unaccompanied not only by science, but also by art or any other virtue which might allow it to be demonstrated or communicated. This connatural wisdom may be purely natural, i.e., based on right action within the ordinary scope of human nature, or it may be supernatural, based on action which not only aims at the promotion of complex organization in the universe, but which does so because we have come to love such organization, and the God who ultimately calls it into being, for their own sake. In this later case, the wisdom in question is caritative and forms the basis for the mystical union with God.

But connatural wisdom (either natural or supernatural) can be joined with other virtues in a way which radically augment its nature. Specifically, wisdom can be joined with either tecnh (specifically one of the fine arts) or with science. Where it is joined with a fine art it becomes the basis for *mythopoesis* (where the wisdom in question is purely natural) or for *imaginative prophecy* (where it is supernatural). Where wisdom is joined with science it becomes the basis either for *philosophy* (where the wisdom in question is natural) or for *intellectual prophecy* (where the wisdom in question is supernatural).

The line between the natural and the supernatural is simply the line between that which human beings can comprehend and demonstrate and that which (while it can become a principle in terms of which other things are explained or demonstrated) cannot itself be comprehended and thus is not susceptible to proof. Over the long haul of human history this line tends to recede. This is, perhaps, best demonstrated by an example. Originally, Israel gained knowledge of God in the struggle to liberate itself from the warlords of Canaan and their Egyptian overlords. Initially this knowledge was purely natural, and was communicated imaginatively through images of God as a warrior who differed from his Canaanite counterpart largely because he fought on the side of the poor. Thus the origin of the specifically Jewish name for God (YHWH) is probably as a title of the West Semitic El: specifically *'el yahwi sabaoth yisrael*— God who brings into being the armies of Israel (Gottwald 1979). As this struggle progressed and the people flourished, they realized that this God who had brought them what could only seem like miraculous victories over superior enemies is in fact also the God who brings all things into

Being—the causative power of Being itself, which is what YHWH actually means. Initially this idea is experienced as revealed—as somehow known but beyond demonstration. And it must be said that even in Plato and Aristotle we do not really get an *argument* for the first principle as Being as such, but only a dim vision that there must be some power behind the material world. Indeed, it is only by *living* the struggle for justice for many centuries that later Jewish, Christian, and Islamic philosophers[4] eventually come to the point of making an argument for, and thus *comprehending*, what Israel first knew supernaturally and without argument.

This does not, mean, to be sure, that the supernatural disappears. Gradually, in the course of the struggle to build a just society—i.e., a society which promoted the full development of human capacities—the people of Israel found themselves stretched beyond the limits of the purely human. The end or terminus of their struggle for liberation, it turned out, was not to be purely and simply a Jewish state, but a much larger epic of liberation of which they were to be catalysts, but which would require of them superhuman sacrifices. This experience then leads in various ways to the development of the Kaballah, with its claim that the struggles of the Jewish people are part of a larger process of *tikkun 'olam*, of the mending of the universe, as well as to Christianity and Islam.

Similar arguments might be made with regard to other traditions. For the Buddha the doctrine of dependent origination (the idea that everything is dependent on everything else and that nothing, therefore, is *inherently* real) is an insight which stretches the very limits of humanity, a vision of a supreme spiritual truth arrived at not through dialectics but rather through years of spiritual struggle which carried him to the very borderlands of humanity. Later Buddhism, living this doctrine, is able to actually understand it and makes it the basis of (competing) metaphysical schools. The cutting edge of human development recedes and the greatest calling is no longer that of the *ahrat*, or enlightened individual, but rather that of the *bodhisattva*, who devotes herself to the liberation of humanity as a whole. Veneration of the historic Buddha, Gautama Siddhartha,

---

4. The first to make such an argument was, in this case, probably the Islamic philosopher Ibn Sina, whose argument for the "Necessary Existent" in the *Danish*, represents the first point at which an essentially Aristotelian argument for the unmoved mover is recognized as terminating not merely in the God of Abraham, but in the God who Moses met as he was preparing to head his people on the long march toward liberation. Moses ben Maimon and Thomas Aquinas then refine this argument further.

gives way to worship of *Prajnaparamita*, the Supreme Wisdom who is the Mother of all Buddhas (Williams 1989, Kalupahana 1992).

It might be asked where the discipline of theology, which has historically been regarded as a wisdom, fits within this framework. Strictly speaking the term *theology* is fully defined only within a Christian context, where it refers to the rational explanation of revealed doctrines regarded as in themselves beyond comprehension or demonstration. The Islamic *kalam* is similar, and catalyzed the development of comparable sorts of reflection within Judaism. In other traditions the line between natural and supernatural is not so clearly demarcated. In Buddhism and Hinduism, for example, scriptural commentary and metaphysical speculation are interwoven in a way which ends up looking a great deal like theology, but without a sharp distinction between revealed and acquired truths.

Theology, from the standpoint of the perspective being developed here, is fundamentally what a community does as it is struggling to live out, and thus to understand, truths which it experiences as still beyond comprehension. Authentic theology is thus organically linked to the life of a definite religious community. Its content generally looks like a mixture of imaginative and intellectual prophecy on the one hand and philosophy on the other hand, with the latter used to elucidate the former. The truths in question, however, are no longer presented as radically new, and the aim is not just to communicate them and render them intelligible, but rather to draw out their implications for the life of the community, so that living them they community can grow in knowledge of God. Theology is thus the highest of the *ordinary* disciplines, because it leads humanity in its day-to-day struggle to become more than human, as philosophy leads it in the struggle to become fully human. Prophetic authority, on the other hand, is *extraordinary* and arises only in moments of crisis and transformation.

Virtues of the Practical Intellect

It should be apparent from what has been said thus far that the virtues of the theoretical intellect are at once ordered to and dependent on action. Indeed, any consideration of them apart from the virtues of practical intellect is artificial, since the theoretical and practical virtues in fact always arise together. Historically the virtues of the practical intellect were treated under two separate headings: that of tecnh or art and that of fronηsiV or prudence. There are two reasons for this division. First, according to Aristotle, while it is possible to have a science of nature (including mineral, vegetable, animal, and even human psychic realities) it is not possible to have a science of human action, since actions are free and thus cannot be deterministically explained. This means that the principles governing making, which works on a raw material which can be scientifically understood, and the principles governing actions, which works on a raw material which cannot be scientifically understood, will be rather different. Second, Aristotle associated making with servile or at least less developed human labor and action with the free participation of citizens in the public arena.

We reject both reasons for making a sharp division between art and prudence. We have already demonstrated that a science of human society is, in fact, possible, and while that science is not deterministic, it is not entirely clear that physical and biological systems are wholly deterministic either, something which does not prevent us from making practical use of the knowledge we have of the laws which govern their operation. Second, while political participation is, in general, a higher exercise of human capacities than making, and while there is a specific political prudence which pertains to particular callings, every human being possesses reason and thus the capacity to deliberate regarding the Common Good, and thus every human being has a right to some significant degree of political participation. With this right comes the responsibility to cultivate political prudence. Finally, at least some of the arts—specifically the liberal arts—pertain at least in part to making and evaluating arguments in the public arena and are thus closely associated with political prudence. We will thus treat the virtues of the practical intellect in an integrated manner, showing that politics is in fact an art—specifically the making of a just community.

Now art involves three distinct aspects:

- First, it is necessary to understand the underlying matter on which one is working. This understanding may take the form of an informal empirical lore or it may take the form of science.
- Second, it is necessary to understand both the proximate and the ultimate ends towards which one is working. This is why art must always be informed by wisdom of some sort, as well as of the practical needs of the persons or community one serves.

- Finally, one must understand how to cultivate the latent potential of the matter in question in order to realize the ends in question.

It is only this latter aspect which constitutes art proper, but this is quite impossible apart from the other two. Together all three aspects define what we call a *technological regime.*

All human societies have had some knowledge of how the universe works. Initially this knowledge consisted simply of what we call an *empirical lore*, i.e., accumulated observations regarding empirical patterns, without a great deal of formalization or explanation. Of particular importance was an understanding of the empirical conditions under which growth and development become possible: e.g., which geometric forms lead to stable buildings, when to plant and how to supplement the water and nutrients naturally available in the soil. This empirical lore was, in fact, sufficient to produce the technological advances on which human civilization is based: the cultivation of plants and animals, irrigation, road building, the smelting and alloying of metals, complex masonry, etc. This technological regime we call *hortic*, from the Latin *hortare* to encourage, because it focused on the encouragement of already existing and poorly understood processes of growth and development.

Gradually, with the advent of petty commodity production after the eighth century BCE this knowledge was enriched by mathematical formalizations and by a formal effort to understand why things are they way they are. This led to the development of various scientific paradigms, the most important of which are the Aristotelian paradigm in the Mediterranean Basin, the Vedic in India, and the yin-yang and five elements paradigms in China, both of which were eventually incorporated into Taoism and ultimately into the Neo-Confucian synthesis of the Song dynasty. All of these paradigms were essentially teleological, in the sense that they understood the material universe as in some sense ordered to an ultimately spiritual end.[5]

---

5. There are, to be sure, Vedic schools, such as the Vaisheshika and Nyaya which uphold an atomistic cosmology, but the most influential school, the Samkya, understands the universe as a process of progressive spiritualization resulting from the creative interaction of *purusa* or consciousness and *prakriti* or matter. The other *darshanas* have tended to adopt this evolutionary view as their own, even while differing from the Samkya school on other points of epistemology, cosmology, and metaphysics.

Closely associated with this teleological science was a technological regime which we will call *alchemical* because it reached its highest development in the medieval discipline called by that name. Alchemy is nothing more or less than an attempt to understand and reproduce the process by which the heavenly bodies exercise their influence so as to be able to produce changes in material systems. In this sense alchemy is very much the sort of tecnh that we today call technology, i.e., a tecnh based on a scientific understanding of how natural process work, as opposed to arts which have developed on the basis of a purely empirical lore uninformed by any explanatory-deductive theory. What sets alchemy part from modern technology, however, is not simply a different understanding of particular natural processes, but rather the larger teleological system in which it understood its activity to be situated. The drive to produce gold, with which alchemy is traditionally associated, while it was certainly not unaffected by the promise of material gain for those who might succeed, was in reality simply a part of this drive towards perfection, gold being regarded as more perfect than the other metals in virtue of its relative immunity to corrosion or other corruption. The real aim of most scholarly alchemists was to create the Philosopher's Stone, "a certain pure matter which, being discovered and brought by Art to perfection, converts to itself proportionally all imperfect bodies that it touches" (Arnold of Villanova in Read 1957: 28). As James Elkins puts it, alchemy's work "was God's and it was the ongoing perfection of the world" (Elkins 1999: 73)

The crisis of teleological science, which we analyzed above, led to a simultaneous crisis for alchemical technology and the mechanistic science which has been dominant since the seventeenth century has been closely associated with the rise of a very specific sort of technological regime: what we generally call *modern industry*. The development of modern industry is typically marked by the invention of the steam engine and the advent of the technical division of labor—i.e., the division of the productive process into minute, relatively unskilled tasks. A more formal definition is possible only by comparison with earlier technological regimes. Where hortic and alchemical technologies sought to understand and help along processes of development which were already at work in the natural world—the growth of a seed, the development of metals underneath the earth—industry begins by breaking down existing forms of organization—burning coal or oil for example, or catalyzing nuclear fission—and using the energy which is released to reorganize matter in accord with the wishes of those who have the resources to pay for the transformation. Industry treats social matter in the same way. Rather than tapping into and attempting to cultivate the already existing knowledge of peasant communities or artisan guilds, it destroys these forms of organization and then uses their component parts—deskilled human "atoms"—in accord with a plan imposed from the outside.

We should note that (unlike alchemy) modern industry has no substantive principles of value to guide decisions about what is made and how. In the absence of a global cosmic teleology there can be no question of some common end to which all things are ordered. This is why "liberal" ethics of the natural rights, social contract, utilitarian, or formalist variety is simply about finding a way to adjudicate conflicting claims on resources. The assumption is always that we will produce as much as possible to satisfy the desires of as many as possible. And Marxism offers only a partial solution to this problem. The drive to promote "development of the productive forces" provides a kind of teleological ordering, but there is no real sense of the place that this plays in a larger project of human development, must less in the cosmohistorical evolutionary process as a whole. The result of both capitalist and socialist industrialism is an extraordinarily high degree of productivity, understood in terms of the energy harnessed for human purposes. But the cost in terms of ecosystem integrity and human development is enormous.

Mechanistic science may itself be approaching a point of crisis, as we suggested in an earlier chapter. It has been remarkably successful at producing formal descriptions of physical systems. But the fact is that it has not been any more successful than was Aristotelian science at producing a unified theory of motion, nor is it able to describe—much less explain—anything like the full range of natural phenomena. We also suggested that recent scientific results, especially findings regarding cosmological fine-tuning and certain aspects of complex systems theory, point to a resurgence of teleological explanation in the sciences. What does this imply for our understanding of tecnh and for our understanding of the proper relationship between humanity and nature in general?

Two points are in order. First, the approach which we are suggesting excludes the static vision of the Deep Ecologists, who seem to value diversity and complexity *except* when it is a human product. The fact is that every organism which has ever lived on the face of this planet has changed it, and some organisms have changed the ecosystem profoundly.

Thus the role of green plants in increasing the oxygen level and making animal life possible. Also excluded is the claim that all elements in an ecosystem have equal rights or equal value. Value is a measure of complexity and organization. The deep ecologists are quite right in claiming that everything in the universe has *intrinsic* value. But more complex systems have more value than less complex and we should not feel badly about combating the AIDS virus or, for that matter, about eating at least some other organisms.

Anthropocentric approaches are, however, equally excluded. Everything does indeed have a purpose, but we are not it. We are, rather, participants in a cosmohistorical evolutionary process which points beyond us, and indeed beyond any finite system, towards God. This is not merely a matter of transcending liberal or neoliberal individualism in favor of a more collective vision. Each system has its own latent potential and its own role in the cosmohistorical evolutionary process and it is our task, as intelligent participants in the process, to understand that role and to help cultivate the garden in which we have grown up. It is only by attention to the immanent purpose of each particular system that we can be certain we will actually increase the overall complexity of the ecosystem, and not fall into the trap of a technological, collectivist utopianism.

It is here that the concept of a neo-alchemical technology becomes so attractive. What alchemy did was to attempt to understand just how each element fit into the organization of the universe as a whole, and to determine how to use its specific latent potentials to serve that purpose.

We are not, to be sure, advocating a revival of the specific theories and techniques of medieval alchemy, any more than we argue for a restoration of the *specifics* of Aristotelian physics. Above and beyond the changes in cosmography which have taken place in the past several hundred years, which we regard as basically valid, humanity has discovered that growth and development takes place in the system as a whole, and not just in individual organisms. Thermodynamics, complex systems theory, evolutionary biology, and historical materialism have all, also, pointed to the critical role of chaos, struggle, and disintegration in the evolutionary process. This changes somewhat the way in which we understand the aim of cultivation and alchemical transformation. The new Philosopher's Stone will not confer on all things the incorruptibility of the divine, but rather help each system not only realize its latent potential, but also—perhaps through a process which involves considerable struggle and even death—

to transcend the limits of what it is and to become something new and still more beautiful. Labor thus becomes a liturgy, and humanity realizes itself as a real participant in the creative life of God.

We humans are not, however, called simply to help physical and biological matter along in its development towards God. Rather, our highest calling consists in promoting our own development and that of our fellow human beings, both as individuals and collectively. This brings us, therefore, to the fine and liberal arts and to the virtue of prudence.

The fine arts represent in this sense a sort of transition. The fine arts are fine not in the sense of refinement, but in the sense of producing something which (unlike the product of instrumental tecnh), is an end in itself: i.e., something which is beautiful. They work, at least directly, not on the social form of matter but rather on something physical or biological. But because they aim at the creation of beauty they also aim, at least, at affecting human beings and at promoting their growth and development.

In our analysis of the transcendental qualities of being, we argued that everything which is, is beautiful. Being, realized as organization, necessarily possesses *integrity*, which unites the various elements of a system into a single whole, *harmony*, which holds diverse elements in a creative tension so that each element mutually determines the other and helps to make it what it is, and *clarity*, which makes the form or structure a window, as it were on the True. In this sense, aesthetics, or the science of the beautiful, is not primarily about the fine arts, but rather about being in general, and thus forms a part of metaphysics. At the same time, things which are made partake in being, and thus in beauty. Thus the beauty of a plowed field or of a well designed bridge. There is, however, a class of things which are produced by human beings add to the overall level of organization of the universe principally and exclusively because of their beauty, and which designed primarily to be beautiful, rather than merely useful. These are the objects produced by the fine arts.

In order to be beautiful, a work of art must reflect the three principal determinations of the concept of beauty: integrity, harmony, and clarity. The integrity of a work of art is its aesthetic unity. This means bringing diverse elements together into a coherent whole. Works of art which are excessively simple—a canvass which is painted in only one color, a song with only one note, a poem with only one word—lack the internal differentiation necessary to display authentic aesthetic unity. At the same time it is possible for a work of art to contain a rich diversity of elements but to fail to really hang together. We thus complain that a painting or a church is too "busy," that a symphony does not hold together, or that a novel is "picaresque."

A work of art exhibits harmony when it exhibits a unity in tension. Consider, for example, a painting which exhibits many different colors all of which, however, are simply shades of green or orange. The lack of tension in the use of color would make such a painting uninteresting. If, on the other hand, a painting simply juxtaposed vastly different colors—say green and orange—without some structure or context which resolved the tension between these two colors, then the result would be merely dissonant. Similarly, a song which uses only one chord creates, and thus resolves, no tension, as would a "novel" in which it is clear from the very beginning that nothing of moment is going to happen and that everything is and will be "all right." Mere dissonance or conflict, on the other hand, is not beautiful either. The work of art, by creating and resolving tension, contributes to our own ability to bring into harmony the diverse imperatives of Being as such.

Clarity in a work of art refers to the work's ability to manifest the form of the object in question. There are, therefore, three fundamentally distinct degrees of clarity. A work of art may manifest a purely sensible form and thus be beautiful, without, however, manifesting any intelligible form or meaning. This, lower, kind of beauty is typical of much purely ornamental art, and of those schools of painting such as impressionism which make no effort to convey a higher truth. Second, art may manifest an abstract, mathematical form, but still lack discursive meaning. This degree of clarity is most typical of great music, but it may also be found in certain types of abstract visual art, architecture, etc. (The profound connection between the beautify of the mathematical forms conveyed in music, and the impact of the musical manifestation of these forms on the passions, remains a mystery.) Finally, art may use sensible forms to convey some intelligible meaning, as when the images in a painting refer to the sacred or tell a story of political-theological significance, or when a novel creates an entire universe, and thus attempts to say something about the actual universe in which we live. This, clearly, is the highest kind of art—the art representing in painting by such works as Rafaello Sanzio's *School of Athens* and *The Great Disputation*, or by Diego Rivera's murals in the *Secretaría de Educación Pública*, in music like Beethoven's Ninth Symphony and in literature by the novels of Dostoevsky or the epic poetry of Dante or Cardenal.

It might be useful at this point to say something about the tension between the finality of the fine arts and their ultimate ordering to higher ends: i.e., to promoting the development of human capacities. This is, in fact, a false dilemma. The fine arts properly promote human development in and through their beauty. Art which sacrifices beauty in order to make a political, philosophical, or theological point sacrifices its very character as art. At the same time the beauty of a work of art is dependent not only on its technical qualities (its integrity and harmony, i.e., its capacity to integrate diverse elements, intrinsically in tension with each other, into a unified whole) but also on its *claritas*, the sense in which and the extent to which it is a real window on higher truth. This is why a painting by Diego Rivera is more beautiful than the decorative motifs on the museum which houses them and why the novels of Silone are more beautiful than even really well written pulp fiction (and there *is* such a thing). The whole doctrine of "art for art's sake," is less a reaction to second rate didactic art, which has always been around and is not an invention of the socialist realists, but rather a response to the larger crisis of meaning in the nineteenth century. In the absence of *transcendental* principles of value (Beauty, Truth, Good) the humanly created beauty of the arts enters a sort of contest as it were with the humanly created truth of the scientist and the humanly created good of the social revolutionary. All three attempts at creating value are authentic, but all three suffer from a failure to understand properly the transcendental ends to which they are ordered. Thus the tragic sense which infuses all three. And thus the collapse of nineteenth century aestheticism and the cult of intentional ugliness in much twentieth century art.

The very best art is, in a sense, therefore, always religious. At its highest level art is infused with the gift of prophetic wisdom, and mediates to us truths which cannot be rationally comprehended or even discursively explained, but only experienced by entering into the imaginative world of a sacred space, a sacred song, a poem, or a novel.

At the same time, the fine arts always suffer from a distinct limitation: they cannot argue their case. There is no way to tell, simply by experiencing a proposed truth through the medium of one or more fine arts, whether or not it is really a truth or simply a seductive falsehood. So long as we are under the influence of powerful images, which may or may not point us towards transcendental principles of value, we are, in a sense, slaves, both to our own passions and to those who would use images to manipulate our passions and cause us to do their bidding. Thus the importance of the liberal arts—the arts which make us free.

The question of course, is just what we can make which, in the very act of making us, makes us free. The liberal arts train us to make arguments, and to evaluate arguments made by others, and thus put us in a position to make decisions for ourselves. In the Middle Ages the liberal arts included the *trivium* (whence the term "trivia") and the *quadrivium*. The first three disciplines pertain to the construction of arguments using natural languages. Grammar pertains to the internal structure of natural languages, mastery of which is necessary if the language is to be used in a way which is both rhetorically and logically compelling. While the liberal art of grammar may be informed by linguistics, which is a social science, it is distinct from it, in that it is less interested in how languages are actually structured, than in promoting the use of the language in accord with its proper structure. Rhetoric, the art of persuasion, certainly provides prudence with a valuable instrument, but it does not by itself teach us how to build and exercise power in service of the common good. Indeed, it was the confusion of rhetoric with prudence which first led Socrates into the public arena, and catalyzed the birth of the discipline of philosophy. Rhetoric (by itself) knows nothing of the ends of human life, and nothing of the way in which those ends are secured. Rather, it knows only how ideas—relatively true or relatively false—can be explained clearly and in a way which appeals to the intellect and the passions. Logic, finally, concerns itself with making valid arguments. This is not the same thing as making true arguments. In order to be true an argument must be valid, but logical validity is not by itself sufficient for truth. If all canines are herbivores, and dogs are canines, then dogs are herbivores.

This said, we must point out that the liberal arts, like all of the arts, involve real knowledge. Just as the craftsman or engineer must possess real knowledge of both his material and the uses which his product will serve, and the musician must possess real knowledge of the musical system, so to, the master of the *trivium* authentically knows something of the structure of the universe—something which is reflected in the fabric of natural languages, and which is not merely a matter of local convention. Different languages may, to be sure, disclose different aspects of the truth. The sense of time in Hebrew is not that in Hellenic or Hopi. But in learning to use these different languages we learn to see something new about the universe. Similarly, the rules of logic are what they are because the universe is what it is. New logics (transcendental, dialectical) do not merely contradict the old, but rather reflect a new and more profound grasp of the nature of truth itself.

The *quadrivium* historically included pure and applied mathematics: arithmetic, geometry, harmonics, and astronomy. What this means, of course, is that mathematics is fundamentally an art and not a science. What it does is to join the rules of logic (usually formal, though there is no reason why there cannot be a dialectical mathematics) with a formal object (usually set theory), and then constructs a complex system of mathematical categories including every imaginable sort of object, as well as many that cannot be imagined.[6] Pure mathematics then studies the rationally demonstrable properties of these objects and their interrelations with each other. Applied mathematics (mathematical physics, biology, or sociology) then uses some of these objects to model actually existing systems, much as a qualitative scientists might construct a model using a natural language, modified to include a scientific terminology, etc. Like the models created by the qualitative researcher, these mathematical models are always and only better and worse approximations—but they can be applied, with varying results, to every conceivable sort of system. In neither case is there an actual explanation of some phenomenon, which is what we mean by science—though it is, as we suggested above, entirely possible that physical systems might be explained as in some sense mathematically necessary, i.e., as structured in the only way it is logically possible for such systems to be structured.

There was, however, always a deeper significance to study of the *quadrivium* than learning to make mathematical arguments in support of the sciences. The *quadrivium* constituted the "higher" liberal arts because they represented a further step on the journey of the dialectic. Understanding the mathematical structure of the universe was an integral step along the way towards explaining it, and thus towards acquired wisdom. Just how this ascent worked varied form one system to the text. Thus, for Platonic thinkers such as Augustine and Boethius, mathematics is first and fore-

---

6. The question of whether or not a mathematical object must be intuitively constructible—i.e., imaginable—is one of the most controverted questions in the philosophy of mathematics, with the "intuitivist" school and most moderate realists arguing that they must be, and most of the others arguing that they need not be. At stake are concepts like "actual infinity" as well as many of the more exotic creations of modern mathematical physics (Koerner 1968).

most a science of measure. Geometry, which measured "inert, inorganic, sublunary spaces", was the lowest of the mathematical disciplines. Music, which "measured the relationship between the soul and the body" came next, then astronomy, which "measured the time and movements of the heavenly bodies." "Arithmetic, the most abstract, was the science of numbers in themselves. The order of these disciplines—the higher liberal arts—ascended through increasing degrees of abstraction from material to incorporeal contemplation, encouraging the knower towards the vision of God" (Pickstock 1999). This reflects the Platonic understanding of mathematical objects as existing apart from matter, in the mind of God. Aristotle, on the other hand, regarded astronomy as the most divine of the sciences after metaphysics, because it is on the basis of an explanation of the motions of the heavenly bodies that we arrive, at long last, at knowledge of the Unmoved Mover (Aristotle, *Metaphysics* XII.7).

Today we understand the liberal arts more broadly, to include an introduction to the scientific disciplines (physical, biological, and social), as well as to philosophy and other "wisdoms,"[7] sufficient to allow the student, if not to actually practice these disciplines, then at least to make and evaluate arguments which draw on them at a level sufficient to permit them to participate fully in the public arena and to make informed decisions regarding fundamental questions of meaning and value. We also generally include sufficient training in the hermeneutic or interpretive disciplines to allow them to approach both secular and religious literature and the other fine arts as a font of meaning[8]. Social scientific training should, furthermore, be understood broadly enough to include at least basic training in politics—the art of building and exercising power in the public arena on behalf of the Common Good.

---

7. By a "wisdom" we mean any discipline which leads us to knowledge of first principles of explanation and/or action. Philosophy does this by means of the dialectic, ascending rationally to first principles. Other wisdoms claim inspired or revealed knowledge of first principles, which they sometimes acknowledge must be subject to disciplined interpretation and combined with dialectic to produce a rational theology.

8. Music theory, and an historical and theoretical introduction to the fine arts generally, form part of the liberal arts; simply learning to paint or make music, or even to write poetry or fiction does not. This is because one could excel at the latter tasks, at least in a technical sense, while producing art which contributed not to human freedom and development, but rather to human bondage. It is only when we understand how the fine arts work to promote human development that we can really become free artists and not merely servants of the ruling classes.

Now a liberal arts education was not *always* the necessary precondition for authentic freedom and political participation. This is because Philosophy, the way of Wisdom for which the liberal arts prepare us, is not the only way of Wisdom, nor is the formal study of the social sciences the only way to acquire political prudence. On the contrary, as we demonstrated above, we human beings have, since the very beginning of our history, risen to first principles by means of a variety of religious disciplines many of which have enduring value both to the communities which developed them and to humanity at large. And even apart from these formal religious disciplines it is possible for human beings to achieve a preconceptual, connatural knowledge of first principles simply by living a life of justice. Being good, they know the Good, even if they cannot define it, or indeed speak about it at all. Two points are, however, in order here. First, in a pluralistic society traditional religious disciplines and/or preconceptual, connatural knowledge are not sufficient. We need to be able to talk to each other about what is Beautiful, True, and Good, and this requires both a common language and common standards of argument. It is not reasonable to tell a Hindu that if he wants to understand God he needs to keep kosher and attend a Yeshiva. But the Hindu and the Jew—and the Muslim, and the Christian, and the Confucian, and the Taoist, and the Buddhist, and the practitioner of indigenous African, American, or Australian religions, will all approach the public arena with a different view of the world, and a different sense of the Good and how to realize it. Philosophy generally and the *via dialectica* in particular, provide a common ground on which fundamental questions of meaning and value can be explored and debated so as to inform both personal and public decisions.

Second, the market order forms human beings in a way which tends to degrade both traditional wisdoms and the preconceptual, connatural wisdom which comes from living a just life. When people grow up and live in a village community or one of the old urban neighborhoods which conserves much of the structure of a village community they have a day to day experience of a system ordered to an end and thus a basis in experience for thinking in terms of the end or teloV of things. They are also disciplined by the community to act in a way which promotes the Common Good. This is the social basis for both traditional and connatural wisdoms, both theoretical and practical. In a market society, on the other hand, there is no global end towards which the system is ordered, but only the individual and competing ends of buyers and sellers. And the market rewards behavior which is narrowly self-seeking rather than behavior which helps individuals—both oneself and others—grow towards the Common Good. It forms people for vice rather than for virtue, for injustice rather than justice (Mansueto 1999b, forthcoming).

It should come as no surprise that dialectics first emerged in humanity's first market society and that the first discourse on liberal education—Plato's *Republic*—was first and foremost a response to the development of petty commodity production, as we demonstrated in an earlier chapter (Plato, *Republic* 376e–412b, 521c–541b). In a pluralistic, market society, it is only by means of the *via dialectica* that people can ascend to first principles, and only by means of dialectic that they can communicate between traditions regarding fundamental questions of meaning and value. This means that people must learn to make and evaluate philosophical arguments. And—given philosophy's reliance on the arts and sciences—this requires a liberal arts education.

Plato himself could not imagine a philosophical democracy. This is because, given the low level of development of the productive forces, it was inconceivable that the whole population might take the time to travel far enough along the *via dialectica* to make possible authentic political deliberation. The same was true of Marx and Lenin, for whom universal philosophical education was a characteristic only of the far distant communist future. In the meanwhile only a few could be expected to advance far enough to actually understand the aims and means of the revolutionary process. Our own situation is quite different. Especially in the advanced industrial countries we are devoting an ever-larger share of our resources to higher education, which is increasingly seen as a condition for productive membership in a society which requires a highly skilled workforce. Unfortunately the education which most receive is technical rather than liberal, or makes merely attempts to "expose" students to a smattering of general culture, without giving them the tools they need to participate actively in the ongoing dialogue of human civilization. It is neither possible nor desirable for everyone in our society to become a professional philosopher or scientist, artist or literary critic. These are noble callings, but so too is the calling of the artisan, technician, or manual laborer who by means of his technical skill and bodily strength creates something new, thus participating in the creative power of the universe itself. Indeed, from the standpoint of those traditions which conceive the divine first and foremost as creative it is the latter who is more god-like. The question, however, is just what to make. Without a liberal arts education which permits him to make and evaluate arguments regarding the first principles in terms of which decisions regarding resource allocation might be adjudicated, the practitioner of one of the instrumental arts, no matter how skilled, is at the mercy of either market imperatives, which make the decision agnostically, without reference to any principle of value, or of Capital and its agents, who are themselves ultimately at the mercy of these same imperatives.

Technical Training without Liberal Arts Education Is Education for Slaves.

This is, of course, just what Capital and its agents want. They need, to be sure, a senior staff which is trained in the liberal arts which can help them guide their corporations and their other institutions. And they are happy to recruit a few members of oppressed nationalities and a few (but fewer) members of the working class into the ranks of this staff, so long as their cadre core comes from socially reliable backgrounds. They are even willing to tolerate a certain amount of ideological dissent in order to get and maintain the support of that staff. That is why they fund elite liberal arts colleges and research universities. But they do not want a society in which the whole body of the working class and the middle strata has the intellectual tools necessary to make and evaluate arguments regarding fundamental questions of meaning and value, and thus to call into question the market allocation of resources. *The liberal arts are subversive.* Capital wants a highly skilled but ideologically and politically compliant working class. That is why education in community colleges and other institutions which serve the working class is merely a pale imitation of the education which is available at elite institutions. And it is this, precisely, which we must remedy.

The whole complex of the intellectual virtues is ordered ultimately to right action. And while it is the virtue of wisdom which allows us to know the Good as such, it belongs to the virtue of *prudence* to know what is right in a specific situation. The scholastic tradition regarded prudence as excellence in knowing the means to the ends of human life. This meant knowledge regarding the means of securing both our ultimate end—knowledge of God in Her essence—and more proximate ends, e.g., civilizational progress, the cultivation of the acquired virtues, etc.

The scholastics also distinguished between monastic prudence or excellence in knowing the means to the ends of one's own life, political or pastoral prudence, or excellence in knowing the means to the end of whole communities, and specific forms of prudence associated with various particular callings (e.g., the prudence appropriate to an entrepreneur or a spiritual director).

Now monastic prudence was historically understood primarily as a matter of applying universal moral principles in particular situations in a way which helps to realize the Good. Discussion of the dynamics of power and leadership, if they were addressed at all, were generally reserved for discussions of political, pastoral, or other special forms of prudence. But this distinction is artificial and reflects an assumption that the goods pursued by ordinary people are purely private and can, somehow, be achieved without the collaboration of others. Now it should be clear that this was never true. Even those whose lives have the very narrowest scope are called to productive labor of some sort, which involves ascertaining the needs of others and collaborating with others in the labor process. Most, furthermore, are called to participate in some way in rearing children, and must both secure the resources necessary for this task and determine how to act in order to promote the development of another human being. Even casuistry, which has historically been considered a significant part of monastic prudence, is fundamentally about how to make moral principles effective, and this in turn involves a consideration of power. And in a democracy or a republic, of course, there are no "purely private" persons. Citizens are charged with making determinations regarding the common good, something which makes the obligation to cultivate political prudence, at least in some degree, universal.

We would like to suggest, therefore, that prudence is, fundamentally, excellence in building and exercising power in service to the common good. And the dynamics of prudence are, as we will see, fundamentally the same whether we are acting within a fairly narrow scope or on a truly global scale.

By power we mean the capacity to get things done. Thus the Latin *potere*: to be able to. This always involves, even in the case of monastic prudence, the ability to get other people to do things. It is important to distinguish properly, however, between power and control. Control, while sometimes necessary, is quite different from power and has to do with keeping things from happening. If we seek to build power, we must ask ourselves:

- What are my interests?
- Who else is involved?
- What are their interests? And
- How can I build realize my interests and build my power?[9]

The first of these questions must be answered partly in reference to ethical principles and partly in reference to an honest appraisal of our own aims. On the one hand, action in contradiction with moral principles can never be prudent, because it does not help us to realize the true ends of human life. On the other hand, we cannot impose on ourselves, any more than we can impose on others, aims which are in excess of our (or their) real level of development. The Hindu concept of the four proper aims of life is useful here. According to Hindu teaching, while *moksa* or liberation is highest aim of human life, pleasure, wealth, and moral conduct are also legitimate aims. So long as we seek these in accord with *dharma* or moral law, aiming for these ends is quite permissible. Only over the course of many lifetimes do we come to authentically desire liberation. It is one thing to challenge ourselves to seek higher ends; it is quite another to deprive ourselves of the lesser goods we require in order to take joy in life at our present level of development and be really effective in the highest order tasks of which we are currently capable. Every authentic good, even the most elemental, helps us to grow and develop. At the same time, it is also true that limiting our enjoyment of lesser goods can help focus us on higher goods for which we are just beginning to develop a taste. Sometimes it also happens that we will choose a life which deprives us of lesser or intermediate goods we still crave precisely in order to discipline ourselves become more focused on higher goods.

Prudence, therefore, begins with a careful and honest appraisal of our own interests. There are a number of different ways we can do this. Knowing what we enjoy and what we do not, and where we are effective and where we are not is absolutely fundamental. It is also helpful, however, in gaining a realistic appraisal of our own interests, to analyze the interests of others—something which is, in any case, the next step in

9. This discussion of power is derived from the organizer and leadership training used by the Industrial Areas Foundation and other interfaith organizing institutes.

building and exercising the power necessary to realize the ends of human life. The best way to do this is through ordinary dialogue between people, formal or informal, intentional or spontaneous. Dialogue—or the dialectic—moves through several distinct stages. We begin by connecting with someone around a common point of interest, and then begin to draw the person out through a series of agitational questions which allows us to identify their principal capacities, interests, and relationships. Further questioning draws out the implications and internal contradictions of the person's ideas, and points towards a higher synthesis. If the relationship is to develop, this process must be reciprocal, and each person must learn as much about themselves as they do about the other person. Building and exercising power effectively, even the ordinary power of someone who is not a leader, requires hundreds and even thousands of such encounters. This is how we make friends and meet our spouses, how we get to know our children and our parents, continuously widening and deepening the web of interconnections which binds us to other people. But it is also the foundation on which authentic leadership arises. And as we tell our stories and listen to those of others our interests and those of the people we engage expand, so that even at the most rudimentary level of development the dialectic serves as a sort of spiritual discipline.

In analyzing the interests and abilities of other people it is important to take into account not only what people say but also what they do. More or less verifiable stories are worth far more than broad statements about values. Once we think we know what interests someone we can invite them to act together with us on something of mutual importance. This can be as small a step as going to the movies or it can be something of much greater moment, though generally one wants to avoid relying on untested relationships. If the person comes through we know that what they said or we inferred was important to them really is. If they do not come through then we need to ask why. As we do this we will begin to test our own self-interest in much the same way. What do we actually value enough to put time into when we are not being coerced? What matters enough to us that other people can use the promise or threat of it to coerce us?

In the course of making this analysis it is also important to assess what we—and others—are actually good at. Generally speaking we will be good at things which interest us, but sometimes people are just beginning to develop an ability and show greater passion than skill in its exercise. In these cases it is good to provide an opportunity for cultivation of the skill, but not to rely on the result. And in some cases, especially among the very young, people may *think* they want to do something but have no real understanding of what is involved.

It is useful to actually map out our own interests and those of the people we are involved with, as it will help us to see possibilities which might otherwise have missed, while making it clear why some things which we thought easy enough to accomplish simply aren't going to happen.

As we begin to decide to whom we want to relate it is important to keep in mind that the purpose of relationships is to help us accomplish our aims in life. This is true even of marriage and close friendships. While it would be a mistake to marry someone we do not like, or who does not like us, and while everyone has a need for a certain amount of affection, the whole aim of relating to other people is to be able to accomplish things which we cannot do ourselves. Sometimes this is simply a question of numbers, but most often we need to connect with people who have somewhat different abilities than we do, and thus different interests. The more someone is able to add to our capacities, the more likely they are to challenge us as well, and at times even to create considerable tension. Especially as we look out beyond the inner circle of people with whom we share our day-to-day lives, we need to remember that it is far more important to be respected than to be liked, and that reliability and accountability are far more important than good feelings. And even within our inner circle, we need people who can hold us accountable—whose criticisms we have to take seriously because they demonstrate again and again that they really appreciate our strengths, and do not simply find us annoying or distasteful.

What one looks for in analyzing a network is potential organization. A really advanced leader can meet most of his or her psychic needs internally, and has already built the networks necessary to meet those needs which cannot be met internally: food, shelter, clothing, etc. The prudent leader does not come to a network of people with fixed requirements and then try to persuade them to do what he wishes, but rather looks at the various ways in which people in a network can be brought together to create new possibilities, and accomplish things which even the most visionary leaders might not even have imagined. At the same time, a good leader also knows not to attempt to lead people in a cause in which he or she is not vitally interested, even if it is intrinsically valuable. If something really needs doing, the right leader will emerge.

Once we know our own interests and those of the people around us, we are in a position to act. This involves a judgment regarding how best to bring together the people within a particular network or cluster of networks in order to promote the development of human capacities and add something to the universe. This judgment may be exercised at three different levels: tactical, operational, and strategic.

The word strategy comes from the Hellenic stratego V, or "general." Strategy is the part of prudence which concerns the formation of an overall plan for identifying, organizing, developing, and deploying the resources necessary to carry out our mission., i.e., to realize our aims in life. It is possible, in turn, to distinguish several different levels of strategic thinking. Strategic judgments must be made not just by organizations and their leaders but by individuals as well. Everyone who is free, i.e., who has both the subjective capacity and material resources necessary to make their own decisions regarding what aims to pursue in life and how, must make what amount to *portfolio, positioning,* and *functional* decisions. By *portfolio* decisions we mean decisions regarding what activities to engage in and which to leave to one side. This involves, for individuals, decisions regarding profession, marriage, friendships, and forms of participation in the public arena (political, religious, etc.) For organizations it involves what businesses or other activities to pursue. By *positioning* decisions we mean decisions about how to pursue these activities so that our approach is unique. The classic positioning decision is the choice between competing on quality and competing on price, but there are far more subtle ways for an organization or an individual to set themselves apart. Both portfolio and positioning decisions should be made by balancing two principles: the principle of comparative advantage and the principle of the cutting edge. On the one hand, we should generally choose activities in which we are not only interested and capable, but have the potential to excel and even become the best, at least in some arena. Only if we are the best in some area will we really be able to lead and promote the development of others. At the same time, we also need to choose at least a few activities and relationships which challenge us to develop emerging capacities, without so over-taxing us that we fall flat on our faces.

Where portfolio and positioning decisions have to do with what is specific about our activities, functional strategy has to do with things everyone must take into consideration: making money, building relationships, developing ourselves intellectually and spiritually, etc., or in the case of an organization research, recruitment, training, liaison, operations, finance, etc. Functional decisions should always be formed by portfolio and positioning decisions. We need to have a way to make money, but the way in which we make money should be shaped and constrained by larger decisions about what we are going to do, not the other way around. We should not, similarly, pursue a particular friendship or a spiritual path just because we know that everyone needs friends who hold them accountable and something to challenge them spiritually, and let that shape our choice of profession or marriage partner without serious reflection regarding the nature of our specific calling. Functional strategy has to do with conditions and constraints, not the leading edge. It should play a strictly subordinate role. A focus on functional strategy is one of the ways in which people miss the opportunity to be free—though it is also sometimes a sign that someone is called primarily to a life of service. Such individuals should be directed to organizations where their particular skills, be they financial, organizational, intellectual, or spiritual, can be linked to some higher aim.

Grand strategy involves the exercise of all of the different levels of strategy over a protracted period of time, generally in a way that accesses, cultivates, and deploys the resources of other actors as well as one's own. An organization may decide for example that it is better at developing a vision and training leaders than it is at mass organizing and make a portfolio decision to forgo the latter activity for present, with the expectation that it will be able to train leaders who will penetrate and eventually come to lead mass organizations, which they will then bring into its fold or that it will build strategic partnerships with other organizations which excel at building mass organizations. The meaningful development and implementation of grand strategies requires both a high degree of development—one must be able to see beyond one's present strengths and weaknesses and into the distant future—as well as access to significant resources.

Global grand strategy is strategy which takes responsibility for ensuring that all of the tasks of social development are carried out, allocating portfolios to various different organizations over a period of time, as they become capable, or optimally qualified, for filling them. These higher levels of strategy involve the ability to make decisions regarding the comparative advantage and cutting edge not only of one's self and/or one's own organization, but also of other people and other organizations, and of allocating resources and tasks to organizations different than one's own. Generally speaking this part of prudence pertains only to those who have been called to political and/or spiritual leadership which consists, precisely, in taking responsibility for the development of other people and indeed entire communities, as well as oneself. This does not mean, however, that the exercise of global strategy pertains only to those who lead organizations or whose leadership involves action in public networks. A good spiritual director, for example, may only engage individuals and may do so far from the public eye, but she is always looking to cultivate people who can carry out the full range of tasks required by humanity and knows how to help them fulfill *their* callings, and not those of some ideal type of the saint. Someone whose principal calling is writing writes with the aim of affecting a particular group of people who will then affect others—in effect calling people to various activities. Global strategy in the fullest sense, however, is exercised by organizations or networks of individuals who are in contact with each other.

Examples of global grand strategy in the public arena would include the Leninist strategy of building support for a communist vanguard by advancing "transitional demands" such as land reform and democracy, or the U.S. strategy of containing socialism during the Cold War by a combination of nuclear deterrence and civil-military counterinsurgency operations.

Operational decision-making has to do with developing plans for achieving particular objectives which are of strategic significance. At the level of monastic prudence this may mean developing relationships in a particular arena, positioning ourselves within a particular institution, raising a certain amount of money, writing a book, etc. At the political level it might mean a major electoral or issue campaign. In making decisions at the operational level it is especially important to:

- Ensure that the end sought actually fits into our strategy and is not simply a good in general,

- Ensure that due consideration is given to the impact of the campaign on our overall strategic position (funding, relationships, what we will learn, individual and collective spiritual state, etc.)

On the one hand, the fact that we are offered an opportunity—and more especially that we are repeatedly offered a particular sort of opportunity—may tell us something about what we ought to be doing. We need to remember, however, that often this offer is being made by people who are either much less developed than we are or who are too distant from us to understand our actual strengths, weaknesses, and trajectory. People often think that leadership is all of one piece and will ask others to undertake tasks for which they are poorly suited, even if they are well suited for leadership in general.

Tactics—from the Hellenic tassein (to arrange)—has to do with how one (literally or figuratively) orders one's forces on the field. Generally we distinguish two levels of tactical leadership. The first, and most basic, has to do with the choice of basic methods of work. The choice of a particular production technique, of a certain type of assault, or of a certain method of applying political pressure (strike, boycott, election, demonstration), a certain method of teaching, or a certain turn of phrase are all tactical decisions, as is a pastor's decision to address a particular problem in the community through individual meetings and counseling, say, rather than a series of sermons, or a researcher's decision to use a certain kind of research method. Generally in making tactical decisions one is looking for a particular reaction and chooses tactics which have a reasonable probability of getting that reaction, based on an analysis of the individuals involved. As with operational decisions, one wants to make sure that the aim sought fits into one's overall plan, and that one's overall strategic position is improved rather than harmed by the action. In the case of tactical decisions, however, the aim in question is generally operational rather than strategic. In adversarial or competitive situations it is wise to choose tactics with which one's own organization is familiar and comfortable, but which will catch competitors or adversaries by surprise, and at which they are incompetent or unpracticed. Basic tactical leadership thus involves training people in the tactics which will be employed.

Higher tactics involves determination of the principal task in a particular period. Assume a given strategy which calls for carrying out a number of different tasks over a long period of time: raising capital, research and development, production, marketing, etc.; building a mass constituency, building a leadership organization, developing a vision, positioning in key institutions, applying pressure and winning partial concessions, responding to an expected systemic crisis, etc. It may seem that there is a unique logical sequence in which these tasks must be carried out, and clearly one cannot, for example apply political pressure without a mass base. But changing political circumstances often create challenges and opportunities which require one to carry out tasks out of sequence. A systemic crisis may make it possible to build a mass base and a leadership core quickly—though then it will still be necessary to train them, unite them around a common vision and strategy, etc. Knowing what part of a strategy to carry out when is a central part of prudence. It is vitally important in such cases to be aware that one may well have been propelled into a position of leadership for which one is not yet ready, either subjectively or in terms of material resources and relationships, and it may be necessary to play catch-up in order to rise to the challenges ahead. This does not mean that one should not take advantage of such opportunities, but it is important, once again, to make sure that they actually serve longer-term strategic goals and do not distract from what is really important. Failure to do this is a particular characteristic of Leninism. Lenin was a master of grand tactics and knew how to take advantage of conjunctural opportunities, but he devoted almost no time to thinking about long-range strategic imperatives. The result is an approach to politics which is characterized by opportunistic shifts in stance which have essentially no end in mind but the power—or rather the positioning—of the party. The party ends up in some sense on top, but unable to carry out its real mission, which requires material and spiritual resources it never bothered to develop.

We should note that the development of high order strategic capacities involves certain institutional conditions, which we will analyze in greater detail when we discuss social justice. For now it is enough to note that excessive centralization makes positioning and portfolio decisions impossible, because there are no other organizations to take on tasks of which one's own organization is incapable. In order to lead in a perfectly centralized social system, one must, like Kojeve's Spinoza, have been God from all eternity. Clearly anyone who sees him/herself that way is not qualified to lead. Thus prudence involves respecting and valuing subsidiarity. At the same time, effective strategic leadership also requires some element of centralization. A radical dispersal of power also makes it impossible for any organization to have much choice regarding positioning, portfolio, etc. And it is vitally important that there be some structure responsible for "grand" and "global" strategy, even if these structures have only limited authority. One does not want to turn the orchestra into a one-man band, but it is, nonetheless, necessary to have a good conductor.

What about the supernatural degrees of the virtues of the practical intellect? Here Thomas distinguishes two distinct gifts of the Holy Spirit: *counsel*, which perfects practical apprehension, and *knowledge*, which perfects practical judgment (Thomas, *Summa Theologiae*, I–II.68.4, II–II.9). Counsel involves seeing the matter we are called on to cultivate more nearly as God sees it: to look beyond our narrow human perspective and see potential where otherwise we might not, while placing limitations in their proper context. Knowledge, similarly, involves making strategic, operational, and tactical judgments from a larger than merely human perspective. This means, above all, fixing aims and choosing means from the standpoint of caritative rather than merely acquired wisdom.

Counsel and knowledge may concern physical and biological as well as social phenomena and technological as well as political decisions. It is thus possible, for example to explain a seemingly regressive law, such as the Second Law of Thermodynamics, as necessary in order to weed out less adequate forms of organization and apply pressure for innovation and progress. The same thing might be done with social scientific laws which point to the tendency of social structures to eventually become obstacles to human development and civilizational progress, requiring revolutionary transformations which often require tragic loss and sacrifice. This sort of reasoning is still natural, and forms part of a philosophically informed cosmology or sociology. But suppose the understanding of the first principle which informs our explanation of the particular things in the world is supernatural—beyond what can currently be comprehended. Such was the case, for example, with the prophetic "explanation" of Israel's sufferings at the hands of the great empires; such was the case with the Buddhist insight into the origins of suffering generally. Now on the basis of this sort of wisdom, our natural desire to overcome the Second Law of Thermodynamics and to "take control" of the universe and its evolution, while understandable, can be seen to be ultimately misguided. It is thus possible to make a prophetic judgment against technologies and technological regimes which point in this direction. Similarly, Jeremiah counseled Israel to accept Babylonian rule, not because he thought it was just, but because he saw it as part of God's larger plan for his people in a way that would not have been possible on the basis of a purely natural wisdom or political science, for which (given the experience of other small states which succumbed to imperial rule in this period) it could only have seemed like a sentence of extinction as a people (Jeremiah 40–45).

Ordinarily the exercise of counsel and knowledge takes the form of an applied—political or pastoral—theology. In the modern era, partly due to the disenchantment of the world by mathematical physics, something we have argued elsewhere is not wholly legitimate, and partly due to the elaboration of a specifically modern and intellectually untenable fundamentalist discourse regarding "miracles" we are a bit nervous about seeking religious meaning—especially supernatural religious meaning—in natural events. Perhaps theological reflection on the ecological crisis and a re-evaluation of such ancient disciplines as astrology can correct this. But for the present, exercise of applied theology is primarily with respect to human (personal and social) realities. In extraordinary times, when new insights are required, the supernatural degree of science is exercised in the form of political prophecy, which is in fact the most common form of prophecy, as insights into the divine nature are few and far between.

If wisdom is based on living justly, then counsel and knowledge in the spiritual and supernatural sense are based on living a life of hope. It is the practice of continuing to hope when things seem hopeless, because we *know* that the world is drawn into Being by the incredible Beauty of God, who always awaits us at the end of our journeys, which allows us to see meaning and thus potential in events which might otherwise seem meaningless and to ascertain why things are the way the are and not some other, perhaps more convenient or transparently meaningful, way. Living a live of hope, we live the ordering of particular things to an ultimate end in terms of which they will ultimately come to be understood as meaningful. And eventually we come to see this meaning and know what to do with it. This is why the gift of knowledge was historically associated with the theological virtue of hope.

THE MORAL VIRTUES

Matter is the drive towards higher levels of organization. In intelligent systems this expresses itself in, among other things, the capacity to reflect in itself the organizing principles of other systems, and to use this knowledge of organizing principles to create new, still more complex forms of organization. This is what we have called intelligence. But the intelligent system is not merely capacity, it is drive. Intellect is not merely capable of creating higher forms of organization; it is actually ordered to those forms, both on the theoretical side, where it is informed by them in sensation and understanding, and on the practical side as it struggles to bring them into being. Intelligence is, in other words, inconceivable without appetite.

Now we have already seen that specifically human intelligence emerges on the basis of a complex and sophisticated kind of sensation, and operates only and always in conjunction with our sensory powers. Much the same is true of the appetites. On the one hand, we humans are ordered to systems more complex than ourselves, and ultimately to God, which is not a sensible but rather an intelligible object. This ordering to an intelligible good we call will, or the intellectual appetite. On the other hand, just as we know God not immediately, as a result of direct rational intuition, but rather mediately, by abstraction and inference from the sensible universe, so too we will God not immediately, through the exercise of a purely autonomous will, but rather mediately, in virtue of a higher organization of our sensual appetites. Will, in other words, grows up on the basis of the sensual appetites, which are always present in the act of willing, even when the object of the will is not sensible but rather intelligible. Moral virtue, or excellence in the appetites, thus includes excellence in the sensual as well as the intellectual appetites.

We have already analyzed in an earlier chapter the organization of these appetites. Here we offer only a brief summary. Human beings, like all matter, are driven to connect, to combine, to integrate—and to abhor isolation, separation, and disintegration. The unique complexity of the human affects derives from the fact that as highly organized systems we experience this drive at several different levels: physical, chemical, biological, and social. For the most part the merely physical and chemical forms of these drives do not come to consciousness. We are, however, intensely aware of a wide range of different biological feelings which incline us to eat, to seek warmth and shelter against the cold, to exercise, etc. and thus to maintain and develop the biological integrity of our bodies, as well as a desire for nonsexual affection and sexual intimacy, and an inclination to care for other animals, not only those of our own species, which we perceive as somehow vulnerable. These drives, all of which impel us to maintain the integrity of our organisms, either directly, by consuming in order to survive, or indirectly, by reproducing and caring for our young, we call desire. We are also aware of an equally wide range of negative feelings, which lead us to avoid things which are bad for us—pain, cold, poison, etc. These negative feelings we call aversion. Similarly, when we connect with something which is good for us we experience joy; when we are separated from it we experience sadness. And even at the sensual level we seek the good of that which is good for us (sensual love) and the destruction of that which is not (sensual hatred) Together desire and aversion, joy and sadness, love and hatred are passions of the faculty which the scholastics called concupiscible.

Now those the resources and relationships we need in order to conserve the integrity of our organisms do not always come easily, and threats to that integrity are not always easily avoided. Our single, fundamental, underlying drive towards organization therefore also expresses itself in a capacity for irascibility: the drive to fight and/or flee. It is our irascibility which gives us the fight to pursue goods which are won only at a cost, and which impels us to flee evils which we could not otherwise effectively resist. It is also our irascibility which enables us to hope in what is difficult to achieve, to despair at what we know is impossible and to feel anger at present evils.

Freud, who placed nearly as much emphasis on the irascible as on the concupiscible passions, had them all wrong. Irascibility is not aggressiveness or a drive towards destruction. The basis of his error is not difficult to see. The market system requires of the vast majority of the people—even among the ruling classes—a willingness to submit to inscrutable forces beyond our understanding or control (the laws of the marketplace). Irascibility, which resists evil, is thus a danger to the market system and (from the standpoint of a good bourgeois like Freud) essentially destructive. From our standpoint, however, irascibility is essential if structural obstacles to growth and development are to be removed.

The will arises on the basis of the concupiscible and irascible faculties in much the same way that the intellect arises on the basis of sensation. In order to understand this process it is necessary to keep in mind that we are dealing not with "parts" of a substance, but with powers of a single, highly organized system. As human beings become increasingly interconnected with each other, and as those interconnections are recorded in our complex neural nets, we learn to "see" increasingly complex, more purely intelligible patterns—or more precisely to abstract those patterns from the mass of sensory data we receive. Thus we come to know higher systems. And since these higher systems integrate a wider range of capacities into a more organized form than lesser, sensible systems, they are, because of that more desirable, and give rise to an act of the intellectual appetite or the will—i.e., love. Or, conversely, we may become aware of a dynamic of disintegration which is not visible to the senses but which leads to the loss of higher order intelligible capacities. This gives rise to another act of the will—hatred.

Now, in so far as our knowledge of intelligible goods is based on knowledge of sensible goods—in fact it *is* knowledge of a higher order organization of those sensible goods—our appetite for intelligible goods is always accompanied by an appetite for the sensible goods on the basis of which the intelligible arise. The same is true of hatred of an intelligible evil. Thus our love for social justice, i.e., a system which unleashes the full development of human social capacities is accompanied by—even filled with—a sensual love of the goods which social justice makes possible. Our hatred of capitalism is filled with an aversion to the bourgeoisie which sustains and benefits from it. Our hope in a just future is filled with both a sensual yearning for the distant goods which a just order will bring, and a visceral anger at those who stand in the way of human development. We see a similar movement when we consider the theological or supernatural virtues. Our love of God is filled not only with a love of proximate intelligible goods—e.g., social justice—but also with a sensual love of the whole creation. Our hope in God is filled with our hope for victory in every proximate battle, and in visceral anger at those who would detain us. This is why, as Aquinas put it, no just act, indeed, no virtuous act at all, is possible without passion.

This analysis of the organization of the appetites gives us a basis on which to understand the nature of moral virtue. Moral virtue consists in the habitual right ordering of the appetites, in real excellence in bringing all our desire and all our striving, all our aversion and all our fear and all our anger together in such a way as to order us ultimately to the highest good, and to all proximate goods in a accord with their value. This does not, strictly speaking, mean loving higher things more and lower things less, but rather ordering our love of lower things, in all its intensity, to our love of the higher, so that passion serves intellectual love and drives us on towards the good.

Let us now consider each of the moral virtues in some detail.

Temperance

The first of the moral virtues is temperance. Temperance is excellence in the exercise of our concupiscible appetite. This means, first of all, the development of our capacity for desire in all of its intensity—the desire for shelter, clothing, food, sex, etc. Sensual love is set in motion by a perception of beauty in the object, whether this beauty is a harmony, integrity and clarity seen, heard, tasted, smelled, etc. And beauty, we have seen, is a transcendental, something which discloses being itself and is thus a window on God. It is thus possible—indeed necessary—to find God in sensible things, and to desire Her there. And this seeing and desiring is not limited to those "higher sensibles" which are most often considered to be the locus of religious experience—the beauty of nature, of high art, etc. It is quite possible, indeed, necessary to see and to desire God in sexual intercourse, in a plate of couscous—even, as Julian of Norwich taught us, in a bowel movement which, since it restores the internal harmony and integrity of the body, has its own sort of beauty. Temperance always involves an intensification, and never a weakening, of our sensual desires. Similarly, we must feel aversion to evil with the greatest intensity of which we are capable.

What then is a "right ordering" or our concupiscible appetite? Two points are in order here. First, at the most basic level, consumption must serve reproduction and production, and not the other way around. This is true at both the biological and the social levels. We appreciate good food because it is good for us. We desire sexual intercourse in order to reproduce and to build relationships with other human beings. Disorders at this level generally arise as a result of some prior or present deprivation. We overeat when we believe, at some level, that food generally, or some kind of food we especially like, is apt to be in short supply. We become sexually promiscuous when we are denied physical affection, and come to believe sexual intercourse is the only way to get it.

At the social level, this principle means that our consumption must increase our capacities, and not become simply an end in itself. Thus, owning a few nice paintings, some music, and having the resources to travel, and even to indulge in an occasional fine meal is not luxury consumption, but rather the satisfaction of a virtuous love of the sensuous beauty in which we meet the divine. Living for these things, on the other hand, makes them luxuries and thus an obstacle to the right ordering of the appetites.

While the intemperance of luxury is not, strictly speaking, a matter of sheer quantity, it is also wrong to say that is simply a matter of attitude. The fact of the matter is that good things are difficult to acquire, and if one has many of them one is probably spending too much time working to get them and not enough on other things—a sure sign of disordered appetites.

The second dimension of "right ordering" has to do with making sure that our sensual desires fill higher order appetites, and do not simply sit alongside them, as a kind of potential distraction. This happens most often when we become convinced, due to an ideological defect, that our sensual appetites are either evil, or have nothing to do with higher goods, or that there is no transcendental Good to which they might point. The result is that our higher appetites are lacking in warmth and passion. We become lukewarm, and God wants to spit us out. It is in this sense quite possible, to value everything in proportion to its worth and still be intemperate if we do not see the higher *in* the lower. Consider someone who loves painting, and who is also dedicated to social justice. He knows that social justice is a higher good than his art—if only because it would make even more art possible. He thus orders his priorities in such a way as to give priority to his political activity. But he does not see the higher good of social justice in his paintings, which he regards as a kind of self-indulgent recreation. Gradually his devotion to social justice fades. He becomes burned out more and more easily, and needs more time "away" to restore himself, until eventually he abandons the struggle altogether, not because of disillusionment or a change in convictions, but simply because he just does not want to—no, cannot make himself—do it anymore. If only he had seen the struggle for social justice in his paintings! He would have drawn strength from his work—would probably have done work better suited to his talents—and would never have grown bitter and dry.

This ordering of lower to higher goods is also essential to the proper enjoyment of the lower goods themselves. Someone who lives exclusively to consume, or whose sensual appetites do not fill their higher appetites, however strong those higher appetites may appear to be, will eventually find their lower appetites decaying, either through boredom or disuse. And since the higher appetites are built out of the lower, the result will be disinterest, and ultimately a lack of motivation to strive for the good.

Is there a supernatural or theological degree of temperance? This is an interesting question. Historically there has been no theological virtue recognized which pertains specifically to the concupiscible passions. There is, however, the gift of fear—which Thomas says guards us against an inordinate lust for pleasures (Thomas. *Summa Theologiae* I–II.68.4), the evangelical counsel of poverty, as well as an associated beatitude: "Blessed are you poor, for yours is the Kingdom."

This way of construing the problem seems to use to reflect a residual Augustinianism. The danger here is that *supernatural* temperance and simply *greater* temperance will be confused—that the definition of such a virtue will turn into a justification for extreme asceticism. This is certainly what happened in the Franciscan tradition, and one can see similar excesses in other traditions: the *Jaina* for example. What would make temperance supernatural, rather is, on the one hand, the character of the higher goods to which the sensual appetites are being ordered and, on the other hand, the extent to which the joy one takes in these goods comes not from possessing or consuming them but rather in producing them, in furthering their well being, or simply knowing that they exist. On the one hand, therefore, supernatural temperance involves an ordering of our sensual desires to spiritual ends so that in enjoying a sensual good it becomes for us a window on the divine. Supernatural temperance in this sense involves the transformation of everything into a sacrament. At the same time, it is always better to create than to consume. Creating sensual goods with the understanding that they are a real participation in the life of God, rather than merely consuming them, thus constitutes the second dimension of supernatural temperance. This sacramental sensibility (and not some rejection of the senses) is why the virtue of temperance is properly associated with the ascent to mystical contemplation.[10]

10. It is true, to be sure, that disciplining the senses can help one focus on higher goods. But real mystical union involves periods during which one is deprived not just of joy in sensual goods, but also of joy in spiritual goods themselves. This is the significance of the "dark nights" of the soul which mark the passage from lower to higher degrees of spiritual development. Whenever we discover a new and higher beauty our first reaction is infatuation. We want it; indeed we want more and more of it and we want it for ourselves. This is as true of God, or rather of some new and higher appreciation of God, as it is of anything else. Such love, however, is rather primitive. As Meister Eckhart put it, we love God first the way we love a cow: for its milk. This love must be disciplined and the only way for this to happen is for our enjoyment of it to be withdrawn, so that love of enjoyment can give way to love of benevolence. But then our enjoyment of the love of benevolence must itself be withdrawn ... It is rather like the flowers on an apricot tree falling off in order to give way to the fruit, which is a higher good, and the fruit giving way to the autumn leaves. Eventually the sun itself, which made those leaves visible, is withdrawn so that we can see the beauty of the night sky. The dialectic of the discovery higher goods and the withdrawal of our enjoyment of them as we enter new dark nights is perpetual. The aim, however, is not the extinction of desire but rather its refinement, as the fire of our love is fed by still more subtle fuels and its flame burns ever more intensely.

Now this flame itself pertains to charity, which is the supernatural or theological degree of justice, the virtue of the will, but the capacity to enter willingly and endure the

Fortitude and Hope

The second of the moral virtues is fortitude, or excellence in the exercise of the irascible appetite. The irascible appetite, we have noted, is an expression of the drive of matter towards higher levels of organization under conditions in which that aim is difficult to achieve, or is threatened by danger and disintegration. Under these circumstances we react with hope that our difficult struggle will succeed, while despairing of lesser goods which must be sacrificed in the process. We dare to prosecute the struggle while fearing for our very lives and fearing that we may not succeed. And we feel anger at the forces which hold us back or threaten our very survival. Fortitude involves an exercise of these passions in such a way that we are, as it were, strengthened for battle, without thereby becoming foolhardy, rash, or wantonly violent.

In just what does the right ordering of the irascible faculty consist? First, it must be noted, that just as temperance does not involve a diminishment of our sensual desires, fortitude does not involve any lessening or diminishment of our hope or despair, our daring or fear, or our anger. On the contrary, in order to be excellent in this arena, we must have a keenly developed capacity for these passions, able to feel with full intensity the surge of hope at new possibilities and despair at our losses, the daring we feel as we begin a battle and the fear which grips us when we and those we care for are in danger, and the anger which rises up whenever we confront wrong injustice. This means not losing touch with what we personally have at stake in the struggle for higher goods, and more generally with the material basis of that struggle. A just society will make possible greater creativity. It means that I can eat, and make love, and write, and have children. Capitalism means that I have to sell my labor power to some money-making devil who will take my precious time and force me to produce junk so that he can by a BMW. Irascibility, furthermore, is by nature personal. Anger, as a sensual passion, is directed first and foremost only at sensibles, not at intelligibles. It is not, strictly speaking possible to be angry at the marketplace, or even at the bourgeoisie, but only at actual people. Capitalists are unjust and it is right for us to be angry with them.

The right ordering of these passions means that they must *serve* and *fill* higher order appetites. For our irascible appetites to serve higher

---

dark nights which make the flame of love burn ever hotter, and to do so without becoming dry and depressed, might also be consider a part of supernatural temperance.

order appetites means that hope in the good things which a just society will bring, fear that we may fail in creating a just society, and anger at present evils must form the basis for an active willing of justice itself, which is an intelligible and not a sensible good. Hope and fear and anger must not become ends in themselves, or means to actions which do not serve the struggle, but must always orient us towards effective action on behalf of the good. There is no virtue in being angry with my boss if that anger simply serves to make me bitter, or leads to rash and foolish action that accomplishes nothing. In order for this happen my anger must be formed by higher order appetites—or rather must not eclipse our love of the higher order goods the arduous pursuit of which mobilized our irascibility in the first place.

Similarly, as was the case with temperance, our irascible passions must fill our higher order appetites. The danger here is, once again, mostly ideological. People become convinced that their hopes and fears and anger have nothing to do with the struggle for the good. They aim for "inner peace" or "indifference." The difficulty is that we are not at peace, but rather at war, and inner peace is neither appropriate nor, strictly speaking, possible. On the contrary, aiming for inner peace usually means a dulling of the irascible appetite, and a tendency to keep our personal anger out of our work. The result is that we lose our motivation to work while, at the same time, building up a reservoir of irascibility which has no outlets—or which we turn against ourselves. The irascibility is there for a reason. We need to let it do its work.

The leading element in fortitude is hope—not foolish hope in things which will never come to pass, but rather a well grounded confidence in the absolutely necessary motion of matter to higher ends. This hope is closely linked to a just will which values most the more important things which will be accomplished and can let go of the less important things which may not be. It is hope which *both* gives us confidence that what we do will make a difference *and* reminds us that because matter's growth towards God is necessary and inevitable, the fate of the world does not in fact depend on us, allowing us to let go of struggles which have become unproductive without feeling crushed by the defeat.

It is for this same reason that supernatural excellence in the ordering of the irascible passions has traditionally been called hope. At this level, of course, the hope in question is in specifically in goods the realization of which transcends finite human capacities. It is hope in our own achievement of the beatific vision, or rather our own unending growth and development towards God, and hope in the divinization of matter generally. Hope of this sort, even more so than natural hope, tends to put our other struggles in perspective. On the one hand, *knowing* that we will, eventually, come to know and love God in ways we cannot now even imagine, and *knowing* that all flesh, indeed all matter, will share in this knowledge and love, gives us the strength we need to fight on, in order to develop ourselves and help others develop the capacities which they need in order to realize their potential. At the same time, it relativizes all finite struggles and makes the inevitable losses we will suffer seem paltry by comparison with the victory we already have in hand. This in turn helps to prevent inordinate daring or fear or anger.

Theological hope has traditionally been associated with the gift of "the fear of God." This may seem a bit paradoxical, given what we have said about the inevitability of matter's motion towards God. There is, however, nothing inevitable about the *pace* or the *path* of our development. Wrong choices are disciplined, if in no other way than the fact that they do not lead to true joy. And the worst mistakes are not those made out of an excess of concupiscence, but rather those made out of fear: fear that by pursing higher goods we will lose our security and stability, our friends and family, even our lives. *Fearing God* means recognizes that such losses, while real and tragic (and actually also inevitable—we all do die) are nothing by comparison with the loss we experience when we take the easy road and avoid risks in an attempt to preserve those finite goods for just a little while longer. At the end of such a road lies *real* loss: i.e., loss of the growth which would have taken place, both in us and in the communities of which we are a part, had we made the hard choices and taken the risks necessary in order to move forward. As Ignazio Silone said, "spiritual growth and securing are incompatible" (Silone 1955).

When we take the role of theological hope and the gift of fear in account, of course, the distance between our position and the Buddhist position, with its emphasis on detachment, diminishes some. Detachment is not an end in itself, but a certain measure of detachment from finite goods is an inevitable result of the perfection of the irascible passions by theological hope and the gift of fear. We continue to experience daring and fear, hope and despair, and anger, but we experience them as motivators which order us towards higher ends. They cease to rule and control us.

A word is in order here about the relationship between temperance and fortitude and the underlying passions which they perfect. The right ordering of the sensual passions involves not only an ordering of these passions to the will, but also a kind of harmony and balance between the concupiscible and irascible faculties. For it is, in part, a desire for an enjoyment of beauty which keeps our anger from consuming us and making us bitter or unduly warlike, and our anger which keeps us from becoming self-indulgent aesthetes or epicureans. This is not to suggest that virtue is possible simply on the basis of such a balance, but only that it is essential to the development of virtue. To be temperate I must have a powerful desire for the beauty I perceive in the world, but also an intense anger at those who keep me from that beauty. To have fortitude I must have enough hope and daring and anger to fight, but a sufficiently powerful sense of the beauty which already exists that I do not become lost in false hopes or consumed by anger.

Justice and Charity

The third and final of the cardinal moral virtues is that of justice. By justice considered as a virtue (as opposed to social justice or the right organization of human society) we mean excellence in the operations of the will—i.e., willing things in accord with their value, and thus being able to act fully in accord with cosmic law. Now the will is moved by a complex configuration of forces, including

- sensible and intelligible goods themselves,
- the senses, which know the sensible goods directly and which garner the images from which we abstract knowledge of intelligible goods,
- the intellect, which knows intelligible goods,
- the will itself, which wills the means to goods it already wills, and
- the passions of the sensual appetites, which may either second the choice of the will or draw it away from its intended object.

Excellence in willing thus presupposes, first of all, intellectual excellence—specifically the capacity to know intelligible goods and the means necessary to achieve them. Knowledge of the Good itself is wisdom, and knowledge of particular intelligible goods is part of theoretical ethics, whereas knowledge of the means to the ends of human life is prudence. While it is, strictly speaking, possible to know the Good and the means of achieving it simply by being taught it and by accepting it on faith, this knowledge will be dim and far from compelling. The highest degrees of justice thus presuppose wisdom of some sort (connatural or theoretical) as well as prudence. This is why ideological questions bear directly on the question of justice. It is impossible to be just without knowing higher goods, and this, in turn, is affected by ideology. The worker who knows only the good of his family -their survival, and the hope that his children might get a better education—is less capable of justice than the worker who knows the higher good of a just society. The worker who understands that a just society is one which, in addition to promoting human development and civilizational progress in general, helps people develop spiritually, is more capable of justice than one who does not. The communist worker, in other words, is more capable of justice than the ordinary good provider and the religious communist is more capable of justice than the secular communist.

At the same time, it is quite impossible to know the Good without becoming habituated to its pursuit. This is because the abstraction necessary to produce theoretical knowledge of the Good takes place only when the images we garner from the senses are illuminated by a connatural knowledge of the Good based on the just act—something we already explained briefly in a previous chapter, but will review here for the sake of clarity.

The clearest example is the cult of *yhwh*. Product of successful peasant resistance to the Canaan warlords and their Egyptian overlords during the late bronze age (Gottwald 1979), this cult took the Canaanite high god (*'El*, the father of *ba'al*, and a rather remote and insignificant figure in most Canaanite religious practice) and transformed him into *'El yahwi sabaoth yisrael*—El who brings into being the armies of Israel. The struggle to build a just society—which was, perhaps originally just accidentally such a struggle, born out of resistance to particular evils—Yahwism gave birth to a tradition which put the struggle for justice against overwhelming odds at the very center of religious life. This, in turn, opened up the possibility of a new kind of religious knowledge. Thus when the prophets speak of *da'ath 'elohim* (knowledge of God) they are not speaking of something theoretical, but rather an experiential knowledge which we gain in actually realizing the divine will.

> Hear the word of YHWH, O Israel;
> for YHWH has a charge to bring against the people of the land;
> There is no faith or mutual trust,
> no knowledge of God (*da'ath 'elohim*) in the land,
> oaths are imposed and broken, they kill and rob;
> there is nothing but adultery and license,
> one deed of blood after another. (Hos 4:1–2 NEB)

> Let us humble ourselves, let us strive to know YHWH,
> whose justice dawns like morning light,
> and its dawning is as sure as the sunrise.
> It will come to us like a shower,
> like spring rains that water the earth. (Hos 6:3 NEB)

Now we have already discussed above the role of connaturality in the production of knowledge. We have argued that society itself is the Agent Intellect. Participation in definite social structures creates in us a direct experience of, for example, classification or certain mathematical formalisms. We experience ourselves as members of a definite class and are thus able to classify other objects. We experience ourselves as functions of complex variables and are thus able to formalize our experience in mathematical terms. The same is true at the level of transcendental abstraction. By *living* judgment we know experientially the principle of judgment and can thus apply it to any range of concrete circumstances. The difference, of course, is that here the principle known connaturally is nothing other than Divine Justice and thus God Himself, vindicating His people in the struggle against their oppressors. In the just act we have an immediate, if still radically imperfect, knowledge of the first principle.

This connatural knowledge of God in the just act is no more conceptual than the connatural knowledge which the Australian aborigine possesses of the principles of classification or the connatural knowledge which a shopkeeper has of the mathematical formalisms which govern the operation of the market system. But like these other, lesser forms of connatural knowledge, it illuminates the images which we garner from experience and allow us to see in the mirror of creatures the creative principle itself. Thus Israel soon began to understand that its revolutionary warrior God brought into being not only the armies of Israel, but in fact the cosmos as a whole, and did so in a single unified movement, so that creation and redemption were not radically distinguished. And in this insight Israel achieves an insight into the divine nature—that is, Being

Itself. Thus the name '*yhwh*" is the causative form of the Hebrew verb "to be." In this sense one could argue, using the language of later dialectics, that the judgment of justice and thus of the Good led ineluctably to the judgment of Being with which it is convertible. This is true in spite of the fact that Israel remained skeptical about elaborate cognitive claims regarding God, rejecting not only representations of the divine nature, but even pronunciation of the divine name outside of the most solemn context of the cult.

Knowledge of the Good is not, however, sufficient for justice. It is necessary, second, that the sensual appetites be are formed and mobilized in service of the intellectual. In willing the struggle, we will a love of beauty, but also a willingness to forego it, we will the defeat of our adversaries, something which mobilizes our anger, but also restraint. Justice, in other words, presupposes temperance and fortitude and builds on them.

It is necessary, finally, that the internal operations of the will to be in good order. A well developed will automatically moves towards the highest good of which the intellect is aware. This means that it wills the means to those higher goods, even where they may involve forgoing lesser goods, sensual or intellectual, or undergoing hardship, suffering, etc. Thus, to will creation of a just society is to will a long and difficult struggle, which will require us to forgo other goods, including prosperity, security, and possibly even our lives. The just decision requires the capacity to will the struggle as well as the end. If we are not practiced in the exercise of the will, this may become difficult.

The interplay of the intellect and of the sensual appetites is especially important in this regard. On the one hand, we must come to the willing of difficult means with a vivid understanding of the higher good, otherwise we may find that it pales by comparison to lesser, but more proximate goods which we see more clearly, be they sensual or intellectual. The creation of a just social order may seem like something distant and far off by comparison with a new scheme for classifying organisms, a better school funding plan, or a new house. It cannot be. We must see it as vividly as the objects which stand before us at this very moment. On the other hand, we must see the higher goods in the lesser. A just society will make possible new theories, and better education, and housing. And it means fighting our adversaries—albeit in a way which serves the larger struggle. In this way both the intellect and the senses collaborate in making the higher good vivid and present and thus make less difficult the choice of difficult means.

The highest, supernatural degree of justice is the theological virtue of *charity*. Now the relationship between justice and charity is the object of considerable confusion. It is often presupposed that justice seeks and gives what is due, while charity demands nothing and gives more than is required. This approach presupposes an approach to ethics which is utterly foreign to the natural law tradition. Ethics is not about adjudicating conflicting claims over resources, but rather about ordering our wills and our social structure toward higher ends. If something is really and truly someone's due, in the sense that it is necessary for the full development of their capacities, then it is wrong for them to forgo that good. Similarly, if something contributes to someone's development then giving it is a matter of justice and not of charity. Nor does the difference have to do with the object of the will, with justice bearing on willing the good for human beings and charity having to do with the love of God. There is a part of justice, known as the virtue of *religion* which has to do with giving God Her due, or rather loving God above all else, because it is God which makes possible all other goods.

The difference between justice and charity, rather, has to do with the precise form of the will. Justice wills what contributes to the full development of human capacities and to the development of complex organization in the universe generally. It does so because the just person is also prudent and knows that his or her own development is dependent on the development of all. Charity, on the other hand, wills the full development of human capacities and the development of complex organization in the universe *as ends in themselves*. Justice, or more specifically religion, loves God as our benefactor, much as we would love a cow. Charity loves God for Her own sake.

Let us look more closely at this distinction.

'El yahwi sabaoth yisrael, God known through natural connaturality as the condition of the people's liberation, is recognized by the ordinary transcendental abstraction which arises on the basis of this connaturality as Being itself, the first principle of explanation and of action, the arch and telos of the universe and of human life. But as the struggle for justice passes over into a pursuit of something which transcends any merely human development, we achieve a supernatural connaturality with God, and on the basis of this advance to the "superabstraction" of revelation— to a wordless knowledge beyond all concepts, a knowledge of the great Unnamable-Bringing-into-Being, which at once awakens and satisfies the deepest and most burning fires of love.

What happens here is that the will is formed by habituation, at first simply to the struggle for justice, as a means to the realization of one's own latent potential and that of the people to whom one is connected. But as one participates in this struggle, it becomes clear that often, from an individual standpoint, more is lost than is gained. And this experience is not just individual. It is collective as well. No sooner had the people of Israel recognized the hand of God in their amazing victories over enemies which far outmatched them in terms of military might, than that hand was withdrawn, or extended in ways that seemed directed to some end other than their own temporal well-being. It is at this point that one realizes that the struggle is not about me, that it is not even about us, if indeed it is about anything at all, and that any attempt to name what it is about, while necessary and even, within limits, satisfying, risks limiting its scope in a way which will inevitably lead to idolatry and disappointment. The struggle is about this Unnameable-Bringing-Into-Being which we experience in being called each and every day to become more than we are and which we learn to discover as much in the disappointments as in the successes, as these point us towards an ever deeper appreciation of divine nature. It is in this way that the divine name, *yhwh*, is revealed.

In this sense, it is quite correct to say that the movement from natural to revealed knowledge of God, and thus from justice to charity, always involves a negative moment, that for growth towards the higher degrees of the spiritual life the *via negativa* is indispensable. In following the light we are always and only drawn into what at first seems like darkness. Gradually, to be sure, we become habituated to this new and more subtle light, and learn a free and easy love for the objects it reveals to us. But even so, if we are not to stagnate, we are always and only called to move on, to penetrate ever deeper into mysteries which are deeper and harder and which stretch us until we become, ever so gradually, something more than merely human. This is the significance of the "dark nights" of which John of the Cross speaks and of which all authentic mystics are deeply and profoundly aware.

Similar dynamics can be found in other traditions. Thus the *Magna Mater*, symbolic expression of humanity's enduring faith in the ultimate meaningfulness of the universe, is not only the alluring maiden and nurturing mother, but also the Crone, who reminds us that in time we must let go of all finite goods—including our own life and even our personal identity—if we are to become what we are meant to be, and to know the principle which gave meaning to our lives and our identities in the first place. Thus the transition in Indian religion from the Vedic cults centered in inner-worldly goods to the later Buddhist and Hindu focus on transcending the ego. And in China the Tao appears both as a principle the partial comprehension of which can help us achieve finite, worldly aims, and as a Way which far transcends all such aims, which it ultimately washes over in pursuit of its own mysterious End, which is also our own.

One note of caution is in order. This higher love to which we are called and in which we are schooled by the trials and tribulations of living out our vocation to justice is not a self-sacrificial love and it is not pitted against the natural desire to realize our own potential. It merely exceeds it. It is a dedication to life which runs over the limits of our own finite living and finds rest only in the living God. Negativity is never an end in itself; there is no merit in continuing to follow in darkness when light and comprehension are within our reach.

This danger is greatest in Christianity, which has historically focused on the cross as the principal locus for the revelation of a divine justice which transcends mere human fulfillment. Israel was seeking liberation from Rome; Jesus (the story goes) demanded that his disciples take up the cross. But this focus on the cross is very dangerous and can give rise to the gravest spiritual and political disorders. If we pit the cross against our own struggle for liberation and development, we can be deceived into believing that loving God means hating ourselves and all of our finite gifts and aspirations, hating them even to the point of death—even, if we follow out the logic of this kind of Christianity, as Samuel Hopkins did, to the point of eternal damnation.[11] The result is that we end up hating everybody and everything and thus hating God as well. And hatred, as we know, has definite political consequences. It is precisely in those times and places where Christianity has become most focused on self-sacrificial love that its capacity for violence has been greatest. And the victims of this violence have, more often than not, been the Jews. Israel's own insights into the way in which divine justice at once includes and transcends our own are obscured and, in the Christian imagination, the Jews are trans-

---

11. Samuel Hopkins, an important late eighteenth century Reformed theologian, was a student of Jonathan Edwards and one of the founders of the abolitionist movement in the United States. He taught that only those who were willing to be damned for the greater glory of God had sufficient evidence of their salvation to be admitted to full communion in the Church. Needless to say he found himself pastoring a very small congregation.

formed into those who uphold justice over love, human liberation, and development over God's mysterious plan for humanity. The religion of *self*-sacrifice paves the way for a Holocaust of Christianity's Other.

The authentic meaning of the cross can be understood only in the context of Israel's long history of struggle and long history of tribulations. It has meaning only for those who, like Mary, hoped that in this new human being which God was drawing forth from her He really did mean to "cast down monarchs from their thrones and lift the humble high, fill the hungry with good things and send the rich away empty" (Luke 1:52–53), and who like the disciples on the road to Emmaus really did "hope that he [Jesus] would be the one to liberate Israel" (Luke 24:21). And it has meaning only if we continue to believe that these are legitimate—no, Holy—aims. To those who shared these hopes, and who were close to Jesus of Nazareth, the cross may indeed have seemed like the culmination of Israel's tribulations, and the Resurrection like the vindication of her millennium of struggle. But to suggest this after the horrors of the Jewish War, much less the Shoah, is nothing short of blasphemous. The cross is legitimately central for Christians because and only because it is through Jesus of Nazareth that we came to share the light of the Law and the Prophets—and because the crucifixion of Jesus thus serves *for Christians* as a reminder of the same lesson which Israel has learned better and more often than others have: that God is calling us to a higher Justice than we can know except in doing it and which, therefore, we cannot name.

Once we have achieved this supernatural justice—once we will the Good for its own sake—and have ordered all of our passions to the service of the Good, we become more than merely human. We live for and take joy first and foremost from cultivating—or as the Buddhists are wont to say "ripening"—other beings. This is the great ideal of the *tzadik*, the saint, or the Bodhisattva. We are inclined today to be skeptical about the claims made on behalf of such figures in the Hasidic literature, or in Christian hagiography, or in Buddhist texts such as the *Dasabhumika* Sutra, and perhaps it is best to regard miracle stories and accounts of Bodhisattvas reincarnating as cats as just a symbolic way of communicating the extent to which those with supernatural justice go to promote the full development of others. But we have already seen how it is the just act which confers on us the power of wisdom and the supernaturally just act which makes it possible to participate, even in this live, in an authentic, connatural knowledge of God. By just act we tap into the power of Being itself.

This is the highest alchemy. Who knows what other powers supernatural justice bestows on us?

What this all makes clear, of course, is that the cultivation of justice, like the cultivation of the other virtues, depends on habituation even where it also depends on knowledge. This habituation takes the form both of the nurturing love of a supportive community and of discipline and hard struggle. In either case it is intimately bound up with the question of social justice, both as the object of that hard struggle and as the community which, to the extent that we can create it, helps nurture us as discipline us. It is to the nature of the just society that we must know turn.

5

Social Justice

WE HAVE DEMONSTRATED IN previous chapters that it is, in fact, possible to rise rationally to transcendental first principles on the basis of which we can not only explain the universe, in at least a preliminary and tentative way, but also order human action. In order to be able to carry out this latter task, however, it has been necessary to define with some precision the nature of the human vocation. We have discovered that human beings are defined by a very specific mode of participation in *esse:* where minerals simply persist in being by taking advantage of the Boltzmann Order Principle in order to conserve their form, and plants and animals use complex organic-chemical reactions to reproduce themselves, we humans actually bring into Being new and more complex forms of organization, thus sharing in the creative activity which is *Esse*. In the process we are stretched to grow beyond our humanity, towards God. This process is, furthermore, by no means solitary. It presupposes, rather, a whole complex of social relationships which are necessary for human development and civilizational progress.

This brings us, then, to the final and most important question we must address in this work: just what sort of social structure best promotes the development of human capacities, both individual and collective? This is a complex question for three reasons. First, resolving it requires that we bring together both general principles and concrete social realities so that, just as we drew on psychology in our discussion of virtue, it will be necessary to draw on social theory in our discussion of social justice. Second, social structure itself has a number of distinct but related dimensions: technology, economics, politics, and culture. Third, we will show that the question itself can never be definitively answered. The ongoing development of human capacities itself changes the conditions for further development requiring new structures and new forms of social organization. Any credible social ethics must at once outline general principles which are universally valid for all human societies and provide a method for addressing the specific questions facing us in the present period.

We begin by outlining some general principles—both ethical principles derived from the natural law theory we have already laid out and social scientific principles which will help us apply the natural law to specific situations. We will then turn to an analysis of the current situation, something which will point us, in the end, to some very specific directions for the present period.

PHILOSOPHICAL PRINCIPLES

The Concept of Law

The general principles governing systems—physical, biological, or social—we call laws. Historically, the natural law tradition has distinguished between various types of law based on their degrees of generality and the way in which we come to know them. Thomas, for example, distinguishes between eternal law, natural law, divine law, human law and the "law in the fomes of sin."

By *eternal law* we mean the law governing the cosmos as a whole across space and time and all other possible dimensions, and thus encoding the rules which govern the action of all possible systems—something we have shown constitutes an actual infinity of relationships ordered to a single final cause. In so far as it takes all dimensions simultaneously as it were, the eternal law knows the structure of all things and is thus a perfect order. In so far as it encodes all of the different forms of organization—something we experience as a temporal sequence of wrenchingly difficult and violent transformations—it knows and conserves the creative power of chaos. And in so far as embraces an actual infinity of different forms of organization it is the end or *telos* towards which all finite, contingent organization is ordered.

This eternal law is, in fact, simply *esse* or Being as such—the end which all forms of organization seek, each in their own way, in proportion to their level of development and according to their specific structures. This end is radically beyond our comprehension. As contingent beings we do not understand the power of Being itself, but only finite strategies for persisting and growing in Being. Being as such thus *orders* our actions and functions as an absolute law, while at the same time remaining hidden and mysterious and radically transcendent.

By *natural law* we mean that portion of the eternal law understood by intelligent systems at a given level of development. It is called natural because the portion of eternal law accessible to a system depends on its nature, essence, or structure. It thus follows that different intelligent systems may have a different understanding of eternal law, and that these different understandings may be better (more complete), worse (less complete), simply different (reflecting different aspects of reality), or both better or worse and different (i.e., globally more or less complete, but lacking some element perceived by another otherwise less developed system, or containing some element not perceived by an otherwise more developed system). All intelligent systems are under an obligation to act in accord with natural law as they understand it.

By *divine law* we mean law which is known on the basis of revelation. We have shown in an earlier work (Mansueto 2002b) that revelation comes about not by the direct illumination of the intellect by God, but rather by participation in transhistorical structures which transcend the social intellect which is the ordinary agent of abstraction. This participation leads to insights into fundamental questions of meaning and value which do not contradict reason, but which cannot, for all that, be rigorously demonstrated, at least at our current level of development. All intelligent systems are obliged to act in accord with divine law, to the extent to which they share the underlying insights on which that law is based.

By *human law* we mean the law framed by intelligent systems in accord with and on the basis of their grasp of natural or divine law to govern emerging forms of organization. Human law is derived from these higher principles in the sense that valid laws reflect the system's best grasp of the progressive dynamic of the cosmohistorical evolutionary process —i.e., its best understanding of just how to promote the development of complex organization—but this process of derivation is prudential and creative, not deductive. When we say that the derivation of human law from higher principles is prudential we mean it depends on an estimate of the particular situation in which the laws are to apply and of the rules most likely to encourage development under those specific conditions. When we say that it is creative we mean that human law is intended to create new structures which have never existed before and are not fully understood (indeed may be very poorly understood) by the systems which create them. All intelligent systems are under an obligation to act in accord with the human laws of their societies unless those laws conflict with the natural or divine law as they understand it.

Now human laws are, generally speaking of two types: civil and religious. The difference is simply that where civil law is derived from natural law religious law is derived from divine law. Civil law has as its aim the cultivation of our natural capacities, religious law the cultivation of supernatural capacities, i.e., the theological virtues. In both cases it is important to make a distinction between the fundamental principles, which are essentially unchanging, but too broad to provide specific and direct guidance to human conduct, and the specific norms, which are the result of finite human judgments made under specific situations, and thus always subject to change and correction.

As we noted in our discussion of virtue, the distinction between natural and supernatural concerns not so much different spheres of life as it does different degrees of development. We will, therefore, address natural and divine, civil and religious law together, noting as we proceed which principles are natural and thus universally binding and which derive from principles specific to particular religious traditions pertain only those who follow that way.

By the *law in the fomes of sin* we mean laws which govern the development of systems organized by backward or distorted structures. Historically, the scholastics took this mean action in accord with sensuality —a lower principle of action which could distract human beings from their true good, knowable only on the basis of the intellect—but which nonetheless has a law-like character, governed by biological structures. The concept may be expanded, however, to include action in accord with social structures which have become an obstacle to social progress, or which permit progress only in a distorted way. This permits us to theorize such principles as the law of value, the laws of capital accumulation, and the law of the declining rate of profit, as authentic laws even though they are embedded in unjust structures. The law in the fomes of sin carries no obligation—though action in accord with it may not constitute a wrong if it remains the only or best path open for further development.

Now we have, in the course of our investigation, identified a principle which meets precisely the definition of law: the tendency for all systems to move, under the attractive power of God, from lower to higher levels of organization, thus realizing their latent potential. This general principle has, furthermore, a number of more specific applications. On the one hand, the development of complex organization presupposes certain principles of order: i.e., the underlying structure of space-time, the laws governing gravitational, electromagnetic, and the strong and weak nuclear interactions. Actual organization, however, emerges through a process of symmetry-breaking. Quantitative changes accumulate until they give rise to qualitative difference. Qualitative differences give rise to complex interactions which render existing structures unstable, which in turn gives rise to new structures and new interactions. Conflict, struggle, decay, and disintegration, the inevitability of which is ensured by the Second Law of Thermodynamics, play a critical role in this process of development, weeding out less adequate forms of organization and making room for the new, ensuring that systems which are stable but finite do not stagnate, but are, rather, forced to begin again, reaching every higher, towards Being as such. As layer upon layer of qualitatively different forms of interaction become superimposed one on the other, systems become more highly organized and more highly organizing: i.e., they order an increasingly diverse range of elements (subsystems) to an increasingly unified end or purpose, seeking Being in ever more complex ways, now in the stability of mineral forms, then in nutrition, growth and reproduction, then in sensation and locomotion, and ultimately in the intellect and will, which allow us to participate conscious and actively in the creative activity of the divine. These same laws apply to human societies, which depend on a certain order for their growth and development but as they pursue Being eventually develop in ways which become incompatible with that order, which becomes an obstacle and must be transcended. Indeed, it is just precisely the fact that the law of the universe is all about reaching beyond present capacities and thus present structures that it takes on the character of a moral imperative at all, i.e., that it takes the form, which we already noted in an earlier chapter—"Act in such way as to promote the emergence of ever more complex forms of organization," rather than only the indicative: "Systems act in such a way as to promote the emergence of ever more complex forms of organization."

More specifically, in so far as the development of complex organization seems to imply an underlying order, a radical openness to change, and an ordering to higher ends, it is possible to identify three distinct principles, which also noted briefly in an earlier chapter, but which we must now discuss in greater depth:

Social Justice

- *the principle of public order*, which guarantees the basic conditions for human social existence,
- *the principle of subsidiarity*, which guarantees the space necessary for the emergence of new forms of organization, and
- *the principle of hierarchy*, which insures ordering of lower forms of organization to higher ones.

Let us consider each of theses different forms of right in turn.

THE PRINCIPLE OF PUBLIC ORDER

In order for the emergence of complex organization to be possible, there must be some regular pattern or structure of social interactions which provides individuals and organizations with a greater or lesser space in which they can predict the overall action of the social system. Without this, effective action becomes impossible and no new organization can emerge.

Concretely, the principle of public order requires that persons (individuals and organizations) act in accord with custom, with rules, regulations and procedures, and with positive law, unless some higher principle requires them to do otherwise. We are thus under an obligation to use a language which others can understand in our communications, to drive on the right side of the road (unless we are in, say, England, in which case we must drive on the left) ... and in general comply with the ordinary and established way of doing things.

The principles of public order are simply a formalization of the forms of organization already achieved by a particular system. They may include rules which have little or no intrinsic validity, but exist simply because there must be some one way people do things in order for there to be any organization at all (driving on the right), but they may also include customs and/or laws which formalize centuries or even millennia of experience about "what works." In order to form part of the right of public order, a principle must meet the following conditions. First, it must be promulgated, either by the public authorities or through the emergence of a custom which has become widely known. Second, it must in fact by followed by the vast majority of people, so that a failure to follow it would disrupt the ordinary flow of social intercourse. Third, it must clearly support the creation of higher forms of organization. The right of public order is the lowest form of right and is always and everywhere superceded by the principle of subsidiarity and the principle of hierarchy. Order is the precondition for organization, but cannot substitute for it. Indeed, every innovation in some sense constitutes a breach of public order, because it entails a different way of doing things. The principle of public order obliges us to ensure that these breaches promote creativity and development, and are not merely random or unnecessarily destabilizing, but cannot be used to block progressive new initiatives.

THE PRINCIPLE OF SUBSIDIARITY

We have seen that organization emerges through qualitative differentiation, which leads to symmetry-breaking, instability, and new forms of interaction. This means that the structure on any given system must not be so rigid as the prevent differentiation, symmetry-breaking, instability, etc. It is the rigidity of certain kinds of structure that binds systems in the current state and leads to stagnation. Thus the ionic bonds which constitute certain salts—e.g., NaCl—are so rigid that it is difficult for these salts to dissolve and recombine in more interesting and complex ways. The covalent bonds which constitute certain organic compounds, on the other hand, are weaker but also more flexible and thus give more scope for the emergence of complex organization.

This same principle applies within social systems. Structures must not be so rigid as to prevent innovation or so brittle that every innovation constitutes a threat to global public order. In so far as social systems are constituted by intelligent organisms, it is especially important to safeguard the possibility of the emergence of new forms of organization which no single member of the system, individual or organization has thus far envisioned, no matter how advanced they may be by comparison with other members of the system. Thus the importance of the principle of subsidiarity: Particular systems have the right to develop, exercise, and reap the rewards of their own capacities, unless and until such development, exercise, and/or enjoyment violates cosmic law—i.e., fails to best promote the development of complex organization.

The principle of subsidiarity may be divided into three parts, which correspond to the three levels at which intelligent organisms and social systems organize: the biological, the social, and the supersocial.

The principle of subsidiarity implies that all systems have a right and obligation to conserve the integrity of their existing organization, which is the precondition for the emergence of all higher forms. This means they have a right to protection against murder and against the destruction of the general conditions of life—i.e., a stable ecosystem in which biological functions can be carried out. This right is, however, not purely negative. Systems also have a positive claim on the resources they need in order to survive; a claim which is not mitigated by failure at one or another point to use those resources productively. To deprive someone of the resources they need to survive is tantamount to murder. This means that all social systems must provide their members with basic subsistence guarantees. For those able to work this means subsistence land rights or guaranteed employment at a living wage. A living wage is a wage sufficient to support an entire family on one income, so that children can claim attention equivalent to the full time effort of one parent. The wage must provide for training the children at the same level as the parents, without leaving them with a debt burden, etc. Any part of the living wage may be provided in the form of state subsidies for basic needs, education, etc. For those unable to work—for whatever reason—it means guarantees for food, housing, clothing, medical care, and social contact equivalent to that provided in a living wage etc. as well as the means of self-development appropriate to the conditions of the person in question..

This "right to life" is not something that belongs uniquely to human beings, or even to intelligent organisms. On the contrary, there is a general presumption against the destruction of any organized system, no matter how simple, a presumption which provides *prima facie* protection for all organisms, and even for mineral formations, etc. Similarly, organizations formed by groups of intelligent organisms also have a claim on the resources they need to survive. The presumption is thus always in favor of the continued existence of a business, a nonprofit organization, etc., which, whatever its weaknesses or limitations hitherto, holds the promise of adding something to the universe at some point in the future.

There are, to be sure, limits to this right to life. First of all, some higher order systems are so structured as to consume lower order systems. The lion has a hierarchical right to eat the lamb. It must be noted, however, that this limitation operates only at the biological level, for it is only at the biological level that higher organization emerges through consumption, metabolism, etc. In social systems, we will see, new organization emerges through production, of which consumption is merely a precondition. More developed individuals, organizations, etc. therefore, do not enjoy a parallel right to consume, or otherwise use, less developed individuals and organizations to realize their own interests. On the contrary, being more developed means precisely being able to develop in a way which contributes to, rather than taking away from, the development of others.

Second, the right to life is superceded whenever doing so results in a net gain in the overall level of organization, or a lesser net loss. This is a simple principle of triage. It is permissible—even obligatory—to kill or let one die in order to save many, unless that one possesses capacities greater than the many which might be saved. This same principle applies to organizations. There is no obligation to subsidize organizations when more is lost to the universe by doing so than is gained, and there is no way to rectify this situation. Indeed, under such circumstances subsidy is wrong.

It must be stressed, however, that this limitation on the right to life should be applied with the greatest caution, lest the whole principle be obviated. There are often situations when disrupting and dissolving whole communities, even at the cost of great loss of life, seems advantageous for social progress. There is a real danger, however, that more is being lost than we may realize at the time—capacities which may not currently seem particularly interesting or important, but which may well be vital for the further development of civilization. It is against precisely such errors that the subsidiary right to life of organizations is intended to protect. A judgment to sacrifice existing organization must always be made with great trepidation.

Now the right of life is simply the foundation of subsidiary right. Subsidiary right proper consists of those claims which intelligent organisms and/or organizations make as a precondition of their effective participation in the cosmohistorical evolutionary process. Once again, these claims take both negative and positive forms. Negatively, all intelligent organisms and organizations enjoy a right to the free exercise of the intellect and will, and freedom from unnecessary restrictions on activities rooted in the exercise of the intellect and will. This means that there should be no unnecessary restrictions on invention, economic initiative, assembly and political organization, the expression of ideas and desires, etc. These freedoms are grounded in two established results. First, we know that all systems tend towards the good, and there is thus a presumption against restriction on their action. Second, new forms of organization emerge from complex, even apparently chaotic new interactions, the space for which must therefore be protected by law.

It must be pointed out, that unlike liberal theorists, we do not ground these rights in the individual, but rather in the larger self-organizing dynamic of the cosmos itself. We have already established, in our cosmology, that all systems tend toward the good, and that the emergence of complex organization requires space for difference, instability, etc. Respect for difference and instability is not something society owes to individuals and organizations, but rather something which individuals and organizations owe to society and to each other.

The right of sociality, however, is not limited to negative guarantees. All intelligent organisms and organizations have a positive claim on the resources they need in order to grow and develop and thus make a positive contribution to the cosmohistorical civilizational project. This means, first of all, a right to the kind of intact social fabric which is necessary for the cultivation of human social capacities. There is an old African proverb which says "it takes a whole village to raise a child." One might add that it takes network of villages to raise a teacher, and networks upon networks to raise a philosopher. Intellect and will develop across a complex network of social relationships, apart from which we are inevitably crippled and fail to make a full and complete contribution to the cosmos.

Second, all intelligent organisms and organizations have a legitimate claim to retain part of the social surplus they produce, and to allocate as they see fit, so long as it promotes their development or that of another. We will speak later of the importance of centralizing surplus for investment in higher order projects which extend the capacity of the whole system. But the fact remains that even the wisest leaders cannot foresee all possible avenues of innovation, nor can they know along which path precisely particular individuals or organisms can best develop. There must, therefore, be room for individuals and organizations to invest in their own development, as well as room for them to invest in innovations which the public authorities do not yet, and perhaps should not yet, buy.

There are a number of ways to ensure that individuals and organizations have access to a share of the surplus they produce. In agrarian societies it may mean simply guaranteeing the leisure time necessary to tinker with crafts, to form new relationships, to study, etc. But it may also be necessary to make sure that another share of surplus is allocated "close to home," to support village priests, teachers, and other local authorities who can help build local capacity. If the first tithe belongs to the poor, the second belongs to the village "priest." In more complex societies, a share of surplus may similarly be guaranteed by providing time for developmental sabbaticals as well as recreational vacation. All individuals have a right and an obligation to pursue the highest level of training from which they can benefit, in those fields where they can make the best relative contribution. Above and beyond this, individuals and organizations have a right to a share of the profits of enterprise, (this applies to workers as well as to entrepreneurs) to royalties on innovations, etc. There is, however, no legitimate claim which arises simply from providing land or capital, the possession of which was originally the result of an act contrary to law (even if this act took place many generations ago). Rents, interest, dividends, speculative profits on capital gains, etc., are all illicit and claims to them are invalid and not covered by subsidiarity.

The right of subsidiary sociality is limited by hierarchical claims on resources for investment. As in the case of the subsidiary right of life, the standard here is that of optimum growth. It is permissible (in fact required) to violate the presumption of subsidiarity when and only when cosmos will gain more by doing so than by not doing so. At the same time, caution must be exercised that valuable but currently invisible capacities are not being sacrificed in the process.

The social form of matter is, by nature, a form of transition, a motion towards higher forms of organization which we cannot as yet even imagine. And yet we try. To be human is to aspire to be more than human —even to be God.

We have already analyzed above the nature of human spirituality, grounded as it is in our ability to see, however dimly, truths too complex for us to prove or fully comprehend, and thus to pursue goods the reality or value of which is not yet fully established. This means, first of all, that spiritual development presupposes the possibility of free exploration— and also that some spiritual claims, in so far as they are not subject to rigorous proof, cannot become the basis of obligatory assent of the intellect and/or will. It is on this basis that we are able to define a subsidiary right of spirituality—i.e., the right of religious freedom. Individuals and organizations have a right to freedom from unnecessary restrictions on religious organization, expression, etc. No one religious community can monopolize the public square, so that participation therein is contingent on membership in that community or conformity to its norms. This does not, however, mean, that the public square is by nature a secular space. It is, rather, a space in which various communities, both religious and secular, contend with (and hopefully learn from) each other in an ongoing debate regarding fundamental questions of meaning and value. This, in turn, however, presupposes certain institutional conditions. Individuals must have the leisure to celebrate holy days, to set aside periods for retreat and meditation, etc. They must also have access to a local religious community which can actively promote spiritual growth and development—something which in turn presupposes the allocation of resources to this community.

Religious freedom is limited in the same way as other subsidiary rights: by the principle of hierarchy which we shall explore later on. Religious freedom may be restricted when religious institutions themselves become so powerful as to constrain the free development of the intellect or when, by compelling religious assent of the intellect or will, more development is encouraged than is lost by the affront to the ordinary path along which intellect and will develop. Once again, such restrictions must be imposed only with great caution, when the fulfillment of cosmic law clearly requires it and when due care has been taken to ensure that hidden but valuable insights are not being lost.

Subsidiary right is grounded in the actual capacity of the system in question to act in such a way which best promotes the development of complex organization. Specific rights may and in fact must be codified in positive law and sanctioned by the public authorities. Respect for these positively defined rights is then required under the right of public order. At the same time, the failure of the public authorities to properly define rights in positive law does not obviate the existence of these rights. On the other hand, the fact that a right has been defined in positive law does not by itself create that right. The existence of a right requires the latent potential in which that right is grounded as well as actual exercise of that capacity in accord with cosmic law. Those who engage in unjust acts, therefore, cannot rely on the fact that those acts may have been legal under positive law. The right of public order stands as nothing before the right of subsidiarity, which always takes precedence over it.

It should be clear in conclusion that the principle of subsidiarity creates no absolute property rights for either individuals or communities, but simply protects the space necessary for initiative and instability.

THE PRINCIPLE OF HIERARCHICAL RIGHT

We have already introduced, without adequately defining it, the concept of hierarchical right in suggesting that "higher order" activities have a superior claim on resources, and in general on intellectual, moral, and spiritual assent those which are in some sense "lower order." We now need to define more rigorously the concept of hierarchy, and to explain just precisely what we mean by "hierarchical right."

The universe realized as an organized system is ordered to a final cause, which we have identified as *esse* or "Being as such," the fully realized capacity to generate an actual infinity of different forms of organization. Movement towards this final cause consists in nothing more or less than increased organizing capacity, so that higher order systems express the underlying organizing principle of the universe (organization as such) more adequately than lower order systems. Higher order systems, in other words, are more creative, powerful, knowing, loving, etc. than lower order systems. The existence of different levels of development does not, to be sure, constitute a total order by inclusion. Higher order systems do not necessarily possess all the capacities of lower order systems. One need only put an unarmed philosopher on the savannah with a pride of lions to discover that. There are also systems which are simply different, but at roughly equal levels of development. Even these systems, however, are organized into collectivities (ecosystems, societies, etc.) which taken together embrace a far wider range of capacities than any single system—and in this case there may well be a total order by inclusion. By hierarchy we mean nothing other than this diversity in kind and level of development, coupled with a grouping into collectivities and an ordering to final cause.

It follows from the existence of this hierarchical ordering that some systems are in a better position to make decisions regarding the allocation of resources, the nature of the first principle, the ordering of our affections etc. than are others. This can happen in two ways: either because the system is larger and more diverse and thus accesses more information, or because it is more capable and thus able to analyze that information and draw conclusions more adequately. And in the most organized systems, including most social systems, both of these dynamics are at work. Mechanisms exist to consult widely, centralizing the information accessed by individuals and organizations. The most advanced then develop mission, strategy, and tactics on the basis of that information and then feed it back to the larger system to be tested, revised, etc. Hierarchical right is, in other words, the principle which defines the government of human communities.

Now, in so far as the fundamental principle of cosmic law requires the development of all systems from lower to higher levels or organization, it also requires that all acts be ordered the highest purposes possible—i.e., the highest purposes consistent with their current level of development. This means, specifically,

- seeking wisdom, i.e., exploring fundamental questions of meaning and value in order to arrive at knowledge of the first principle, and applying the answers which result from that search to our lives together—what we call the *magisterium*,
- ordering affections from lower order to higher order goods— what we call the right of *sanctification*, and
- transferring resources (including human labor) from lower order to higher order activities—what we call the right of *dominion*.

We need to consider each of these rights in turn.

If systems are to develop, and make a contribution to the development of the universe, they must be ordered to more highly organized systems, and ultimately to Being itself. In the case of intelligent systems, this involves an act of the intellect, whereby the less developed system perceives, and grasps the essence of the more developed system (however dimly and inadequately), which thus becomes an end or a lure for its own growth and development. In so far as some systems are already more developed than others, they will have a better grasp of even higher order systems, and thus of the Truth in general, which is nothing but Being itself understood by the intellect. These systems are thus in a position to promote the intellectual development of lower order systems, and thus lead them to the truth. This capacity defines a right and an obligation —that of the *magisterium*, which is the principle form of the exercise of hierarchical right.

The exercise of the magisterium consists of three distinct but related activates:

- active pursuit of wisdom through scholarship, research, and other creative activities,
- the work of teaching, and
- prophetic interventions intended to challenge ideological distortions and the injustice they promote.

The search for wisdom is the foundation of the exercise of the magisterium, since it produces the knowledge in the name of which magisterial right is exercised. It is, furthermore, through ongoing search for truth that the most intellectually developed individuals, who cannot themselves be regularly taught through the ordinary magisterium, are forced to run up continuously against the limits of their own grasp of the truth, and find themselves always and forever ordered to a truth which they never fully comprehend.

This search for truth is itself hierarchically ordered, both with respect to the relationships between the various disciplines and with respect to the relationship between scholarship, teaching, and prophetic intervention. Seeking Wisdom presupposes, first of all, a mastery of the liberal arts, which are the tools, as it were, out of which knowledge and wisdom are constructed. Second, it requires an ongoing effort both to explain the universe and to interpret it's meaning. This is the place of the sciences on the one hand and of the fine arts and the hermeneutic disciplines, which serve as a window on truth and allow us to see through the image to the meaning, on the other hand. Finally, it is necessary to draw conclusions, however, tentative, from our understanding of the universe and from humanity's imaginative window on God, regarding fundamental questions of meaning and value. In this sense the "sacred sciences"—philosophy, theology, and politics and the law—depend on the other disciplines, the free and autonomous development of which is the precondition of an informed exploration of fundamental questions of meaning and value. At the same time, however, this autonomy is subsidiary and not absolute. While the liberal arts, the fine arts, the sciences, and the hermeneutic disciplines may well have legitimate ends other than the service of the sacred sciences this is their *highest* end, and the end to which their development must ultimately be ordered. And any practical implications, in so far as they bear on the ordering of human action, must be mediated by the sacred sciences.

Similarly, while every human being participates in the search for knowledge and wisdom, and while every human being has a subsidiary right to draw their own conclusions regarding the results of this search, the search takes place properly and legitimately only under the guidance of teachers who can lead it. These teachers have an obligation to listen to the people, who may well have insights superior to their own. This is especially true given the possibility of connatural knowledge and *caritative wisdom*, which make it possible for those without formal education to know first principles, or indeed any other sort of principle, preconceptually and experientially to be sure, but nonetheless better and more completely than the scientist, philosopher, or theologian. At the same time, the people must also listen to their teachers, and cannot claim to make judgments for which their education is inadequate. Wisdom, which orders all things, is an acquired virtue that comes as the result of much discipline. It is one thing to be unpersuaded by a sophisticated philosophical or theological argument; it is another thing to say that one has no need to be instructed by such arguments. The same is true of subsidiary disciplines. This rules out the sort of anti-intellectualist fundamentalism which rejects dialogue with literary-critical or sociohistorical-critical scholarship of the scriptures or with the results of the modern sciences.

The ordinary exercise of the *magisterium* thus takes the form of public deliberation regarding fundamental questions of meaning and value. This dialogue is led by teachers with the full participation of the people. In this deliberation, teachers of the sacred sciences take precedence over those of other disciplines, and those who teach teachers and who themselves add to knowledge and wisdom take precedence over mere tradents. But wisdom speaks in many and varied voices, and we must listen to everyone.

Legislation, in the natural law tradition, is essentially just an extension of the magisterium. Human law, as we have seen, is simply an interpretation and application of the natural and divine laws. While the principle of public order requires that there be recognized public authorities which formalize our interpretation of these higher principles, and while communities will generally want to provide some regular mechanism for carrying out this work, it is the relative truth value of an interpretation which gives it the authority to order action, not the status of the person(s) making it or the process which was followed in arriving at it (Thomas, *Summa Theologiae*, I–II 95:2). Even so, there are certain principles to which any legislative process must conform if it is to generate wise and prudent decisions. First, it must provide for the broadest possible popular consultation, and must not promulgate new human laws without the consent of those to whom they apply, except under the most unusual circumstances, and then only for so long as those special circumstances endure. Second, it must provide a recognized place for the wisest members of the community. Valid human laws are framed, as Isidore says, by the people and their elders together (Isidore *Etymologies* v:10, Thomas, *Summa Theologiae*, I–II 90:3, 95:4). Third, it must provide for some process by which human laws or applications thereof which are contrary to the natural or divine law may be abrogated.

This last criterion presents special problems. The principle of public order requires that, wherever possible, such abrogation of laws take place within the existing legal structure. This means that the council of elders—or rather of the wise—must double as kind of supreme court. But this same council will itself have been involved in framing the very laws which it now reviews for their conformity with the principles of reason. Any other panel with the capacities required would, furthermore, be drawn from essentially same social categories. What this means is that the authority to rule on the justice of human laws must ultimately lie outside the human law itself, in the extraordinary magisterium exercised by prophets whose claim to be heard rests exclusively on the quality of what they say. The fact that their authority lies outside of human law, does not, however, make it any less fully *legal* authority. On the contrary, the obligation to obey an authentic prophet supercedes all other legal obligations.

Human beings are rational animals and, as we have seen, willing follows naturally on knowing. Human beings, in other words, naturally will the highest good they know, except in so far as that willing is constrained by force of habit or by the force of inordinate passions. This means that task of ordering human action is first and foremost the work of teaching, of cultivating knowledge of ever higher goods, and thus eliciting ever higher loves. Both the passions, however, and the force of habit are very real and because of this the *magisterium* requires the assistance of a lesser office which acts on the passions and which cultivates the formation of good habits.

How, precisely, does one act on the passions, other than through the intellect which rightly governs them? The passions, we must remember, are natural responses to sensory stimuli. This means that they can be affected by means of a direct appeal to the senses which, at the same time, encodes the higher principle to which they should be ordered. This is why the sanctifying office acts first and foremost through *ritual* and more broadly through the fine arts. How, precisely, does this work?

Beauty, we will remember, is one of the transcendental properties of Being. Specifically, it is Being as an object of perception, sensual, or intellectual. More specifically, it has the qualities of integrity, harmony, and clarity. By integrity we mean that all of the aspects of the beautiful object form part of a single, integrated whole, such that the removal of any one of them would diminish the whole in a qualitative manner. By harmony we mean the ability of the object to whole together diverse elements which are in tension with each other. By clarity, we mean that the object in question is a window on the Truth, and thus on Being as such. The beautiful object, precisely because of its beauty, elicits desire and thus orders the appetites to itself, and thus to Being as such, with which it is convertible.

The *original* and *ordinary* locus of this action is public ritual and the public sacred space in which the ritual takes place. The gradual differentiation of the fine arts from the matrix of ritual is largely a result of the emergence of competing interpretations of the dominant social myths during the axial age, and later of growing skepticism regarding religious claims generally during the modern era. The emergence of plural perspectives regarding fundamental questions of meaning and value means that human societies can no longer have a single ritual cycle in which everyone participates and that public spaces can no longer be constructed in such a way as to carry a single, hegemonic complex of meanings. This does not, however, mean, that public space-time should attempt to be neutral. The aim, rather, should be the construction of a public space-time in which the *commons* or public square is itself an intersection of competing sacred spaces and public time (i.e., the calendar) is defined by competing and overlapping ritual cycles, so that the question of meaning (for meaning has indeed become *the* question of our time) is always drawn to the forefront. Living in a world which is meaning-laden naturally lifts the appetites towards a higher good; living in a world in which meaning is a question naturally stimulates the intellect.

There are two ways to act directly on the will. It is possible, on the one hand, to analyze the factors which contribute to the development of particular habits and thus to empower individuals to change them.

Understanding why we are choosing a lesser good even when we know the higher can help us to choose the goods we actually desire rather than those to which we have become habituated. This is the work of counseling and spiritual direction. It is, on the other hand, sometimes necessary to impose external discipline which helps those stuck in bad habits to break them or to assist those who aspire to perfection to make progress along their path. Here it is important to distinguish between the internal and external forums and between sanctions which are backed by coercion and those that are not. Generally speaking public sanctions backed by coercion can be imposed only in order to enforce human laws which are clearly derived from natural law and do not require assent to revealed principles. Individuals can be subjected to religious law only with their consent.

Preaching stands in an ambiguous position with respect to the magisterium and the right of sanctification. On the one hand, because it conveys to the people the results of the sacred sciences, it is an authentic act of teaching and thus participates in the magisterium. On the other hand, where teaching appeals primarily to the intellect, preaching appeals at least in significant measure to the passions, through the art of *rhetoric*. To the extent that it forms the passions directly it is an exercise of the sanctifying office.

There are definite limits on the exercise of the right of sanctification. Ritual acts appealing to the senses and the passions must be ordered to the truth, and the work of liturgists, therefore, is always subject to the supervision of philosophers and theologians. Attempts to discipline the appetites must not interfere with the freedom necessary for long-term development. The Good is infinite and incapable of definitive penetration, and we must always be aware of the possibility that what seems to us like a lesser good, may simply be a higher good which we do not understand. Similarly, the mode of restriction must be such as to respect the dignity and latent potential of the individual or organization restricted. In particular, discipline which undermines self-esteem and fosters a conviction of depravity or inability to do good is contrary to the principle of sanctification itself.

If systems are to develop, then it is not sufficient to allocate resources to conserve and develop capacity among individuals and organizations, along the lines we have specified in our discussion of subsidiary right. On the one hand, the organizing capacity of individuals and particular organizations is limited and larger projects are beyond their scope. On the other hand, the most advanced and thus valuable activities are those which are most complex and thus beyond the comprehension of the vast majority. Indeed, the most valuable activities in the cosmos are by definition those which are so complex as to be beyond the capacity of any mind which has yet emerged, individual or collective, and thus beyond any conceivable willing. It is thus necessary for a system to have mechanisms by which resources can be centralized for larger scale or more advanced initiatives—including those which the vast majority may be unable to comprehend, and thus unable to explicitly endorse—and to forbid allocations of resources contrary to the principle of cosmic

There are any number of legitimate ways in which a system can do this. The most effective, because it directly engages the creativity and initiative of the people, and helps develop their capacity to understand more fully the activities they are supporting, is through liturgies. The word "liturgy" comes from the Hellenic *laitreia* (worship) and *ergon* (work), and originally meant work offered for the gods, or more immediately for the temple establishments. In this context we mean by liturgies direct labor levies, accompanied by extensive training, debate, discussion etc. In principle all labor should be a liturgy offered freely to the cosmos. Special liturgies should be offered to support advanced projects which fundamentally extend the capacity of the system in question. This may mean a group of villages working together to build an irrigation system or a network of roads, a temple or an observatory—or it may mean engaging citizens in direct labor to support mass literacy programs, local childcare networks, construction of the "information superhighway," or space exploration.

Where liturgies are not possible, dominion may be exercised through the imposition of taxes in kind or cash. Taxation generally does less to promote development and capacity building than do liturgies, because the people can simply pay the tax and forget about the project. There is a tendency for people to gradually lose sight of—or never really even begin to understand—the purpose for which they are paying the tax, and to fall into a cycle of resentment and resistance. It is thus very important that taxation be accompanied by in-depth, detailed accounting of the way in which the resources are being used, the results obtained, etc. Taxes in kind are preferable to taxes in cash, because people feel that some part of them, at least, is directly involved in the project.

It is, finally, permissible to centralize resources for investment by directly retaining a portion of the surplus produced by the workers within one's own organization. This may be done both by state enterprises and by nonstate organizations. As in the case of liturgies and taxes, the case for the retention of the surplus must be explained, and the workers engaged to at least some degree in making decisions on just how the resources are to be used.

This said, there are a number of limits on the right of dominion. First and foremost, the level of surplus extraction must not be so great as to undermine the integrity of the ecosystem and the social fabric, and thus the conditions for the reproduction of existing capacity. Similarly, it must not, except under conditions of the greatest necessity, deprive individuals and subsidiary organizations of the share of surplus which they need in order to develop. This is particularly important when the organization of production makes extraction through liturgies difficult or impossible, and where surplus extracted thus not, therefore, directly benefit those who are producing it.

Second, the method of surplus extraction itself must not contribute to the destruction of the productive forces. This rules out forced labor levies and taxes in cash or kind which are imposed in such a way as to brutalize the population, as well as temple sacrifices which are extracted using religious mystification (as opposed to rituals which actually expand the capacities of participants). It also rules out slavery, which violates the principle of subsidiarity.

Finally, exercise of the right of dominion must allocate resources to higher order activities, not just accidentally, but through the application of necessary rules. This means that extraction of surplus through market mechanisms—interest, dividends, and rents—is illicit because this surplus is allocated to individual consumption or capital accumulation rather than capacity building. Similarly, it must be clear that dominion is not in any sense a consumption right, but a right to resources for production. Systems at a higher level of development have no greater claim on consumption than those at a lower level of development, and attempting to increase consumption constitutes a wrong and is *prima facie* evidence that the system in question is, in fact, operating at a very low level of development.

We should note, finally, that it is possible for the right of dominion to come into conflict with the right of subsidiary sociality. Resolution of this conflict must proceed along the lines of the principle of optimum overall development. Consider, for example the question of the optimum division of surplus between a group of direct producers, who can be counted on the use it productively, to expand their capacities through education, travel, etc. and an advanced research project which will vastly expand human capacities, but which very few people understand, and thus very few can actively support. The only general rule in this case is that both activities merit some share of the surplus. The optimum allocation depends on a prudential judgment regarding just what combination of investments will, over the infinite totality of space and time, lead to the highest overall level of development. In making this determination it is necessary to take into account not only estimates of the relative gains from each activity considered in isolation, but also positive and negative feedbacks between the activities. Taxing people against their will in order to support a research project they do not understand may, for example, encourage passivity or resentment, and thus hold back the political development of the people. But the project might also open up new opportunities for the people which they hitherto never imagined. Similarly, restricting opportunities for advanced research might discourage people from entering that sort of work, and thus have repercussions far beyond a decision not to fund a specific project. But higher levels of education and culture might also create a broader constituency for advanced research, and create a larger pool of people thinking creatively about higher order problems.

Hierarchical right is grounded in the actual capacity of the system in question to act in such a way which best promotes the development of complex organization. Specific rights may and in fact must be codified in positive law and sanctioned by the public authorities. Respect for these positively defined rights is then required under the right of public order. At the same time, the failure of the public authorities to properly define rights in positive law does not obviate the existence of these rights. On the other hand, the fact that a right has been defined in positive law does not by itself create that right. The existence of a right requires the latent potential in which that right is grounded as well as actual exercise of that capacity in accord with cosmic law. The fact that a right was defined in positive law offers no protection to those who exercise it if it turns out that no such right actually existed.

Similarly, the right of hierarchy may and indeed must be violated where doing so best serves the interests of promoting the development of complex organization. While in principle hierarchy transcends and takes precedence over subsidiarity, both are simply applications of the larger principle of cosmic law, which must always be kept in mind as the real criterion of action.

It should be clear, in conclusion, that the principle of hierarchy creates no absolute claims on the part of individuals or organizations, whether to resources, or to assent of the intellect and/or will. Hierarchy is a regulative principle, balancing that of subsidiarity, which is intended to promote the development of complex organization. The only absolute claim is that of Being as such, and after that of Cosmos herself, and all systems within her, to grow and develop.

SOCIAL SCIENTIFIC PRINCIPLES

Theoretical Foundations

The principles which we have identified above are universally valid for all human societies. They can be properly applied, however, only on the basis of a correct understanding of social conditions. This, in turn, requires that we understand both how human societies in general operate, and also the specific dynamics of the society to which the principles are to be applied. Social ethics, in other words, presupposes not only an ethical theory but also a social theory and a social analysis.

Finding such a theory presents us with more problems than one might imagine. Most liberal and liberationist thought has assumed that it is possible to simply appropriate one of the existing social theories, or else work a sort of synthesis between them (Baum 1976, Segundo 1976). Social theory, after all, is simply a tool for understanding how societies work, and thus for affecting them. The principles which govern our intervention into the public arena will come from another source—from philosophy or theology.

Critics from both the *Communio* and *Radical Orthodoxy* tendencies (Ratzinger 1984, Milbank 1991) have shown convincingly that matters are not nearly so simple. Essentially all modern social theory is constitutively secularist. By this I mean not that it takes for granted the idea that religion will gradually lose its influence in the public arena, and that this is, on the balance, a good thing, but that it *defines* its formal object in such a way as to not only prescind from but actually negate humanity's larger spiritual vocation, even when religion itself is taken seriously as a social force.

This constitutive secularism expresses itself differently in the case of different theoretical perspectives, but the underlying difficulty is the same in all cases. Human society is understood as emerging and developing without respect to any transcendental τελος, and any reference to such a τελος is treated as a means of pursuing some inner-worldly aim. Thus neoliberal theory of the sort developed by F. A. Hayek (Hayek 1988) treats religion as a spontaneous adaptation to certain social environments and thus as having survival value but not truth value. Weberian interpretive sociology (Weber 1921/1968) treats religion as essentially an instrument in an ongoing struggle between civilizations. For Durkheim (Durkheim 1911) religion is first and foremost a symbolic expression of—and a means of reinforcing—solidarity. Religion is, of course, all of these things, but it *matters*, sociologically as well as philosophically or theologically, whether or not one's survival strategy, civilizational ideal, or social bond is based on something *real* and *transcendental*, or is, rather, founded on a misunderstanding which modern social scientists can now correct, and in the process subject human society to the same sort of systematic rational control to which the physical and biological sciences (or rather the τεχνη) based on them, has subjected the rest of the natural world.

It is, interestingly enough, Marx and Engels who are actually *least* secular in that they regard human society as the highest expression of a larger cosmohistorical evolutionary process by which matter develops from lower to higher levels of organization, a process of development which, were it not cut short by the inevitable heat death of the universe, would eventually terminate in—God (Engels 1880/1940). Dialectical materialism is, in this sense, more nearly a sort of interrupted materialist pantheism than it is a true atheism. Following Feuerbach, however, Marx and Engels treat religion as a misunderstanding of this teleological dynamism, a misunderstanding which makes something *immanent* and in its supreme expression *human* into an attraction to something transcendent and divine. This *religious alienation* is the result of exploitative social structures which it helps, at the same time, to reinforce. Authentic liberation is possible only when human beings recognize themselves as not only leading participants in, but actually the masters of, the cosmohistorical evolutionary process.

It is this emphasis on mastery, rather than any specific position on the religious question, which marks modern social theory as constitutively and irreducibly secular. As we have shown in other contexts (Mansueto and Mansueto 2005) this drive towards mastery is not the result of some residual metaphysical impulse, but rather precisely a result of a univocal metaphysics which understands God as the Infinite or as Subject rather than as *Esse* as such, and makes it at least possible that humanity might achieve divinity by means of innerworldly civilizational progress.

Transcending modernity and secularism means doing sociology in a way which takes seriously not only religion, but also its object. This does not mean that sociology must pass judgment on metaphysical or theological questions (quite the contrary), but it must take humanity's ordering to transcendental ends into account as a real factor in human history.

This is (once again paradoxically) most easily accomplished by *correcting* the secularist and modernist errors in historical materialism. Historical materialism regards human society as a result of the interaction between the forces and relations of production—i.e., between technology and economic structure. As new technologies emerge they require new economic structures to organize the productive processes they make possible. Political and ideological forms grow up largely as a way to legitimate these economic structures. New technologies make old economic structures obsolete, resulting in economic crises, class struggles, and eventually social revolutions which clear away old economic structures and make way for new ones.

This is an extraordinarily powerful social theory, the explanatory power of which far exceeds that of its principle competitors. It is also, in many ways, profoundly in accord with our analysis of human nature, which stresses human creativity as a real participation in the life of God. But Marx erred, I would like to suggest, in neglecting material factors which are utterly independent of human action—i.e., the ecosystem—as well as the transcendental end to which human civilization is ordered. It is quite possible to retain both the explanatory power of historical materialism, and its focus on human creativity, while correcting these errors. A complete and rectified dialectical social theory would recognize that human civilizations are nothing more or less than the product of our efforts to achieve definite spiritual ends under definite material conditions, by means of definite social structures, and cannot be properly understood without reference to all three types of factors.

1. The *material* basis for the development of civilization is the human organism and the ecosystem or ecosystems it inhabits,

which constrain profoundly the range of survival strategies which are open to it and thus the whole pattern of social development.

2. The *formal* cause of human civilization is social structure. Social structure includes:

   2.1 *technological structures*, i.e., particular ways of reorganizing physical and biological matter,

   2.2 *economic structures*, i.e., particular ways of organizing human labor and centralizing and allocating resources,

   2.3 *political structures*, i.e., particular ways of building and exercising power,

   2.4 *ideological-cultural structures*, i.e., particular ways of organizing our experience of the universe, including ways of approaching fundamental questions of meaning and value, and

   2.5 *psycho-social structures*, i.e., particular ways of organizing the human psyche to serve the aims of the society in question.

3. The *final* cause of human civilization is *God*. But this is understood in different ways by different civilizations: Thus Medieval Europe understood itself as ordered to *Esse* as such, Medieval India to the union of *Brahman* and *atman*. We call this the civilizational ideal[1]

The lines between material basis and social structure, and social structure and teleological ordering are a bit ambiguous. Absolutely speaking the material basis is confined to the ecosystem. Technology and economics are just as much social products as politics and culture. Relatively speaking, however, the whole "built up" infrastructure of a society, including its technological apparatus and the social surplus it can generate, con-

---

1. This frankly Aristotelian approach is the result of a dual effort to address developments in the sciences which point towards the need to reintegrate teleological thinking into scientific explanation, an argument which I make in outline form in *Knowing God: Restoring Reason in an Age of Doubt* (Mansueto 2002), and will I make at much greater length in its sequel, *Knowing God: The Ultimate Meaningfulness of the Universe*, and an effort to reintegrate both ecological and spiritual considerations into dialectical and historical materialism which, when these are factored back in, *is* Aristotelian.

stitute the material foundation on the basis of which political and cultural realities develop. A religious ideology is, similarly, an integral part of the social structure, i.e., the way a particular society is organized, and not itself an end or teloV. We gain access to the way a society understands its ends, however, by analyzing its ideological-cultural structure. The same is true of the relationship between the various instances of the social structure. Organizing labor and centralizing and allocating resources both involve building and exercising power. Building and exercising power, similarly, generally involves an appeal to fundamental principles and values. This is true even in predominantly secular societies. These categories should thus be used flexibly in a way which serves the purposes of the particular analysis which is being carried out.

Now human societies develop as human beings pursue the Good as they understand it, given the constraints imposed on their perceptions by the material conditions and social structures. They develop social structures in order to make possible the pursuit of the Good under those material conditions. When those structures begin to hold back their ability to pursue the Good they challenge and attempt to modify them, sometimes gradually and incrementally, sometimes through revolutionary upheavals. Particular ways of understanding our End or purpose (i.e., particular ideologies) can serve either as catalysts for change or as means of social control.

In analyzing the dynamics of human societies it is necessary to distinguish between civilizational, structural, periodic, and conjunctural crises.[2] A *civilizational crisis* takes place when, generally after a succession of structural crises, people actually lose faith in a civilizational ideal and stop pursuing it. A *structural crisis*, on the other hand, arises from a contradiction between the social structure or complex of structures by which the civilization organizes its activities on the one hand and the underlying material conditions (i.e., the ecosystem) and/or the real ends to which people aspire. Structural crises can be, but are not always, resolved by fundamental structural change. Anasazi-Pueblo civilization expanded beyond the carrying capacity of the ecological niche it inhabited and responded to the resulting crisis by decentralizing, abandoning large temple complexes of the sort we see at Chaco for the scattered vil-

---

2. These distinctions derive from Louis Althusser and his followers (Althusser and Balibar 1968/1970), but have been modified to reflect the larger approach to social theory outlined above.

lages which we now see among the Puebloan peoples, a shift which may also reflect changes at the religious level (Stuart 2001), but which also reflects significant civilizational continuity. Roman civilization ran into a structural crisis because its basic strategy—using the surplus generated by chattel slavery to buy into the Silk Road trade—ran into insuperable limits. Logistic and ecological factors made further expansion impossible, bringing an end to the wars of conquest which provided a steady supply of slaves. The empire was forced to shift from the use of chattel slaves to the use of settled, dependent peasants, known as *coloni* and to significantly increase rates of exploitation. This exploitation was legitimated as service to the common good using Christian religious ideals, something which allowed the empire, but not, perhaps, Roman Civilization, to persist in parts of the East, where elements of the old structure served a new ideal. In the West and in the *Masreq* and the *Maghreb,* this system lacked credibility and Roman Civilization was displaced by the religious civilizations of Christendom and *Dar-al-Islam,* both of which were inspired by ideals radically different from those which shaped Rome.

Periods are characterized by well-defined approaches to resolving the fundamental tensions or contradictions within a particular social structure. One might, for example, speak of a democratic period in Hellenic Civilization, in which land reform and political concessions helped to ease the contradictions between the Athenian peasantry and the large landowners without, however, fundamentally altering the basic, petty commodity/chattel slave structure of the society. Welfare state capitalism was also such a well-defined period. Periodic crises occur when a given way of containing contradictions stops working without, however, necessitating a global change in social structure. *Subperiods* of various degrees of importance are defined by lesser shifts in strategy by the ruling classes, often in response to the development of new adversaries or competitors.

By a *conjuncture* we mean a definite moment in history defined by a specific constellation of social forces which come together to affect, or attempt to affect, change in the teleological ordering of a society (i.e., a civilizational change), in its underlying structure, or in the strategy of the ruling classes.

The Current Situation

This framework allows us to understand the current situation in a new and more profound way. Specifically, by thematizing the concept of civilizational ideal, we can understand more accurately just what modernity is about—and thus why humanity has been so disappointed by its failure. Far from representing a global abandonment of humanity's transcendental aim, modernity, like all other civilizational ideals, represents a specific way of understanding and achieving those aims. In its dominant forms modernity is founded on a univocal metaphysics which understands the first principle as the infinite or unlimited and specifically as infinite or unlimited knowledge and power. Thus the tendency among modernists not only to *characterize* but actually to *define* God as omniscient and omnipotent and thus as *sovereign*, i.e., as exercising effective control over the universe and its constituent elements. Early (Protestant) modernity recognized the existence of such a divine sovereign and sought for humanity a kind of subaltern sovereignty as His vice-regent. Positivistic high modernism, on the other hand, was skeptical about the existence of such a God precisely because it sought the full measure of divinity for human beings, and sought to achieve this by means of scientific and technological progress—including progress in the social sciences and social engineering. If positivistic modernity was generally hesitant to admit this goal even to itself (though there have always, as we pointed out in an earlier chapter, been "god-builders" and "transhumanists" of various kinds), it is because modern science early on began to generate pessimistic results such as the Second Law of Thermodynamics which almost from the beginning called radically into question the viability of that goal. And yet it could not abandon it completely, because it is what legitimates the sacrifices which modern social structures, both capitalist and socialist, have required of humanity. Humanistic modernism, finally, retained the analogical metaphysics of *Esse* which was dominant in most postaxial civilizations, but sought to transcend *contingency*, and thus implicitly to attain divinity, by means of a philosophical wisdom and revolutionary political practice which elevated humanity to the state of the unique subject-object of the cosmohistorical evolutionary process (Lukacs 1922/1971).

Modernity is in crisis for three principal reasons. First, the pursuit of the modern ideal (and specifically of the scientific modern ideal), far from liberating humanity from finitude and materiality, seems to be generating an ecological crisis of unprecedented proportions—one which may threaten the actual habitability of the earth. This is because modern industrial *techne*, rather than tapping into and nurturing existing dynamics of growth and development, dissolves such dynamics (generally by combustion) in order to release energy and do work. We are quite literally burning up the planet, and suffocating in the resulting smoke.

Second, neither of the two principal economic structures associated with modernity nor the modern sovereign nation state have been able to realize either the positivistic or humanistic variants of the high modern ideal. Both capitalism and socialism are characterized by a way of mobilizing labor—the wage relation—which results in profound alienation, undercutting the humanistic modern ideal of rational autonomy. And both are characterized by internal contradictions which ultimately lead to crisis and stagnation, thereby undercutting the scientific and technological progress which would be necessary to carry humanity beyond finitude by innerworldly means. Capitalism redeploys capital to low wage, low technology activities and drives down wages, undermining both capital formation and effective demand. Attempts to ameliorate these problems require high levels of state spending, which either leads to high deficits and rising interest rates, further undermining capital formation or to high taxes, undercutting attempts to support effective demand. Socialism, while it has demonstrated its effectiveness at carrying out basic development tasks such as ensuring food self-sufficiency and first and second stage industrialization, and at centralizing resources for civilization-building, leads to rising worker incomes coupled with shortages of consumer goods, something which leads inevitably to declining productivity and eventually to permanent stagnation.

Third, the modern sovereign nation state, (or its proxies, such as the Communist Party), to just precisely the extent to which it has attempted to become the vehicle for making humanity or a section thereof into the "unique subject object" of the cosmohistorical process has in fact undermined the most basic conditions for the cultivation of rational autonomy and democratic citizenship. To the extent that it has not aspired to such high ends, and have left room for the cultivation of rational autonomy, it has been largely an instrument of Capital in developing national economies and as such simply a stage along the way in the development of global parastatal structures which show little signs of being democratic.

Third—and most importantly—the modern ideal itself is flawed. Ultimately this flaw is rooted in bad metaphysics. The univocal metaphysics at the core of the Protestant and positivistic variants of the modern ideal understands God as the infinite or the unlimited. This leads either to a spirituality of *authority and submission*, with humanity acting as God's vice-regent, or to an attempt to actually *build* God through scientific and technological progress. In either case, the results are profoundly unsatisfying. This is because what beings actually seek is neither childlike submission nor the "bad infinity" of endless existence and unlimited power, but rather ever fuller participation in the creative power of Being itself. Scientific and technological progress can certainly be such a participation, but modern *techne*, with its effort to consume and combust the earth, and modern science, which always and only serves such *techne* are both ultimately counterfeits. It is not just that modern efforts to build God have failed, but that God cannot be built. God *is*; the divine within us—individually and collectively—must be cultivated.

Humanistic modernism presents different problems entirely. This trend, which has its roots the Radical Aristotelianism of the High Middle Ages, found its highest expression in Hegel and Hegelian Marxism. Unlike the Protestant and scientific modernism, it largely conserves, as we have noted, the analogical metaphysics of the Silk Road Era. What it seeks to transcend is not so much finitude as contingency. For Hegel as for Hegelian Marxists, philosophical wisdom rooted in democratic and/or revolutionary practice allows us to *identify* with the Idea, or with the historical process, becoming, as the early Lukacs put it, "the identical subject-object" of the historical process (Lukacs 1922/1971). In this sense it is very much in continuity with the more mystical strains of Aristotelian and Thomistic philosophy, such as those represented by Meister Eckhart. The difficulty, of course, is that we are, in fact, contingent, and no deepening of philosophical wisdom and no extension of democratic citizenship or revolutionary political practice can overcome that. Lukacs already partly acknowledged this when he argued that it is the *class* (read the Communist Party) and not the *individual* which is the authentic subject object of human history (Lukacs 1922/1971). But of course the proletariat and its political party, even if we argue that they enjoy a certain ontological privilege in virtue of their rootedness in humanity's core activity of creating, are also contingent. Thus humanistic modernism fades over into the urbane despair represented by the Frankfort School and thinkers like Adorno, an attitude which is very close to postmodernism.

This said, there *are* aspects of modernity worth conserving. From scientific modernism, we need to take away a deepened insight into *techne* as a real participation in the self-organizing activity of the cosmos. From humanistic modernism we need to conserve the ideal of rational autonomy and democratic citizenship, and to remember the sane roots of humanistic modernist politicism in the Jewish identification of *da'ath 'elohim* (knowledge of God) and the just act.

The crisis of modernity is, to be sure, only in its incipient stages. Global geopolitical dynamics are still dominated by a struggle between those who are benefiting from the emergence of a unified global market in capital, and those who are not. The former advance an agenda of at least modest ecological responsibility, free trade, investment in science and technology and (among the more progressive) human capital, multilateralism, and cosmopolitan tolerance. The latter mobilize various fundamentalisms, which are actually attempts to revive the early modern ideology of transcendent sovereign God, or religious populisms in order to shore up increasingly irrelevant nation state structures and justify at least partial delinking from the global market. In the long run, however, neither camp will be able to adequately address the crisis of the modern ideal. Neoliberal and neosocialists cosmopolitanism will be unable to answer the question of *meaning*, of what progress is *towards* and *for*; fundamentalism and populism will answer it in a way which so constrains development as to result in stagnation and decay.

It is unclear just how the crisis will unfold. It is conceivable that the party of meaning and of hope will be able to articulate a new civilizational ideal and develop structures which can realize it, reform, revolution, or some combination thereof. But most civilizational crises historically have resulted in a transition by decadence or in civilizational collapse. In the first case new ideals and institutions emerge gradually as the old ones decay. This is what happened with Hellenistic Roman Civilization in Europe. In the latter case there is an actual collapse of urban life and new beginning on the basis of radically new ideals. This has not actually happened in Afro-Eurasia since the crisis of the Late Bronze Age, but it did happen to certain civilizations in the Americas which reached a comparable point in their development at a chronologically later period: i.e., the Maya, the Anasazi, the Mississippians, etc. Total collapse seems unlikely under present conditions apart from a catastrophic war or ecological catastrophe. We need, in any case, to work for a transition by reform and/or revolution while preparing for a transition by decadence or even collapse.

A VISION AND A STRATEGY

Beyond Modernity

The principal task of social ethics in the present period is to develop a concrete vision of a future which rejects decisively the flawed modern ideal of divinization by means of innerworldly civilizational progress while re-grounding the imperative to promote the full development of human capacities—both civilizational and spiritual. This involves nothing short of defining a new civilizational ideal. We have undertaken to do this at length in another work, *Emerging from the Matrix: Spirituality and Politics in an Age of Civilizational Crisis*. Here we will offer only a few general indications.

At the outset of this work we set forth the basic philosophical and theological parameters within which it has been undertaken. At the philosophical level we affirmed a moderate realism enriched by the contributions of neuropsychology, cognitive development theory, and the sociology of knowledge, a teleological cosmology which takes the results of modern science as something which still need to be *explained* and which point toward a universe which is ultimately meaningful and ordered to a transcendental end, a dialectical metaphysics of *Esse* enriched by dialogue with the results of modern science and humanity's diverse wisdom traditions, and a radically historicized natural law ethics. At the political-theological level, we argued that humanity and human civilization are defined by a drive towards divinization, a drive which, while frustrated in each and every specific instance, nonetheless, precisely through this frustration, stretches us towards and beyond full humanity. These philosophical and theological foundations in turn ground a revision of dialectical social theory to take into account the ordering of humanity to transcendental ends and a reading of the human civilizational project which follows from this theory.

We are now in a position to show that this analysis places very specific constraints on what constitutes a viable civilizational ideal at this point in history. Both preaxial and modern civilizations regard meaning as unproblematic. In preaxial societies meaning is embodied in a shared mythos which has not yet been questioned. In modern societies, it is taken for granted that reason can resolve all questions of meaning definitively, by reducing them to purely scientific technical problems. Once those problems are resolved, humanity will enjoy unlimited, effectively divinizing, technological power or else establish itself as Subject of the cosmohistorical evolutionary process, The Axial Age metacivilizational project, on the other hand, was defined by *both* the recognition that meaning has become problematic *and* the conviction that this problematization enriches, rather than circumscribing, our search for meaning, which now gradually penetrates the entire population. It is ordered toward the creation of a public arena which is neither sacral and confessional nor secular, but which is *constituted* by deliberation around fundamental questions of meaning and value, with space for both those who find meaning and those who do not. And it insists that all activity, even the mundane activity of production, has spiritual significance, while rejecting modernist univocity and immanentism, which reduces meaning to a matter of innerworldly progress.

I would like to suggest that the potential of this Axial age project was never really exhausted, and that it in fact constitutes the main stream of the human civilizational project. The protracted process of the problematization of meaning, and of religious rationalization and democratization which defined Axial Age civilizations was cut short by the emergence of modernity. The crisis of modernity means, fundamentally, rejoining this steam.

It is the vocation of the present period to make the axial dialogue *global*, and to engage the *whole people* in deliberation around fundamental questions of meaning and value and in work which is creative and meaningful in the light of whatever principles they rationally embrace. This means, first of all, bringing all of the various axial traditions: Taoism and *dao xue*, Hinduism, Jaina, and Buddhism, Judaism, Christianity, Islam, and the dialectical tradition into dialogue with each other. It means extending what we call sapiential literacy—the ability to make and evaluate arguments regarding fundamental questions of meaning and value and thus to participate in public deliberation around ends to the entire population. It means developing a new political economy which cultivates creativity and autonomy in service to the common good. And it means retheorizing and reconfiguring the way in which we produce as an alchemical cultivation of the properties latent in matter, physical, biological, and social, rather than as a means of building God or consuming finite resources for our own pleasure.

Just what sort of civilizational ideal will emerge out of this process remains to be seen. Civilizational ideals are not, after all, simply *written*. It is, however, possible to make an informed conjecture. Imagine a global dialogue between the great axial age traditions and the principal variants of modernity. And imagine that the participants in that dialogue want to conserve the achievements of modernity while rejecting its key metaphysical error: the univocity of being. Now there have, historically, been two very different ways of rejecting metaphysical univocity: the analogical metaphysics of *Esse* which developed in Christendom and *Dar-al-Islam*, and which, as we have seen, had correlates in India and China, and the analogical metaphysics of *pattica samupadda* which developed in the Buddhist World. The first metaphysics is analogical in the sense that the phenomenal world of contingent beings is regarded as participating in, but only participating in the Necessary Being which grounds the system as a whole. The second metaphysics is analogical in the sense that because everything depends on everything else, *nothing* exists Necessarily in the sense of the Avicennist or Thomistic *Esse*, but participates in the interconnected totality (what the Hua-yen call the "jewel net of Indra") in much the same way that contingent beings participate in *Esse* as such in a Thomistic metaphysics.

While these two metaphysical traditions are diametrically opposed to each other on what is, in a sense, the most fundamental question—that of necessary Being—they both regulate the way in which other fundamental questions can be answered, and constrain those answers in strikingly similar ways. Both the metaphysics of *Esse*, for example, and the metaphysics of *pattica samupadda* at once affirm reason as the first and ordinary way of approaching fundamental questions of meaning and value, and recognize its limits and the possibility of a higher knowledge (prophetic and/or mystical) that builds on reason. Knowledge of the first principle is the logical terminus of the dialectical ascent, and yet this first principle is, itself, beyond comprehension. We cannot say what Being *is*. Nor, for that matter, for most Buddhist traditions, can we really say what *sunyata* or emptiness is. And for both traditions there is a higher sort of knowledge which transcends dialectics, while building on it—a knowledge which is experiential and nonconceptual and rooted in the practice of justice or compassion on the one hand and contemplative or meditative practice on the other.

Similarly, both the metaphysics of *Esse* and the metaphysics of *pattica samupadda* acknowledge a limited meaningfulness for the phenomenal universe. For the metaphysics of *Esse*, contingent beings participate in Being as such in proportion to their essential natures, by conserving form, by nutrition, growth, and reproduction, by sensation and locomotion, and by intellect and will. For the metaphysics of *pattica samupadda*, contingent beings participate in *sunyata* by gradually evolving towards an Enlightenment which permits them to live with joy and actually help ripen other beings. Both steer clear of the twin dangers of god-building and radical acosmism.

Finally, both metaphysical traditions embrace a kind of natural law ethics focused on ripening or cultivating being, even if they understand this ethics somewhat differently. The moral imperative is, in each case, determined by a correct understanding of reality (and not simply, as in modern ethics, by divine command or by an attempt to ground order in a world without God). In both cases, that imperative consists in cultivating intellectual and moral capacities and in building a social structure which does the same.

The next steps in the human civilizational project will, we would like to argue, be focused on a new ideal of cultivating or ripening being, and characterized by a vigorous debate regarding just what that means. The metaphysics of *Esse* and the metaphysics of *pattica samupadda* constitute, in effect, two poles and two starting points for that discussion. In between lie the diverse alternatives presented by Chinese and Hindu metaphysics—the former, as we have argued elsewhere, actually very close to the metaphysics of *Esse*, but informed and moderated by a direct dialogue with Buddhism, the later a conscious step back from Buddhist otherworldliness. The next civilizational ideal will, furthermore, be defined by a *global* debate. It will no longer be possible, in other words, to write Thomism without engaging Buddhist as well as Augustinian critiques. It will no longer be possible to write *dao xue* without engaging *nyaya* and Asharite critiques. And more will be debated than simply principles. Thus the tradition of sharp polemics between clearly defined theoretical alternatives which defines the public arena in the West (here understood to include *Dar-al-Islam*) and *sometimes* China as well, will be challenged by the Hindu and Chinese models of pluralism. In the Hindu tradition, alternative *darshanas* or perspectives are regarded as partly competing and partly as working out a division of labor in which one excels at logic and epistemology, another at cosmology, and still another at metaphysics. Alternative religious aims *moksa* (liberation), *dharma* (right conduct), *artha* (wealth and power), or *kama* (pleasure) are accepted as appropriate to different individuals with different callings or levels of karmic development. And for those who seek *moksa*, there are many different paths open: *jnana* or knowledge, *dharma* or right conduct, and *bhakti* or devotion. In the Chinese tradition various philosophical and theological schools are integrated into a higher synthesis using the Chinese Buddhist practice of *p'an chiao*, in which, with each regarded as representing a partial truth appropriate to beings at a certain stage of spiritual evolution (Williams 1979, Collins 1998).

This new ideal of seeking wisdom and ripening being in a radically pluralistic context will, to be sure, leave plenty of room for those who do not find meaning. Doubt is fundamental to the axial project and respect for those who remain in doubt is the condition of any real progress beyond it. Nor will advocates of the various forms of the modern ideal simply vanish, any more than traditional Hindus or Confucians did in the modern era. But the overall tenor of the society will be very different. Let us see how.

The Structural Dynamics of Ripening Being

Human civilizations pursue their ideals under definite material conditions and using definite social structures. Civilizational ideals do not determine structures, but they do constrain them and, more specifically, define a certain social-structural problematic in the context of which struggles around social structure unfold. The development of these structures is also constrained significantly by what remains from earlier civilizations. The structural dynamics of the next steps in the human civilizational project thus depends significantly on which of the potential scenarios which have identified actually unfolds.

This said, it is, nonetheless, possible to describe in broad outlines the likely structural characteristics of humanity's next civilization. We can do this by reasoning from the constraints under which those structures are likely to emerge. On the one hand, humanity will either be struggling to contain and rectify a profound ecological crisis, or else emerging from a civilizational collapse engendered, at least on part, by an ecological crisis it was unable to contain. Harmony with the ecosystem is thus likely to be a fundamental criterion by which social structures are judged. On the other hand, the next steps in the human civilizational project are likely to be characterized by an ongoing search for meaning and a focus on "ripening being," as well as by vigorous debate regarding just what that means, with a spectrum of interpretations reaching from a Jewish, Christian, or Islamic metaphysics of *Esse* to a Buddhist metaphysics of *pattica samupadda*.

What follows may seem to some to be utopian. It is not, at least in the sense in which that term has been used in the dialectical tradition. It is not, in other words, simply a vision of a world which "ought to be" based on a certain set of ethical presuppositions. It is, rather, a real resolution, or rather a set of parameters for a set of possible resolutions, to the crisis of modernity. As such, while we will not make any claims on behalf of its inevitability (total civilizational collapse *is* possible), it has powerful social forces behind it, forces which will constrain and channel the course of history and shape, if not determine, the next steps in the human civilizational project.

Neoalchemical and Synergistic Technologies

These constraints will be reflected in all of the principal structural spheres, and will result in a fundamental break with modernity. Consider the question of technological regime. We have already noted that one of the most profound dimensions of the current civilizational crisis is the contradiction between industrial technology and the integrity of the ecosystem. This should have come as no surprise. Industry is based, as we have noted above, on breaking down existing forms of organization to release energy and do work. The result will, therefore, almost inevitably be resource depletion as we use up first fossil fuels and then fissionable fuels (what Buckminster Fuller called our planetary trust fund) and global warming and pollution as the waste products accumulate and undermine the integrity of the ecosystem.

This developing ecological crisis has given rise to a number or responses, many of which are merely reformist (Baxter 1974)—suggesting better regulation of industrial technologies—and others which can only be called antihuman. "Deep ecologists" for example, call for reducing the human population planet to essentially Paleolithic levels, on the premise that the planet cannot sustain a higher human population without inevitable damage to its overall ecological viability (Naess 1989). Reformist proposals of the first sort, while they may help stave off crisis until more profound solutions can be developed, fail to address the underlying problem; "deep ecology," on the other hand, is based on an incorrect understanding of all life as essentially equal, a position which is inconsistent in privileging life, but not its more complex and creative forms, and is static, privileging one stage in the evolution of ecosystems over all others.

There is, however, an alternative: a return to an alchemical *techne*, one which cultivates the existing potentials in matter rather that dissolving them to release their energy.

We are not, to be sure, advocating a revival of the specific theories and techniques of medieval alchemy, any more than we argue for a restoration of the specifics of Aristotelian physics. Above and beyond the changes in cosmography which have taken place in the past several hundred years, which we regard as basically valid, humanity has discovered that growth and development takes place in the system as a whole, and not just in individual organisms. Thermodynamics, complex systems theory, evolutionary biology, and dialectical sociology have all, also, pointed to the critical role of chaos, struggle, and disintegration in the evolutionary process. This changes somewhat the way in which we understand the aim of cultivation and alchemical transformation. Rather than seeking a "philosopher's stone" which can confer on all things the incorruptibility of the divine, we seek rather to help each system not only realize its latent potential, but also —perhaps through a process which involves considerable struggle and even death—to transcend the limits of its essence is and to become something new and still more beautiful.

What will this look like in practice? As with all dimensions of social structure, the next technological regime will be characterized by struggle within a new problematic rather than by any one uniform pattern. One tendency will build on and extend the internal dynamics of late modern science, especially those disciplines which challenge the mechanistic paradigm of high modernity, such as relativity, quantum mechanics, complex systems theory, and evolutionary and developmental biology, until it creates a technology which is more alchemical than modern. Another will delve deeply into and attempt to revive the premodern scientific and technological disciplines of many different cultures and extend them using methods and resources which (even when they deny it) will owe much to modernity, discovering, for example, just how Chinese and Ayurvedic medicine work and perfecting new techniques drawing on what seemed the dead end of medieval Christian and Islamic alchemy. In between these two tendencies there will grow up an entire spectrum of new technologies which, like R. Buckminster Fuller's synergetics, integrate modernist elements with ancient (in his case Pythagorean) traditions.

At the beginning of this transition there will appear to be a profound tension between those who "still" want to build starships and those who prefer to tend herb gardens in the shadow of some great cathedral, with only a visionary few understanding that these are and always have been just two dimensions of a single task: that of ripening being. But as the transition proceeds new ways of creating will emerge which break down these barriers. Our road to the stars will turn out to have more to do with the shadow of that old cathedral than we ever imagined, while the new cathedrals we build will be enriched by our journeys to the stars and become true monuments to humanity's evolving participation in the creative life of God.

The Political Economy of Self-cultivation and the Common Good

The economic arena will also be characterized by sharp tensions. Because of its focus on ripening being, the next civilizational ideal will, to a very large extent, require that economic decisions be justified in reference to the common good: i.e., by the promotion of complex organization generally and the cultivation of human capacities and civilizational progress in particular. We will ask, in other words, not "does this structure or policy contribute to economic growth and thus to the (usually hidden) aims of building God by scientific and technological means or of elevating humanity to the level of Subject of the cosmohistorical evolutionary process?" but rather "does this structure or policy contribute to ripening being, individually and collectively?"

Concretely, our break with modernity will be a break with *both* the generalized commodity production *and* centralized bureaucratic planning (although both will likely persist for some time). The rejection of generalized commodity production follows naturally from a recognition of contradictions of capitalism which Marx identified long ago: the alienation engendered by the wage relation and the fact that markets lack any way to access information regarding which activities serve the common good. The rejection of bureaucracy follows from a recognition of the limitations of actually existing socialism (especially the tendency towards a scissors crisis), as well as of the way bureaucracies function within capitalist societies.

The question, of course, is what will replace generalized commodity production and state planning. At the broadest level, we can expect to see a return to regulated petty commodity production: i.e., a system in which there are diverse ways of organizing labor and diverse forms of property which interact freely in an open marketplace, but in which the commodification of labor and capital are excluded and the operation of the system as a whole is regulated in order to promote human development and civilizational progress.

Within this context we can expect to see at least five different ways of organizing resources for production. First, we can simply decentralize the use of what has long been humanity's principal mechanism for centralizing resources for investment in human development and civilizational progress: taxation. While there are, undoubtedly, projects which are so large that they will require an essentially global taxing authority (e.g., space exploration), and while we may want to require that all communities fund certain basic needs and invest in institutions essential to human development, there is no reason why the centralization and allocation of resources by means of taxation cannot be radically decentralized. This is especially true given the relative decline of nation states vis-à-vis cities as the defining units of the global economy. If the principal taxing authority rested with cities, rather than with nation states, there would be far greater diversity in the way resources were deployed.

It is also useful to mention, in this regard, one of the principal economic achievements of the older civilizational tradition we hope to re-engage: the *zakat*, the tax on wealth which forms one of the five pillars of Islam. Because it is a tax on wealth, the poor pay very little, while the rich are compelled to invest their resources in a way that produces growth, lest their patrimonies gradually be taxed away.

A second way to ensure that resources are used in a way which serves the common good without promoting bureaucratic centralization is to endow educational, scientific, charitable, and religious organizations with claims on the surplus generated by particular economic enterprises. This is, of course, already common under capitalism and it was also common in most Silk Road societies, but it is worth considering how the wealth of the nonprofit sector might be expanded. It is important, to be sure, to find ways to protect those who labor for such enterprises. There is no guarantee that a university or a religious institution with claims on the surplus produced by a group of workers will not become exploitative. But this approach does ensure that the surplus will be used in a way which promotes human development and civilizational progress.

Third, we can change that way in which we write corporate charters. We currently require that nonprofit corporations use their resources in a way which serves the "exempt" purpose of the organization. There is no reason why for-profit charters could not gradually be rewritten to contain similar requirements. This means, of course, understanding that the mission of a corporation is to produce some useful good or service, not to make profits for stockholders. The result would be a gradual phasing out of dividend payments, reduction of executive salaries, and so forth, and ultimately the end of the financial markets and the market in capital generally. Banks would be transformed into something more like private foundations. This does not mean, however, that the corporations would fall under state control. Rather, they would be governed as nonprofit corporations are currently governed, with significant leeway as to the way in which they allocate their resources, as well as the right to form strategic alliances, and so forth. Private stockholding would essentially disappear, and corporations would be owned and controlled by their workers, subject to the regulations specified above. We call this the "social charter" system.

These last two approaches are a way to accommodate the likely persistence of larger enterprises in the economy, while encouraging greater social responsibility without bureaucratic centralization.

Fourth, we can re-build the guild system, which linked what was, essentially, the private ownership of small enterprises with collective self-regulation of quality, prices, training, and working conditions. The guild system had the advantage of limiting competition based on price and forcing competition based on quality, something which contributed significantly to helping backward medieval Europe enter the Silk Road economy as an export of high-end manufactured goods. This approach has potential not only in traditional artisanal sectors which have experienced a renaissance in recent years, but in information economy and high technology activities which are characterized by a large number of small firms.

Finally, in some regions and some sectors of the economy (or in the event of a transition by decadence or civilizational collapse, rather than by reform or revolution) still less centralized options exist. Neocommunitarian and neomonastic forms (with or without fully communal living) may be attractive options under certain conditions: a highly productive, intensive agrarian, handicrafts (including "custom high-technology crafts"), and/or service economy (e.g., a residential school) coupled with an intact village or intentional community. The aim here is not complete autarchy. The community provides goods or services to the larger economy, and its charter forbids luxury consumption. It may even pay a tax in cash or kind. And in order to develop, the community would undoubtedly need goods and services from the outside. But because it approaches self-sufficiency, it retains an even greater autonomy in decisions about resource allocation than state or corporate systems, albeit on a much smaller scale.

What we need to keep in mind is that while all five of these structural options centralize and allocate resources for human progress, they will lead to very different trajectories of development. Consider the question of energy sources. Full development of safe fusion energy is likely only under a system with significant state centralization of resources for research and development. Neocommunitarian or neomonastic systems, on the other hand, are likely to favor development of solar energy, because of the greater independence it affords. Social charter systems, or the social charter sector in a larger system, while freed from the market pressures which favor continued use of fossil or fissionable fuels, might tend to be a bit more opportunistic, each organization favoring whatever energy source helped it carry out its own mission. State-centralizing systems make space exploration possible; at least with current technologies neocommunitarian structures do not—but they do conserve social fabric and provide a rich context for certain forms of artistic, scientific, philosophical, and religious development. On the other hand there is little reason why either the state or small communities ought to, or would want to, be involved in making heavy machine tools. Clearly we need some combination of all these systems, and different regions will likely opt for somewhat different combinations. The choice between these different options depends in large part on forces over which we will have at best very limited control: the relative weight of the various social classes within the civilizational bloc, and the conditions under which we are organizing the transition. A revolutionary or reformist transition clearly favors the use of taxation, though there is no reason why it cannot conserve significant social space for the social charter and neocommunitarian options. A transition through decadence and renewal clearly favors the social charter and neo-communitarian options—the latter more strongly the deeper and more rapid the disintegration. Even so, any form of organization will require the existence of some institution which exercises at least minimal political functions: the administration of justice and the defense of the realm, as well as institutions which provide intellectual and moral leadership.

A Public Arena Constituted by Deliberation Around Fundamental Questions of Meaning and Value

The third arena in which humanity will be breaking with distinctly modern structures is that of political authority. This break will occur along two principal axes. First, there will be a global rejection of the sovereign nation state. Sovereignty is, as we noted above, in many ways the constitutive relation of modernity and in rejecting the modern ideal we reject sovereignty as well. In the place of sovereign states we will see, instead, the emergence of complex interpenetrating and overlapping networks of political authority. The most important level of authority will, increasingly, be cities. This is because the city—with its hinterlands—is the natural unit of human civilization and is increasingly the principal unit of the global economy as well. We have already discussed the importance of recognizing for cities the right to tax the way sovereigns currently do. Cities will also play the leading role in developing public educational and cultural institutions. Larger political units—if they are to be relevant at all—will increasingly be collaborations among cities around ecological, technological and economic projects, while nation states, rendered culturally heterogeneous by global migrations and economically heterogeneous by globalization, will become increasingly irrelevant.

This said, we will also witness the emergence of supranational political entities, and especially of an increasingly effective international political authority. This will not be a "world state," and even regional entities like the European Union are likely to become less rather than more state-like. Rather, this political authority will have two principal functions: 1) to address issues and undertake projects which, such as the ecological crisis or space exploration, simply cannot or should not be handled at the local level, and 2) to serve as a final political guarantor for peace and human rights. It will, in effect, establish certain minimum standards which city-states must meet, without telling them how to meet them, and will undertake global projects which smaller jurisdictions cannot handle.

Second, we will witness a fundamental change in the way in which we understand democracy. Up until now, democracy has been primarily a debate about means (i.e., about how to realize the modern ideal). Increasingly it will become a debate around ends (i.e., a debate around fundamental questions of meaning and value). This does not mean that policy level debates will disappear, but rather that we will witness the emergence of a new layer of public discourse. This dynamic will be intensified by global communications and global migrations. The result will be to render essentially impossible a polity that is either secular or confessional, for the simple reason that there will rarely be a majority which accepts either a single religious tradition or one or another variant of secular modernity. It will become necessary, if public discourse is to be meaningful, to address the prior questions—questions about what it means to be human—which even now lie behind public policy debates and render them often unproductive.

This second change will reinforce the first. While the radical pluralism of the emerging civilizational project will inhibit any trend towards theocracy or the sacralization of political authority, it will become increasingly clear that the most important leaders are precisely those who lead public deliberation around fundamental questions. Such leaders will not replace political leaders as we currently understand them—those who focus on building power or on policy questions—but the effect will be to inhibit the formation of *any* sovereign authority. Building and exercising power will become increasingly complex and will require serious engagement with fundamental questions.

A Spirituality of Meaning and Self-Cultivation

The final structural characteristic of humanity's new civilizational project will be the emergence of a spirituality of meaning and self-cultivation. This represents a sharp break with the principal spiritual options presented by modernity: either submission to a sovereign God or the pretense that spirituality is unimportant, *passé*, or even delusional, either as a cover for modernist immanentism and self-divinization or as a result of authentic despair. And it represents a real re-engagement with the spiritual traditions of axial civilizations—but with a powerful difference. In early stages of the axial project, sapiential literacy was limited to a small sector of the population. Even where people aspired to full participation in religious life, this was not a real option for them, and ordinary religious leaders became, in effect, mediators between the elite engaged in axial breakthroughs and the masses that could not really assimilate or understand them. As a result, even traditions which held reason in high respect—dialectical philosophy, Confucianism, Catholicism—often became quite authoritarian.

Today this situation is already changing. Increasingly ordinary people are insisting on making their own decisions regarding fundamental questions of meaning and value. Often, because we have yet to achieve anything like authentic widespread sapiential literacy, this has meant that people become attracted to movements which promise cheap grace (evangelicalism) or cheap wisdom (the New Age). But this simply presents those of us who are the custodians of humanity's spiritual heritage with a new challenge. We must find a way to lead effectively under radically new conditions. And this means, first of all, cultivating real sapiential literacy—an ability to make and evaluate arguments regarding fundamental questions of meaning and value—among the people. It also means respecting the right of people to make their own choices in the spiritual realm.

This need not—indeed must not—entail a derogation of spiritual authority. On the contrary, it demands that spiritual leaders function at a fundamentally higher level of sophistication. It also means that if they can meet this challenge, their influence will, as we suggested in the previous section, expand very significantly. But it does mean that they must actually have something to offer. They must actually lead rather than simple demanding deference.

If these conditions are met—if we can cultivate real sapiential literacy among ever broader sectors of the population, and if we can identify and train spiritual leaders who can lead a literate *laos*, we will soon find people turning away from movements which offer cheap grace and cheap wisdom, and gravitating instead to those institutions which are most demanding but which because of this have the most to offer them. It is just precisely such institutions, I would like to suggest, which will lead the coming transition.

Strategic Directions

Modern Strategic Theory

Most strategic thinking in the modern era has been dominated by *evolutionary* and *revolutionary* approaches to social change. By an evolutionary approach we mean one which regards social change as the result of the gradual development of one or more aspects of the social system. In the modern world this has generally meant scientific and technological progress, though there have been theorists such as Immanuel Kant and Eduard Bernstein who have argued that human history is driven by a sort of moral progress. Evolutionary approaches are incompatible with the dialectical sociology presented in this work for the simple reason that they tend to vastly underplay the importance of fundamental structural obstacles to development and thus to the need for revolutionary ruptures if progress is to continue.

By a revolutionary theory we mean just precisely one which recognizes the necessity of such ruptures as well as the need for conscious leadership in catalyzing and navigating them. The most prominent revolutionary strategy in the modern period was, of course, Lenin's. Lenin argued that generalized commodity production systematically produced ideological deformations which kept the vast majority of the working class from seeing the need for structural change. This made it necessary to form a vanguard of revolutionaries who understand the "line of march, conditions, and ultimate general result" of the struggle, and are thus able to lead it. This vanguard then waits for the development of a revolutionary situation—i.e., a situation in which "the people can no longer live in the old way and the ruling class can no longer rule in the old way." It then puts forward transitional demands—demands that the people fully understand and support, such as "land, bread, and peace" (the demands which the Bolsheviks put forward in 1917) or national liberation and democracy, but which the ruling classes *cannot* meet without threatening their very existence. This allows the vanguard to come power with the full support of the vast majority of the people, without having to actually raise the population to the level of fully communist consciousness.

There are a number of difficulties with this strategy, not least of which is the fact that it makes no real provision for actually including the majority of the people in the revolution which is made in their name. Alternative revolutionary strategies, such as those advanced by Bogdanov and Gramsci attempt to remedy this. Bogdanov, for example, argued that the principle function of the vanguard is to actually educate the people. Gramsci advanced a strategy of cultural hegemony in which the vanguard penetrates cultural institutions and then uses them to create a cultural consensus for revolutionary social transformation, drawing on popular religion, for example, to build a bridge to socialist consciousness.

These culturalist approaches are clearly more compatible with the larger social theory advanced here, which stress the role of civilizational ideals in catalyzing and ordering social progress, but they suffer one very serious difficulty: they remain irreducibly modernist—i.e., they aim at the conquest of sovereignty, even if by less coercive and more inclusive means. This is a mistake not only because sovereignty or state power has proven itself a less effective instrument of social transformation than modern revolutionary theory had hoped, but because it conceals a hidden spiritual aim which is the real object of the struggle for sovereignty. Both Leninism and its culturalist variants are ultimately ordered to divinization by means of revolutionary practice, i.e., by elevating the proletariat, through its vanguard, to the status of Subject of the cosmohistorical evolutionary process. As we have seen this project is fundamentally mistaken, based as it is on bad metaphysics.

RIPENING BEING

But if modern strategic theory is so profoundly mistaken, we will need an alternative. This might seem rather daunting, but both our underlying social theory and our reading of history suggest a clear alternative: a return, albeit on a more conscious basis, to a strategic paradigm more familiar in axial than in modern civilizations, in which religious elites, often organized in orders or schools, made a conscious effort to promote their vision and transform society both through scholarship, teaching, and public debate and through engaging existing institutions (including the dominant political and religious authorities) and building new ones, political, economic, and technological as well as religious, without aiming for or expecting to achieve anything like sovereignty.

Just what would such a strategy look like in the present period? Let us see. We face two principal strategic challenges in the present period. We must, first of all, re-constitute the core disciplines of human civilization—those which order a civilization towards transcendental ends, which we call the *sapiential disciplines*, and rebuild the sapiential institutions and sapiential intelligentsia which cultivate them. More specifically, we need to build, out of the many institutions of civil society currently engaged in the work of civilization building, political-theological organizations which can exercise conscious leadership in the next steps in the human civilizational project. Second, these organizations must then both engage existing institutions and build new ones—institutions which foster a spirituality of meaning and self cultivation, a new public arena constituted by deliberation around fundamental questions of meaning and value and a political economy which is not only in harmony with the ecosystem and with humanity's fundamentally creative nature, but which actually taps into and cultivates the latent potentials of both. Let us look at each task in some detail. Let us look at each task in turn.

Philosophy and theology have been under assault throughout the modern era. Philosophy, which included and built on the sciences and which regulated theological discourse, found itself under attack as early as the thirteenth century (or earlier in *Dar-al-Islam*) by theologians for whom analogical metaphysics represented an assault on their new ideal of the sovereignty of God. The hermeneutic disciplines, formerly an auxiliary to theology concerned with the interpretation of sacred texts, contributing to but not determining theological judgment, became, in the context of Reformation Christianity (and Asharite Islam), essentially the whole of a theology which understood itself as, purely and simply, interpreting the revealed word of God. Those who rejected this theology took refuge in the interpretation of the texts of earlier and other civilizations, now misunderstood as "secular." These two developments together constituted something called "the humanities," a science of meanings which can be rationally investigated and interpreted, but embraced, if at all, only on nonrational grounds. The sciences, meanwhile, abandoned teleological explanation, which had served as a propaedeutic to rational metaphysics, in favor of mathematical formalization, which was the precondition for understanding how the universe worked and thus bringing it under rational human control. Philosophy was reduced to what Roy Bhaskar has called "underlaboring" (Bhaskar 1989, 1993) for other disciplines: investigating the conditions of their possibility, clarifying linguistic confusions, etc. Authentically and organically premodern religious traditions, meanwhile, tended for the most part to regard the extension of modern education as a threat, and turned inward, relying for support on largely preliterate, premodern constituencies. With the exception of a few dissenters operating on the margins of traditional religious institutions (Thomism) or the socialist and communist movements (critical theory) humanity was left without intellectuals capable of leading reflection around fundamental questions of meaning and value.

Our task with respect to this situation is complex and multidimensional. On the one hand, we need to reconstitute philosophy and theology as architectonic disciplines which rationally investigate fundamental questions of meaning and value, drawing on the results of the sciences and the hermeneutic disciplines, but subjecting those results to the scrutiny of a higher rationality—i.e., precisely a rationality focused on questions of ends and purposes. This new philosophy and theology cannot, however, operate any longer within the context of a localized civilizational tradition or even in the context of dialogue with neighboring civilizations. They must, rather, be authentically global in character, with Thomists, as we suggested above, engaging critiques advanced by Hua yen Buddhists and practitioners of Advaita Vedanta answering the objections of practitioners of *dao xue* and Hanafi *fiqh*.

But there is more at stake hear that simply restoring the status of philosophy and theology as intellectual disciplines. We must heal the wounds created by the Augustinian Reaction and the Averroist Counter-Reaction, which gave birth to the Protestant and humanistic modern ideals respectively and thus lead to the marginalization of philosophy and theology in the first place. This means restoring the mutual respect which dialectics on the one hand and supra-rational wisdoms on the other hand owe to each other. No spiritual claim can be legitimate if it contradicts human reason, but there *are* truths which transcend rational demonstration and when reason denies this it either forgoes the possibility of divinization, which is our true end, or else falls into the trap of delusional, purely innerworldly strategies for transcending contingency, strategies which always lead to disappointment.

Reconstituting the sapiential disciplines means reconstituting the sapiential institutions and intelligentsia. Historically, the highest levels of the sapiential intelligentsia have been organized by three principal types of institutions: the monastery or religious order, the university, and the communist party. All three offer useful models but all three also suffer from serious defects. Monasteries and religious orders have recognized the ordering of humanity to transcendental ends and understood correctly their own identity as communities of those seeking perfection. There has been a tendency, however, greater in the case of monastic than of mendicant communities, towards withdrawal from rather than transformation of society. The celibate character of most such communities, in particular, means that they have not been able to offer the people as a whole a credible model of spiritual excellence, which is inevitably pit against worldly engagement and civilization building. Communist parties, on the other hand, have been world-transforming but have denied humanity's transcendental vocation and often failed to cultivate intellectual and moral excellence among their members. And, of course, the ideal of immanentist self-divinization which defines the communist ideal is part of what this work is rejecting.

Universities represent a rather different problem altogether. They are not, strictly speaking, political theological organizations—tertiary social actors which aim at conserving or transforming a civilizational ideal—but rather institutions of civil society, and more specifically collections of guilds *some* of which *historically* cultivated disciplines which by their very nature (philosophy, theology, and to a lesser extent politics and law) conserved and/or transformed civilizational ideals. From the very beginning the university was always in danger of treating the special rights of the professoriate (those associated with academic freedom) as ends, rather than as means to even higher goods essential to the human civilizational project. And universities have, as we have seen, largely fallen from their historic vocation and become specialized research and training institutions serving the needs of global Capital. At the same time, universities *do* offer something which neither the religious order nor the communist party ever had: a culture of ideological pluralism and debate.

As we rebuild the sapiential intelligentsia we will need to find new forms of political theological organization appropriate to the next steps in the human civilizational project. It is not possible to specify in advance what such forms of organization will look like, but only to identify some broad characteristics. They will, first of all, recognize humanity's ordering towards transcendental ends, though they may understand those ends very differently. Second, they will recognize the contributions of both humanity's ancient spiritual traditions (pre- and post-axial) *and* of modernity (both modern science and modern critical humanistic scholarship) and will, therefore, be located and act not so much *within* particular wisdom traditions as in relation to all of them, even when they advocate a specific political-theological position. Third, they will join goals of spiritual perfection and civilizational building, of personal regeneration and revolutionary transformation (though perhaps in varying measures). At least some will attempt to show what it means to seek perfection while living in the world, and will thus include not only as full members but among their highest level leaders individuals who are married as well as those who are single or celibate. While passionately advocating for their own perspectives, they will avoid political monopolism and hegemonism.

Finally, they will conserve the best traditions of both religious orders and the communist movement: conscientious study, service to the common good, a careful balancing of unity and principle, close ties to the people, and the practice of criticism and self-criticism.

Where will these organizations come from? Some may emerge out of the adaptation to traditional religious orders or (less likely) communist or paracommunist organizations. Something like the Turkish-based Gulen movement, for example, seems to be moving in this direction, though it is still far from having all of the characteristics identified above. Others will develop out of research, education, and organizing institutes which also become real religious communities. This is the hope for our own organization, *Seeking Wisdom*.

The members of these organizations must, we should note, not merely *claim* to be humanity's intellectual and moral, and therefore spiritual leaders. They must actually be so. This means that the minimum point of entry must be a demonstrated ability to make and evaluate arguments regarding fundamental questions of meaning and value and to make their principles and values effective in the public arena. They must also soon learn to teach others to do so—to function as effective teachers and organizers. The highest level leaders must actually contribute to humanity's ongoing deliberation regarding fundamental questions and/or be authentic institution builders. Members must also have a real commitment to ongoing spiritual development and follow a spiritual path which they have chosen thoughtfully and on basis of both rational conviction and a developing understanding of their own distinctive strengths, weaknesses and spiritual needs.

This does not, by the way, mean that members of our political theological organizations must hold university degrees. We must aim to revive the tradition of autodidact working class intellectuals and draw from the ranks of community based liberal arts programs as well as those of college and university graduates. And we must always respond with reverence when we find in our midst a true *tzadik* or *bodhisattva*, who may or may not have any formal education, but nonetheless demonstrates a heroic level of wisdom and justice.

Together, these organizations will define the true *universitas* of the new era, partly displacing existing universities from their position of global intellectual leadership and partly challenging them to rediscover their deeper calling. This is critically important. The new generation of political-theological organizations which we envision must scrupulously avoid the sectarian competition which characterized both traditional religious orders and, especially, the communist movement. On the contrary, they must model a form of engagement which is at once principled and passionate but also respectful of the many ways of wisdom. And, above all, they must avoid the illusion that by establishing hegemony and "organizing and directing the cosmohistorical evolutionary process" they can somehow find a shortcut to transcendence.

What about engaging and transforming the institutions of civil society? Formally this means a strategic alliance with procivilizational elements in the bourgeoisie and the traditional religious hierarchies, since it is they who currently control these institutions. This alliance is strategic because we share with these sectors an interest in conserving the integrity of the ecosystem, the social fabric, and humanity's civilizational traditions, including both the authentic contributions of positivistic and humanistic modernity and those of pre-axial and post-axial traditions, and in furthering civilizational progress and spiritual development, even if we are guided by different civilizational ideals. The difficulty of course, is that different elements in the bourgeoisie and religious hierarchies often support different aspects of this agenda. While both are increasingly clear on the need to confront the ecological crisis, the progressive sectors of the bourgeoisie (information, high technology, and allied finance) are more clearly committed to investing resources in developing human capacities (research, education, etc.), and generally respect and defend the value of an open, and pluralistic (if not always engaged) civil society. The religious hierarchies and, to a lesser extent the conservative sectors of the bourgeoisie understand the need to conserve the integrity of social fabric and provide support for conserving older civilizational traditions. In generally alliances with the former will be easier than with the latter, but in places where conservative sectors of the bourgeoisie are trying to transform themselves from an extractive to a knowledge based economy (e.g., the United Arab Emirates), or in situations where religious hierarchies have joined to their concern for the integrity of the social fabric and the conservation of meaning a passion for social justice and a willingness to challenge the market allocation of resources new and interesting strategic options open up. Our watchword must be careful analysis of the local situation and the changing balance of forces and the flexibility to pursue different alliances in different places, or even in the same place simultaneously.

Substantively, engaging and transforming the institutions of civil society means:

1. Promoting socially responsible investment and social entrepreneurship, while strengthening trade unions, peasant leagues, and other organizations which make "low end" ecologically and economically exploitative strategies less attractive to Capital.

2. Active engagement in the public arena, including

    2.1 participation in electoral politics, supporting or forming alliances with the parties most aligned with (and most likely to advance) the principles of strategic alliance outlined above,

    2.2 extra-electoral participation in public life through lobbying, direct action, etc., to advance the same ends.

    2.3 working to reshape public debate and create a public arena *constituted* by deliberation around fundamental questions of meaning and value by helping value based organizations become effective in the public arena through formats such as interfaith congregation based organizing and by creating public fora in which debate around public policy is explicitly linked to deliberation around the fundamental philosophical and theological questions which lie behind those debates,

3. Working within the institutions of civil society to transform them in a way which reflects our emerging civilizational ideal. This means:

    3.1 Working to transform schools and universities so that they make an authentic liberal arts education—one which cultivates free human beings and citizens capable of making and evaluating arguments regarding fundamental questions of meaning and value and public policy—accessible to everyone,

    3.2 Working to transform religious institutions so that they can creatively and effectively meet the spiritual needs of a sapientially literate laity in a post-critical globalized civilization, accepting the authentic contributions of modern science and critical humanistic scholarship as well as the *fact* and the *value* of engagement with spiritual questions in a way which is not only respectful of but actually draws on the wisdom of humanity's diverse civilizational traditions.

Rebuilding civil society, on the other hand, means building new institutions which link our emerging political theological organizations to the working classes in a way which effectively engages them in the work of civilization building. This is important even in the event of a transition by reform, because it is what will give us a mass base of support and thus sufficient weight within the procivilizational alliance advance our emerging civilizational ideal. In the event of a transition through revolution, decadence, or civilizational collapse it will give us the nucleus of a new society. Here there several distinct forms of activity stand out:

1. *We need to build our own enterprises and our own economic base of ecologically sound enterprises which engage ordinary workers in creative labor which provides economic self-sufficiency and sufficient leisure to permit civic participation and intellectual, moral, and spiritual self-cultivation.* The range of economic activities is potentially limitless, but might usefully be divided between traditional agricultural and craft activities which provide new opportunities to create and capture value in the global economy and emerging high technology activities to which our political-theological organizations can bring a distinct new emphasis. Examples of the first might include fair trade coffee, tea, and herb production, ethnobotanicals, or organic truck gardening near major urban centers to supply high-end culinary markets. Examples of the second might include software and game development which services humanistic and social science academic markets or which tells traditional and emerging stories embodying our civilizational ideal in new ways. In between lie the construction and culinary fields to which many immigrant workers bring extraordinary skills.

2. *We need to create a public arena constituted by deliberation around fundamental questions of meaning and value.* This means creating *places* where people from diverse traditions can meet and engage each other around fundamental questions and public policy debates and simply as well as the social space for such deliberation to take place. As we noted in the foregoing analysis, there is significant diversity around the planet with respect to the openness, pluralism, and engagement which characterizes civil society. This is shaped by everything from legal frameworks and political culture through ethnoreligious demographics and urban structure and religious monumentalization. As we are engaging the diverse spaces which already exist we need to create new ones which are characterized by the highest possible degrees of openness, pluralism, and engagement, and populate them with organizations which provide the people with the ability to engage in real deliberation around fundamental questions. Such spaces will be easiest to create in places with a legal framework which protects free expression and with high degrees of ethnoreligious diversity, but even in these settings there remains the difficult work of catalyzing real engagement—an issue we will look at in the next section, which addresses tactics. For now it will suffice to say that we need to create physical spaces where people can come together face to space as well as virtual spaces where they can meet across significant distances. Those spaces need to be structured in a way which promotes dialogue, deliberation, and debate, and be dominated by symbols which mediate our emerging civilizational ideal. It also means actually *organizing* deliberation through individual relational meetings, grassroots programs in the liberal arts and interreligious and intercultural dialogues, and linking this deliberation to action both within and outside existing political structures.

3. *We need to build religious congregations of a new kind which are adapted to a sapientially literate and globalized laity or at least to a laity evolving in this direction.* We have noted before both that the people increasingly aspire to sapiential literacy, to making informed, independent decisions regarding funda-

mental questions of meaning and value and that they address these questions in a way which engages not only their "native" spiritual tradition, but others as well. Congregations rooted in particular traditions will not disappear, both because large sections of the people have not undergone such a transformation and because many who have find their spiritual path and spiritual home within the disciplines of a traditional religious community. But ever broader sections of the population seek a *community* in which they can study and fashion a spiritual path which draws on the wisdom of more than one tradition. On the one hand these communities will be more intellectually focused than earlier types of congregations. On the other hand, people will demand from them what they have always demanded of local shrines and congregations: devotional space, public liturgy, rites of passage, etc.

This is, in many ways, a modest agenda by comparison with that advanced by modern strategic theories, evolutionary and revolutionary. This is not because we are less hopeful, but rather because our hope is both greater and different. We understand that humanity's destiny is not a counterfeit divinization by means of scientific and technological progress or revolutionary practice, but rather a endless journey into a divine the depth and beauty of which we cannot even begin to fathom. There is no "definitive solution to the riddle of history," much less an "end of history," but this does not mean that there is no progress or that history is simply an endless "clash of civilizations," but rather that progress is infinite if also uneven and that, to paraphrase Sandinista leader Ricardo Morales Aviles, while history has only one meaning and one direction, there are always new swords and new ways of holding our heads high.

There can be no doubt that we live in dark times. But those of us who belong to the party of meaning and of hope—which is the only true party of humanity—know that this darkness cannot last forever. The long winter of capitalism and modernity is coming to an end. Socialism was a late winter thaw which at once gave us a respite and taught us the difference between mitigating contradictions and actually resolving them. Now, beyond the present storm, we can see the first signs of spring.

Bibliography

Abu-Lughod, Janet. 1989. *Before European Hegemony: The World System AD 125-1350*. New York: Oxford University Press.
Aglietta, Michel. 1987. *A Theory of Capitalist Regulation*. London: Verso.
Aldaraca, Bridget, et al. 1980. *Nicaragua in Revolution: The Poets Speak*. Minneapolis: Marxist Educational.
Alighieri, Dante. 1300-1318/1969. *De Monarchia*. Indianapolis: Bobbs-Merrill.
———. 1300-1318/1969 *Commedia*. Translated as *The Divine Comedy* and with commentary by John D. Sinclair. New York: Oxford University Press.
Althusser, Louis. 1965/1977. *For Marx*. London: Lane.
———. 1968/1970. *Reading Capital*. London: New Left.
———. 1966-1969/1971. *Lenin and Philosophy*. New York: Monthly Review.
Amin, Samir. 1978. *The Law of Value and Historical Materialism*. New York: Monthly Review.
———. 1979/1980. *Class and Nation, Historically and in the Current Crisis*. New York: Monthly Review.
———. 1988/1989. *Eurocentrism*. New York: Monthly Review.
Anaxagoras. c. 450 BCE/1996. *On Nature*. In *Classical Greek Reader*, edited by Kenneth Atchity and Romsemary McKenna, 122-24. New York: Holt.
Anaximander. c. 560 BCE/1996. *On Nature*. In *Classical Greek Reader*, edited by Kenneth Atchity and Romsemary McKenna, 72-73. New York: Holt.
Anaximenes. c. 545 BCE/1996. *Air*. In *Classical Greek Reader*, edited by Kenneth Atchity and Romsemary McKenna, 74-75. New York: Holt.
Anderson, Perry. 1974. *Passages from Antiquity to Feudalism*. London: New Left Review.
Anselm of Canterbury. c. 1065/1969. *Prologion*. In *A Scholastic Miscellany*, edited and translated by Eugene Fairweatherl, 69-93. New York: Free.
———. c. 1065/1982. *Cur deus homo*. In *A Scholastic Miscellany*, edited and translated by Eugene Fairweather, 100-83. Philadelphia: Westminister.
Aristotle. c. 350 BCE/1946. *Politics*. Translated by Ernest Barker. Oxford: Clardendon.
———. c. 350 BCE/1952. *Metaphysics*. Translated by Richard Hope. New York: Columbia University Press.
———. c. 350 BCE/1973. *De Anima*. In *Introduction to Aristotle*, translated and edited by Richard McKeon, 153-247. Chicago: University of Chicago Press.
———. c. 350 BCE/1973. *Ethics*. In *Introduction to Aristotle*, translated and edited by Richard McKeon, 338-583. Chicago: University of Chicago Press.
———. c. 350 BCE/1973. *Physics*. In *Introduction to Aristotle*, translated and edited by Richard McKeon, 121-45. Chicago: University of Chicago Press.

Aquinas, Thomas. c. 1260/1963. *In Boethius De Trinitate*. Published as *The Division and Methods of the Sciences*, translated and edited by Rose Brennan and Armand Maurer. Accessed at http://dhspriory.org/thomas/BoethiusDeTr.htm.

———. 1272/1952. *Summa Theologiae*. Chicago: Encyclopaedia Britannica.

Arendt, Hannah. 1958. *The Human Condition*. Chicago: University of Chicago Press.

Augustine. 426/1972. *The City of God*. Translated by Henry Bettenson. New York: Penguin.

———. c. 386/1969. *Contra Academicos*. In *Medieval Philosophy*, edited by John Wippel and Alan Wolter, 33–43. New York: Free.

———. c. 395/1969. *De libero arbitrio*. In *Medieval Philosophy*, edited by John Wippel and Alan Wolter, 63–81. New York: Free.

Averroes. c. 1175/1978. *The Incoherence of the Incoherence*. Translated by Van Den Greg. David Brown.

Avicenna. c. 1025/1973. *The Metaphysica*. Translated by Morewedge Parvis. London: Routledge and Kegan Paul.

———. c. 1025/1981. *Psychology*. Translated by F. Rahmah. Westport, CT: Hyperion.

Ayer, A. J. 1937. *Language, Truth, and Logic*. New York: Oxford University Press.

Barrow, John and Frank Tipler. 1986. *Anthropic Cosmological Principle*. Oxford: Oxford University Press

Baum, Gregory. 1976. *Religion and Alienation*. New York: Paulist.

Baxter, William. 1974. *People or Penguins: The Case of Optimal Pollution*. New York: Columbia University Press.

Bennett, Charles. 1987. "Dissipation, Information, Complexity, and Organization." In *Emerging Syntheses in Science*, edited by David Pines, 215–31. New York: Addison Wesley.

Bentley, Jerry. 1993. *Old World Encounters: Cross Cultural Contacts and Exchanges in Pre-Modern Times*. New York: Oxford University Press.

Berkeley, George. 1710/1998. *Three Dialogues Between Hylas and Philnous*. Oxford: Oxford University Press.

Bhaskar, Roy. 1989. *Reclaiming Reality*. London: Verso.

———. 1993. *Dialectic: The Pulse of Freedom*. London: Verso.

Bogdanov, Alexander. 1928/1980. *Tektology*. Intersystems.

Bohm, David. 1980. *Wholeness and the Implicate Order*. London: RKP.

Boler, John. 1993. "Transcending the Natural: Duns Scotus on the Two Affections of the Will." In *American Catholic Philosophical Quarterly* LXVII:1 109–26

Bonaventura. c. 1274/1970. *Quaestiones disputate de Scientia Christi*. In *A Scholastic Miscellany*, edited by Eugene Fairweather, 379–401. New York: Macmillan.

Boniface VIII (Pope). 1296/1960. *Clericis Laicos*. In *Readings in Church History: Volume One: From Pentecost to the Protestant Revolt*, edited by Colman J. Barry, 464. New York: Newman.

———. 1302/1960. *Unam Sanctum*. In *Readings in Church History: Volume One: From Pentecost to the Protestant Revolt*, edited by Colman J. Barry, 465–66. New York: Newman.

Bucher, Martin, Alfred Goldhaber, and Neil Turok. 1995. "Open Universe from Inflation." In *Physical Review D* 52.6, 3314–37.

Bucher, Martin and David Spergel. 1999. "Inflation in a Low-Density Universe." *Scientific American* 280, 63–69.

Budiansky, Stephen. 1992. *The Covenant of the Wild*. New York: Morrow.

Cajetan [Vio, Tommaso de]. 1495/1934. In *De Ente et Essentia*, trans. L. H. Kendzierski and F. C. Wade, *Cajetan: Commentary on "Being and Essence"*, Mediaeval Philosophical Texts in Translation 14, Milwaukee, WI: Marquette University Press, 1964.

———. 1498/1953. *De Nominum Analogia*, trans. A. Bushinski and H. J. Koren, *The Analogy of Names and the Concept of Being*, Pittsburgh: Duquesne University Press.

Calvin, John. 1536/1993. *The Institutes of the Christian Religion*. Grand Rapids: Eerdmans.

Campbell, David. 1989. "Introduction to Nonlinear Phenomena." In *Lectures in the Sciences of Complexity*, edited by Erica Jen, 3–105. New York: Addison-Wesley.

Caputo, John. 1982. *Heidegger and Aquinas: An Essay on Overcoming Metaphysics*. New York: Fordham.

Chaterjee, Satischandra and Dhirendramohan Datta. 1954. *An Introduction to Indian Philosophy*. Calcutta: University of Calcutta.

Childe, V. Gordon. 1851. *Man Makes Himself*. New York: Mentor.

Ching, Julia. 2002. *The Religious Thought of Chu Hsi*. Oxford: Oxford University Press.

Coleman, John. 1991. *One Hundred Years of Catholic Social Teaching*. Maryknoll, NY: Orbis.

Cleary, Thomas. 1990. *The Tao of Politics*. Boston: Shambala.

Collins, Randall. 1998. *The Sociology of Philosophies*. Cambridge, MA: Belknap.

Confucius. c. 500 BCE/1979. *Analects*. Translated by D. C. Lau. New York: Dorset.

Daly, James. 2000. *Marx and the Natural Law Tradition*. London: Greenwich Square.

Daly, Mary. 1984. *Pure Lust*. Boston: Beacon.

———. 1998. *Quintessence*. Boston: Beacon.

Dahm, Helmut. 1988. *Philosophical Sovietology: The Pursuit of A Science*. Dordrecht: Reidel.

Damasio, Antonio. 1994. *Descartes' Error*. New York: Grosset/Putnam.

Darwin, Charles. 1859/1970. *The Origin of Species*. In *Darwin: A Norton Critical Edition*, edited by Philip Appleman. New York: Norton.

Davies, Paul. 1988. *The Cosmic Blueprint*. New York: Simon and Schuster.

———. 1994. *The Last Three Minutes*. New York: Basic.

Davis, Mike. 1986. *Prisoners of the American Dream*. London: Verso.

———. 1930. *Dialectics and Natural Science*. Moscow: n. p.

Deng Ming-Dao. 1990. *Scholar Warrior*. San Francisco: HarperSanFranscisco.

Denton, Michael. 1985. *Evolution: A Theory in Crisis*. New York: Burnett.

Derrida, Jacques. 1967/1978. "Violence and Metaphysics." In *Writing and Difference*, 79–153. Chicago: University of Chicago Press.

———. 1967/1978. "From a Restricted to a General Economy: For an Hegelianism Without Reserve." In *Writing and Difference*. Chicago: University of Chicago Press.

Descartes, René. 1641/1998. *Meditations*. Translated with an introduction by Desmond M. Clarke. New York: Penguin.

Destutt de Tracy, Antoine Louis Claude (Count). 1825–1827. *Elements d'Ideologie*. Laris: Levi.

Duhem, Pierre. 1909. *Etudes sure Léonard de Vinci*. Paris: Hermann.

Duns Scotus, John. 1301/1965. *A Treatise on God as First Principle* (*De Primo Principio*). Translated by Allan Wolter. Chicago: Franciscan Herald.

Dumezil, Georges. 1952/1977. *Les Dieux des Indo-Europeans*. Paris: Gallimar.

Durkheim, Emile. 1911. *Formes elementaires de la vie religieuse*. Paris: Alcan.

Dussel, Enrique. 1998. *Etica de la liberación en la edad de globaización y exclusión*. México: Editorial Trotta.
Eamon, William. 1993. *Science and the Secrets of Nature*. Princeton: Princeton University Press.
Eco, Umberto. 1988. *The Aesthetics of Thomas Aquinas*. New York: Random House.
Edwards, Jonathan. 1746/1957–1989. *A Treatise Concerning Religious Affections*. In *The Works Jonathan Edwards*. Vol. 2, edited by Jon E. Smith. New Haven: Yale University Press.
———. 1754/1957–1989. *The Freedom of the Will*. in *The Works Jonathan Edwards*. Vol. 1, edited by Paul Ramsey. New Haven: Yale University Press.
Elkins, James. 1999. *What Painting Is*. London: Routledge.
Emmanuel, A. 1969/1971. *Unequal Exchange*. New York: Monthly Review.
Empedocles. c. 500 BCE/1996. *On Nature*. In *Classical Greek Reader*, edited by Kenneth Atchity and Romsemary McKenna, 117–121. New York: Holt.
Engels, Frederick. 1880/1940. *The Dialectics of Nature*. New York: International.
Ezcurra, Anna Maria. 1986. *The Vatican and the Reagan Administration*. New York: Circus.
Fang, Thombe. 1981. *Chinese philosophy: Its Spirit and its Development*. Taipei: Linking.
Feuerbach, Ludwig. 1841/1957. *The Essence of Christianity*. New York: Harper.
Foucault, Michel. 1966. *Les mots et les choses*. Paris: Editions Gallimard.
Frank, Andre Gunder. 1998. *ReOrient: Global Economy in the Asian Age*. Berkeley: University of California Press.
Frank, A. G., and B. K. Gills. 1992. "The Five Thousand Year World System: An Introduction." In *Humboldt Journal of Social Relations* 18:1, 1–79.
———. 1993.*The World System: Five Hundred Years or Five Thousand?* London: Routledge.
Frend, W. 1957. *The Donatist Church*. Oxford: Clarendon.
Freud, Sigmund. 1927/1928. *The Future of an Illusion*. New York: Norton.
———. 1930. *Civilization and its Discontents*. New York: Norton.
Friedman, A. 1922. "Über die Krummung des Raumes." *Zeitschrift für Physik* 10, 377–86
Fromm, Erich. 1941. *Escape from Freedom*. New York: Winston.
———. 1947. *Man For Himself*. New York: Winston.
Fuller, Buckminster. 1975–1979. *Synergetics*. New York: MacMillan.
———. 1981. *Critical Path*. New York: St. Martin's.
———. 1992. *Cosmography*. New York: Macmillan.
Fukuyama, Francis. 1989. "The End of History." *The National Interest,* Summer 1989, 3–18.
Gal-Or, Benjamin. 1987. *Cosmology: Physics and Philosophy*. New York: Springer.
Gamwell, Franklin. 1990. *The Divine Good*. New York: Harper.
———. 2000. *Democracy on Purpose*. Washington, DC: Georgetown University Press.
Garrigou-Lagrange, Reginald. 1938a. *Les trois ages de la vie interieure*. Paris: Cerf.
———. 1938b. *La realité du principe de la finalité*. Paris: Cerf.
Gilson, Etienne. 1968. *Dante and Philosophy*. Gloucester, MA: Smith.
———. 1936. *The Spirit of Medieval Philosophy*. New York.
———. 1952. *Being and Some Philosophers*. Toronto: Pontifical Institute of Medieval Studies.
Gilson, Etienne; Langman, Thomas; and Maurer, Armand. 1962. *Recent Philosophy*. New York: Random House.

Goerner, E. A. 1965. *Peter and Caesar*. New York: Herder and Herder.
Gorbachev, Mikhail. 1987. *Perestroika*. London: Collins.
Gottwald, Norman K. 1979. *The Tribes of Yahweh*. Maryknoll, NY: Orbis.
Gramsci, Antonio. 1948. *Il materialismo storico e la filosofia di Benedetto Croce*. Torino: Einaudi.
———. 1949a. *Il Risorgimento*. Torino: Einaudi.
———. 1949b. *Note sul Macchiavelli, sulla politica, e sullo Stato Moderno*. Torino: Einaudi.
———. 1949c. *Gli intelletualli e l'organizzazione di cultura*. Torino: Einaudi.
———. 1950. *Letteratura e vita nazionale*. Torino: Einaudi.
———. 1951. *Passato e presente*. Torino: Einaudi.
———. 1954. *L'Ordine Nuovo*. Torino: Einaudi.
———. 1966. *La questione meridionale*. Roma: Riuniti.
Grant, Edward. 1978. "Cosmology." In *Science in the Middle Ages*, edited by David Lindberg, 265–302. Chicago: University of Chicago Press.
Halliwell, Jonathan. 1991. "Quantum Cosmology and the Creation of the Universe." *Scientific American* 272, 12.
Harris, Errol. 1965. *Foundations of Metaphysics in Science*. London: Allen & Unwin.
———. 1987. *Formal, Transcendental, and Dialectical Thinking*. Albany: State University of New York Press.
———. 1991. *Cosmos and Anthropos*. Atlantic Highlands, NJ: Humanities.
———. 1992. *Cosmos and Theos*. Atlantic Highlands, NJ: Humanities.
Hartle, J. B., and S. W. Hawking. 1983. "The Wave Function of the Universe." *Physical Review D* 28, 12.
Hayek, F. A. 1973. *Law, Liberty, and Legislation. Volume One: Rules and Order*. Chicago: University of Chicago Press.
———. 1988. *The Fatal Conceit*. Chicago: University of Chicago Press.
Hegel, G. W. F. 1807/1967. *Phenomenology of Mind*. Translated by J. B. Baillie. New York: Harper.
———. 1817/1990. *Encyclopaedia of the Philosophical Sciences (Outline)*. Translated by Steven Taubeneck. New York: Continuum.
———. 1830/1971. *Encyclopaedia of the Philosophical Sciences*. Translated by William Wallace. Oxford: Oxford University Press.
Heidegger, Martin. 1928/1968. *Being and Time*. New York: Harper and Row.
———. 1934/1989. *Beitrage sur Philosophie* ("Contributions to Philosophy"). Frankfurt: Klosterman.
———. 1941/1979–1987 *Nietzsche*. San Francisco: Harper & Row.
Heraclitus. c500 BCE/1996. *On Nature*. In *Classical Greek Reader*, edited by Kenneth Atchity and Romsemary McKenna, 111–13. New York: Holt.
Hesiod. c 750 BCE/1988. *Theogony*. Translated with an introduction and notes by M. L. West. Oxford: Oxford University Press.
Ho Ping-ti. 1959. *Studies on the Population of China, 1368–1953*. Cambridge: Harvard University Press.
Hobsbawm, Eric. 1959. *Primitive Rebels*. New York: Norton.
Hume, David. 1777/1886. *Enquiry Concerning Human Understanding*. London: Longmans, Green.
———. 1779. *Dialogues Concerning Natural Religion*. London: Longmans, Green.
Ingham, Mary Elisabeth, CSJ. 1993 "Scotus and the Moral Order." *American Catholic Philosophical Quarterly* 67:1, 127–40.

Innocent III (Pope). 1189. *Sicut universitatis conditor.* In *Readings in Church History: Volume One: From Pentecost to the Protestant Revolt*, edited by Colman J. Barry OSB, 438. New York: Newman, 1960.

———. 1202. *Venerabilem fratrem,* in *Readings in Church History: Volume One: From Pentecost to the Protestant Revolt,* edited by Colman J. Barry OSB, 437. New York: Newman, 1960.

———. 1204. *Novit Ille.* In *Readings in Church History: Volume One: From Pentecost to the Protestant Revolt,* edited by Colman J. Barry OSB, 436. New York: Newman, 1960

Jaki, Stanley. 1988. *The Savior of Science.* Washington, DC: Gateway.

Jaspers, Karl. 1953. *The Origin and Goal of History.* New Haven: Yale University Press.

John Paul II. 1998. *Fides et Ratio* 53. Accessed at http://www.vatican.va/holy_father/john_paul_ii/encyclicals/documents/hf_jp-ii_enc_15101998_fides-et-ratio_en.html.

John of St. Thomas. 1631–1632/1955. *Ars Logica.* Translated by F. C. Wade as *Outline of Formal Logic.* Milwaukee: Marquette University Press.

Joravsky, David. 1961. *Soviet Marxism and Natural Science.* New York: Columbia.

Kalupahana, David. 1992. *Buddhist Philosophy: An Historical Analysis.* Hilo: University of Hawaii Press.

Kant, Immanuel. 1755/1968. *Universal Natural History and Theory of the Heavens.* New York: Greenwood.

———. 1781/1969a. *Foundations of the Metaphysics of Morals.* Translated by Lewis White Beck. Indianapolis: Bobbs-Merrill.

———. 1781/1969b. *Critique of Pure Reason.* Translated by Lewis White Beck. Indianapolis: Bobbs-Merrill.

Kelly, Kevin. 1992. "Deep Evolution: The Emergence of Postdarwinism." *Whole Earth Review* 76, 4–10.

Kierkegaard, Søren. 1843/1971. *Either/Or.* Translated by David F. Swenson and Lillian Marvin Swenson, with revisions and a foreword by Howard A. Johnson. Princeton: Princeton University Press.

———. 1846/1941. *A Concluding Unscientific Postscript.* Translated by Walter Lowrie. Princeton: Princeton University Press.

Konrad, Gyrogy and Ivan Szelenyi. 1967. *Intellectuals on the Road to Class Power.* New York : Harcourt Brace Jovanovich.

Korner, Stephen. 1968. *Philosophy of Mathematics.* New York: Dover.

Krauss, Lawrence and Starkman, Glenn. 1999. "The Fate of Life in the Universe." *Scientific American,* Nov 1999, 51–57.

———. Forthcoming. "Life, the Universe, and Nothing: Life and Death in an Ever-Expanding Universe." *Astrophysical Journal,* available at xxx.lanl.gov/abs/astro-ph/9902189.

Kyrtatas, Dimitris. 1987. *The Social Structure of Early Christian Communities.* London: Verso.

Laclau, Ernesto. 1977. *Politics and Ideology in Marxist Theory.* London: Verso.

Laclau, Ernesto, and Chantal Mouffe. 1985. *Hegemony and Socialist Strategy.* London: Verso.

Lancaster, Roger. 1988. *Thanks to God and the Revolution.* Berkeley: University of California Press.

Langton, Christopher. 1989. *Artificial Life: Proceedings of an Interdisciplinary Workshop on the Synthesis and Simulation of Living Systems.* New York: Addison-Wesley.

Lao Tzu. c. 500/1972. *The Tao Te Ching*. Translated by Gia-fu Feng and Jane English. New York: Vintage.
Laplace, Pierre Simon. 1819/1951. *A Philosophical Essay on Probabilities*. New York: Dover.
———. 1799–1825/1969. *Treatise on Celestial Mechanics*. New York: Chelsea.
Lasch, Christopher. 1977. *Haven in a Heartless World*. New York: Basic.
———. 1979. *The Culture of Narcissism*. New York: Norton.
———. 1990. *The True and Only Heaven*. New York: Norton.
Leibniz, Gottfried von. 1713/1992. *Monadology*. Amherst, NY: Prometheus.
Lenin, V. I. 1902/1929. *What is to Be Done?* New York: International.
———. 1908/1970. *Materialism and Empiriocriticism*. Moscow: Progress.
———. 1916/1976. *Philosophical Notebooks* (Volume 38 of the Collected Works). Moscow: Progress.
Lenski, Gerhard, and Jean Lenski. 1982. *Human Societies*. New York: McGraw Hill.
Lerner, Eric. 1991. *The Big Bang Didn't Happen*. New York: Vintage.
Levi-Strauss, Claude. 1949/1969. *The Elementary Forms of Kinship*. Boston: Beacon.
———. 1958/1963. *Structural Anthropology*. New York: Basic.
Levinas, Emmanuel. 1965. *Totalité et Infini: Essai sur extériorité*. The Hague: Nijhoff.
Lindberg, David. 1978. *Science in the Middle Ages*. Chicago: University of Chicago Press.
———. 1992. *The Beginnings of Western Science*. Chicago: University of Chicago Press.
Linde, Andrei. 1994. "The Self-Reproducing Inflationary Universe." *Scientific American*, November 1994, 98–104.
Locke, John. 1690/1967. *Two Treatises on Government*. London: Cambridge University Press.
———. 1690/1995. *Essay Concerning Human Understanding*. New York: Dutton.
Lonergan, Bernard. *Insight*. New York: Philosophical Library.
Lukacs, Georgi. 1922/1971. *History and Class Consciousness*. Cambridge: MIT.
———. 1953/1980. *The Destruction of Reason* London: Merlin.
Luria, Aleksandr. 1973. *The Working Brain*, New York: Basic.
———. 1974/1976. *Cognitive Development*. Cambridge: Harvard University Press.
Lyotard, Jean Francois. 1979/1984. *The Postmodern Condition*. Minneapolis: University of Minnesota Press.
MacAleer, Graham. 1996. "Saint Anselm: An Ethics of *Caritas* for a Relativist Agent." *American Catholic Philosophical Quarterly* 70, 163–78.
MacIntyre, Alisdair. 1980. *After Virtue*. South Bend, IN: Notre Dame University Press.
———. 1988. *Whose Justice? Whose Rationality?* South Bend, IN: Notre Dame University Press.
Malebranche, Nicolas. 1674/1980. *The Search after Truth*. Translated by Thomas M. Lennon and Paul J. Olscamp. Columbus: Ohio State University Press.
———. 1684/1977. *A Treatise of Morality* [microform]. Translated by James Shipton. Ann Arbor, MI: University Microfilms International.
———. 1687/1980. *Dialogues on Metaphysics*. Translation and introduction by Willis Doney. New York: Abaris.
Mandel, Ernest. 1968. *Marxist Economic Theory*. New York: Monthly Review.
Mannheim, Karl. 1936. *Ideology and Utopia*. New York: Harcourt, Brace, and Co.
Mansueto, Anthony. 1995. *Towards Synergism: The Cosmic Significance of the Human Civilizational Project*. Lanham, MD: University Press of America.
———. 2002a. *Religion and Dialectics*. Lanham, MD: University Press of America.

———. 2002b. *Knowing God: Restoring Reason in an Age of Doubt*. Aldershot, UK: Ashgate.
Mao Tsetung. 1937/1971. "On Contradiction." In *Selected Readings from the Works of Mao Tsetung*, 83–133. Peking: Foreign Languages.
Margulis, Lynn and Fester, Rene. 1991. *Symbiosis as a Source of Evolutionary Innovation*. Cambridge: MIT.
Maritain, Jacques. 1938. *Degrees of Knowledge*. London: Bles.
———. 1951. *Man and the State*. Chicago: University of Chicago Press.
Marx, Karl. 1843/1978. "Contribution to the Critique of Hegel's Philosophy of Right: Introduction." In *Marx-Engels Reader*, edited by Robert C. Tucker, 16–25. New York: Norton.
———. 1844/1978. *Economic and Philosophical Manuscripts* In *Marx-Engels Reader*, edited by Robert C. Tucker, 66–125. New York: Norton.
———. 1846/1978. *The German Ideology*. In *Marx-Engels Reader*, edited by Robert C. Tucker, 146–202. New York: Norton.
———. 1848/1978. *The Communist Manifesto*. In *Marx-Engels Reader*, edited by Robert C. Tucker, 469–500. New York: Norton.
———. 1849/1978. *Wage Labor and Capital*. In *Marx-Engels Reader*, edited by Robert C. Tucker, 203–17. New York: Norton.
———. 1859/1961. *Contribution to the Critique of Political Economy: Preface*. In *Marx's Concept of Man*, by Erich Fromm, 217–20. New York: Continuum.
———. 1867/1977. *Capital*. Volume One. New York: Vintage.
———. 1881/1978. "Letter to Vera Zasulich." In *Marx Engels Reader*, edited by Robert C. Tucker, 665–75. New York: Norton.
———. 1863/1963. *Theories of Surplus Value: Part One*. Moscow: Progress.
———. 1863/1971. *Theories of Surplus Value: Part Two*. Moscow: Progress.
Matthews, Caitlin. 1991. *Sophia: Goddess of Wisdom*. London: Mandala.
Maurer, Armand. 1963. *The Division and Methods of the Sciences*. Toronto: Pontifical Institute of Medieval Studies.
———. 1993. "Thomists and Thomas Aquinas on the Foundation of Mathematics." *Review of Metaphysics* 47, 43–61.
Mayr, Ernst. 1982. *The Growth of Biological Thought*. Cambridge: Harvard University Press.
———. 1988. *Toward a New Philosophy of Biology*. Cambridge: Harvard University Press.
McCool, Gerald. 1977. *Catholic Theology in the Nineteenth Century*. New York: Seabury.
———. 1994. *The Neo-Thomists*. Milwaukee: Marquette University Press.
Meikle, Scott. 1985. *Essentialism in the Thought of Karl Marx*. London: Duckworth.
Mill, J. S. 1848/1965. *Utilitarianism*. Indianapolis: Bobbs-Merrill.
Milbank, John. 1990. *Theology and Social Theory*. London: Blackwell.
———. 1999. "The Theological Critique of Philosophy in Hamman and Jacobi." In *Radical Orthodoxy*, edited by John Milbank, Catherine Pickstock, and Graham Ward, 21–37. London: Routledge.
Merton, Thomas. 1963. *Selected Poems*. New York: New Directions.
Miranda, José Porfirio. 1972. *Marx y la Biblia*. Salamanca: Sigueme.
———. 1973. *El se y el mesias*. Salamanca: Sigueme.
Morrison: Karl. 1975. "Where are the Prophets," Address to the 355th Convocation of the University of Chicago, 29 August 1975, in *The University of Chicago Record*.

Murdoch, John, and Edith Sylla. 1978. "The Science of Motion." In *Science in the Middle Ages*, edited by David Lindberg, 206–64. Chicago: University of Chicago Press.
Naess, Arne. 1989. *Ecology, Community, and Lifestyle*. Cambridge: Cambridge University Press.
Nagarjuna, Siddha. c. 200/1970. *Madhyamakakarika*. Tokyo: Hokuseido Press.
Newton, Isaac. 1700. *The Reasonableness and Certainty of the Christian Religion*. London.
Niebuhr, Reinhold. 1941. *The Nature and Destiny of Man*. New York: Scribners.
Nietzsche, Friedreich. 1889/1968. *The Will to Power*. New York: Random House.
Owens, Joseph. 1980. *St. Thomas Aquinas on the Existence of God*. Edited by John R. Catan. Albany: State University of New York Press.
Paley, William. 1802/1986. *Natural Theology*. Charlottesville, VA: Ibis.
Pawlikowski, John. 1982. *Christ in the Light of Jewish-Christian Dialogue*. New York: Paulist.
Pedersen, Olaf. 1978. "Astronomy." In *Science in the Middle Ages* 303–337, edited by David Lindberg, 303–37. Chicago: University of Chicago Press.
Peifer, John. 1964. *The Mystery of Knowledge*. New York: Magi.
Pickstock, Catherine. 1999. "Soul, City, and Cosmos after Augustine." In *Radical Orthodoxy*, edited by John Milbank et al, 243–77. London: Routledge.
Pines, David (ed.). 1987. *Emerging Syntheses in Science*. New York: Addison-Wesley.
Pixley, Jorge. 1989. *Historia sagrada, historia popular: historia de Israel desde loes pobres 1220 a.C. a 135 d.C.*. San José de Costa Rica: Editorial DEI.
Plato. c. 385 B.C.E./1968. *Republic*. Translated by Alan Bloom. New York: Basic.
———. c. 385 B.C.E./1960. *Timaeus*. New York: Penguin.
Prigogine, Ilya, and G. Nicolis. 1977. *Self-Organization in Non-Equilibrium Systems*. New York: Wiley.
———. 1979. *From Being to Becoming: Time and Complexity in the Physical Sciences*. New York: Freeman.
——— and I. Stengers. 1984. *Order Out of Chaos*. New York: Basic.
——— and Tomio Petrosky. 1988. "An Alternative to Quantum Theory." *Physica* 147A, 461–86.
Pythagoras. c. 530 BCE/1996. *The Golden Verses*. In *Classical Greek Reader*, edited by Kenneth Atchity and Romsemary McKenna, 83–85. New York: Holt.
Radkey, O. 1958. *Agrarian Foes of Bolshevism*. New York: Collier.
———. 1962. *The Hammer Over the Sickle*. New York: Collier.
Rahner, Karl. 1957/1968. *Spirit in the World*. New York: Herder.
———. 1976/1978. *Foundations of Christian Faith*. New York: Seabury.
Ratzinger, Joseph Cardinal. 1984. "Instruction Regarding Certain Aspects of the Theology of Liberation." Washington: United States Catholic Conference.
———. 1986. "Christian Freedom and Liberation." Washington: United States Catholic Conference.
Reich, Robert. 1992. *The Work of Nations*. New York: Vintage.
Roos, Matts. 1994. *Introduction to Cosmology*. New York: Wiley.
Read, John. 1957. *From Alchemy to Chemistry*. London: Bell.
Reith, Herman. 1958. *The Metaphysics of St. Thomas Aquinas*. Milwaukee: Bruce.
Rosmini, Antonio. 1841/1993. *The Essence of Right: Introduction, Moral System*. Translated by Denis Cleary and Terence Watson. Durham: Rosmini House.
Rousseau, Jean-Jacques. 1762/1962. *Le contrat social*. Paris: Freres.
Rowley, David. 1987. *Millenarian Bolshevism*. New York: Garland.

Ruether, Rosemary. 1974. *Faith and Fratricide*. New York: Harper.
———. 1992. *Gaia and God: An Ecofeminist Theology of Earth Healing*. San Francisco: HarperSanFrancisco.
Sacks, Oliver. 1985. *The Man Who Mistook His Wife for a Hat*. New York: HarperCollins.
Rig Veda. 1981. *The Rig Veda*. Translated by Wendy Donger O'Flaherty. New York: Penguin.
Ste. Croix, C. E. M de. 1982. *The Class Struggle in the Ancient Greek World: From the Archaic Age to the Arab Conquests*. London: Duckworth.
Sarkisyanz, E. 1965. *Buddhist Backgrounds of the Burmese Revolution*. The Hague: Nijhoff.
Sartre, Jean Paul. 1943. *L'etre et le néant*. Paris: Gallimard.
———. 1960. *Critique de la raison dialectique*. Paris: Gallimard.
Scheler, Max. c. 1928/1961. *Man's Place in Nature*. Boston: Beacon.
Schelling, Friedrich. 1810/1994. *Stuttgardt Seminars*. In *Idealism and the Endgame of Theory*, edited and translated by Thomas Pfau, 195–286. Albany: State University of New York Press.
Schopenauer, Arthur. 1819/1995. *The World as Will and Idea*. London: Everyman.
Segundo, Juan Luis. 1976. *The Liberation of Theology*. Maryknoll, NY: Orbis.
———. 1985. *Theology and the Church*. New York: Harper & Row.
Seifert, Josef. 1981. *Back to Things in Themselves*. London: Routledge, Keagan, & Paul.
Sewell, William. 1980. *Work and Revolution in France*. New York: Cambridge University Press.
Seyvastyanov, V., A. Ursul, and Yu Shkolenko. 1979. *The Universe and Civilization*. Moscow: Progress.
Sheldrake, Rupert. 1981. *The New Science of Life*. Los Angeles, CA: Tarcher.
———. 1989. *The Presence of the Past*. London: Fontana.
Silone, Ignazio. 1955. *Vino e pane*. Milan: Monadori.
Soloviev, Vladimir. 1878/1995. *Lectures on Divine Humanity*. Translated and edited by Boris Jakim. Hudson, NY: Lindisfarne.
Snodgrass, Anthony. 1981. *Archaic Greece: An Age of Experiment*. London: Dent.
Spinoza, Baruch. 1677/1955. *Ethics*. New York: Dover.
Stone, Merlin. 1976. *When God Was A Woman*. London: Dorset.
Stuart, David. 2001. *Anasazi America*. Albuquerque: University of New Mexico Press.
Thales of Miletus. c. 575 BCE/1996. *Water*. In *Classical Greek Reader*, edited by Kenneth Atchity and Romsemary McKenna, 45. New York: Holt.
Thapar, Romila. 2002. *Early India: From the Origins to 1300*. Berkeley: University of California Press.
Theissen, Gerd. 1982. *The Social Setting of Pauline Christianity*. Philadelphia: Fortress.
Thibault, Paul. 1972. *Savoir et pouvoir: philosophie thomiste et politique cléricale au XIXme siècle*. Quebec: Université de Laval.
Tillich, Paul. 1967. *Systematic Theology*. Chicago: University of Chicago Press.
Tipler, Frank. 1994. *The Physics of Immortality*. New York, Doubleday.
Tracy, Patricia. 1980. *Jonathan Edwards, Pastor: Religion and Society in Eighteenth Century Northampton*. New York: Hill & Wang.
Turnbull, Herbert Westren. 1956. *The Great Mathematicians*. In *The World of Mathematics, Volume One*, edited by James R. Newman, 75–168. New York: Simon & Schuster.
Twetten, David. 1996. "Clearing a 'Way' for Aquinas: How the Proof from Motion Concludes to God." *American Catholic Philosophical Quarterly* 70, 259–78.
Tyler, Hamilton. 1964. *Pueblo Gods and Myths*. Norman: University of Oklahoma Press.

Vatican II. 1966. *The Documents of Vatican II*. New York: Guild.
Venturi, Franco. 1966. *Il popolismo russo*. New York: Grossett & Dunlap.
von Steenberghen, Fernand. 1980a. *Le probléme de l'existence de Dieu dans les écrits de s. Thomas d'Aquin*. Louvain-la-Neuve, Belgium: Éditions de l'Institut Supérieur de Philosophie.
———. 1980b. *Thomas Aquinas and Radical Aristotelianism*. Washington, DC: Catholic University of America Press.
Waddington, C. H. 1957. *The Strategy of the Genes*. London: Allen & Unwin.
Wallerstein, Immanuel. 1974. *The Modern World System Volume I: Capitalist Agriculture and the Origins of the European World Economy in the Sixteenth Century*. New York: Academic.
———. 1980. *The Modern World System Volume II, 1600–1750: Mercantilism and the Consolidation of the European World Economy*. New York: Academic.
———. 1989. *The Modern World System Volume III: The Second Era of Great Expansion of the Capitalist World Economy, 1730–1840s*. New York: Academic.
Waters, Frank. 1963. *The Book of the Hopi*. New York: Viking Penguin.
Weber, Max. 1921/1968. *Economy and Society*. New York: Bedminster.
Wesson, Robert. 1991. *Beyond Natural Selection*. Cambridge: MIT.
Wetter, Gustav. 1952/1958. *Dialectical Materialism*. New York: Praeger.
Wilhelm, R., and C. F. Baynes. 1967. *The I Ching or Book of Changes*. Princeton: Princeton University Press.
Williams, Paul. 1989. *Mahyana Buddhism: The Doctrinal Foundations*. New York: Routledge.
Woods, Richard. 1986. *Eckhart's Way*. Wilmington, DE: Glazier.
Wolf, Eric. 1969. *Peasant Wars of the Twentieth Century*. New York: Harper.
Xenophanes. c. 500/1996. *On Nature*. In *Classical Greek Reader*, edited by Kenneth Atchity and Romsemary McKenna, 86–90. New York: Holt.
Zimmermann, R. E. 1991. "'The Anthropic-Cosmological Principle.' Philosophical Implications of Self-Reference." In *Beyond Belief: Randomness, Prediction, and Explanation in Science*, edited by John Casti and Anders Karlqvist, 14–54. Boca Raton, FL: CRC.
Zurek, Wojcieck Hubert. 1990. *Complexity, Entropy, and the Physics of Information*. New York: Addison-Wesley.

www.ingramcontent.com/pod-product-compliance
Lightning Source LLC
Chambersburg PA
CBHW050346230426
43663CB00010B/2006